Heidegger, Education, and Modernity

Heidegger, Education, and Modernity

Edited by Michael A. Peters

ROWMAN & LITTLEFIELD PUBLISHERS, INC.
Lanham • Boulder • New York • Oxford

ROWMAN & LITTLEFIELD PUBLISHERS, INC.

Published in the United States of America
by Rowman & Littlefield Publishers, Inc.
An Imprint of the Rowman & Littlefield Publishing Group
4720 Boston Way, Lanham, Maryland 20706
www.rowmanlittlefield.com

12 Hid's Copse Road, Cumnor Hill, Oxford OX2 9JJ, England

British Library Cataloguing in Publication Information Available

Library of Congress Cataloging-in-Publication Data

Heidegger, education, and modernity / edited by Michael A. Peters
    p. cm.
  Includes bibliographical references and index.
    ISBN 0-7425-0886-2 (alk. paper)—ISBN 0-7425-0887-0 (pbk. alk. paper)
    1. Heidegger, Martin, 1889–1976—Contributions in education. 2.
  Education—Philosophy. 3. Postmodernism and education. I. Peters, Michael (Michael
  A.), 1948–

LB775 .H44122 H45 2002
370'.1—dc21

2002024820

Printed in the United States of America

♾™ The paper used in this publication meets the minimum requirements of American
National Standard for Information Sciences—Permanence of Paper
for Printed Library Materials, ANSI/NISO Z39.48–1992.

Contents

v

Preface

The full corpus of Heidegger's writings is difficult to gauge not least because much of his work has yet to be published or translated into English. The German edition of his works reputedly will run to over a hundred volumes. Only a fraction of his work has been translated in English. Much of this has only appeared recently in English translation and there has been a delay of many years between the writing and publication of many of Heidegger's texts. His *Nietzsche*, based on lectures he delivered at the University of Freiburg-im-Breisgau during 1936–40, and individual lectures during both the decade 1936–46 and the early 1950s, was not published until 1961. The volumes of the English version appeared only in the years 1979–87. *Contributions to Philosophy (from Enowning)*, widely considered Heidegger's most important work after *Being and Time*, was published in German in 1989 and only translated into English in 1999.

With such a deferral of the publication and translation of his works, Heidegger's philosophy still awaits a full reception even though the outlines of his thought are now well known and its effects have been strongly felt in continental Europe, the English-speaking world, Japan, and other parts of the world for many decades.

In view of this incompleteness, it might be thought that any assessment of the significance of Heidegger's work for education is premature. Certainly, the first English translation of the transcript of his deposition to the Committee on De-Nazification (included in this volume) helps to make

vii

accessible his thought in this area at a particular and painful turning point in his life. This collection of essays can only be seen as a first and tentative attempt to understand and appreciate Heidegger's work in relation to questions of education. It is the first word by way of commentary and interpretation, not the last word.

The collection contains essays by a range of international contributors from Belgium, Ireland, Israel, United Kingdom, United States, Australia, and New Zealand. It focuses on the significance and understanding of Heidegger's philosophy in relation to education within the broad problematic of modernity—a contestable term open to multiple readings.

I would like to thank all the contributors who have had the forbearance to put up with the delay in publishing this collection. Edited collections often take considerable time to bring to publication. The idea for a collection of essays first occurred to me in 1998 and was, in part, inspired by a visit by Hubert Dreyfus to the University of Auckland during that year.

Also I would like to acknowledge the editorial guidance and support of Dean Birkenkamp and Alison Sullenberger at Rowman & Littlefield. Finally, I would like to acknowledge and thank the University of Auckland and the University of Glasgow for granting me the academic support over the past few years so that I might complete this project.

Michael Peters
The University of Glasgow

Introduction

Heidegger, Education, and Modernity

Michael A. Peters

But where the danger is, also grows the saving power.

—Friedrich Hölderlin, *Patmos*

Western history has now begun to enter into the completion of that period we call the *modern*, and which is defined by the fact that man becomes the measure and center of beings. Man is what lies at the bottom of all beings; that is, in modern terms, at bottom of all objectification and representability.

—Heidegger, *Nietzsche*, 2, 61/4: 28

Martin Heidegger (1968, 3) begins his course of lectures—a set of twenty-one lectures—which he delivers to his students during 1951 and 1952, with the following words: "We come to know what it means to think when we ourselves try to think. If the attempt is to be successful, we must be ready to learn thinking." Learning, in other words, is central to understanding thinking. He continues: "In order to be capable of thinking, we need to learn it first. What is learning? Man learns when he disposes everything he does to him at any given moment. We learn to think by giving our mind to what there is to think about" (4). Yet he suggests while there is an interest in philosophy there is no readiness to think. The fact is that, even though we live in the most thought-provoking age, "we are still not thinking" (4). In *What is Called Thinking?* Heidegger is immediately

1

concerned with learning and construes the learner on the model of the apprentice, emphasizing the notion of "relatedness"—of the cabinetmaker's apprentice to the different kinds of wood that sustain the craft. The relatedness of the learner-apprentice to his craft or subject, he determines, will depend on the presence of a teacher. Heidegger then begins a rather long passage on teaching that I have decided to quote in full because it clearly illustrates how important learning and teaching were to Heidegger's philosophy. He writes:

> Teaching is even more difficult than learning. We know that; but we rarely think about it. And why is teaching more difficult than learning? Not because the teacher must have a larger store of information, and have it always ready. Teaching is more difficult than learning because what teaching calls for is this: to let learn. The real teacher, in fact, lets nothing else be learned than—learning. His conduct, therefore, often produces the impression that we properly learn nothing from him, if by "learning" we now suddenly understand merely the procurement of useful information. The teacher is ahead of his apprentices in this alone, that he has still far more to learn than they—he has to learn to let them learn. The teacher must be capable of being more teachable than the apprentices. The teacher is far less assured of his ground than those who learn are of theirs. If the relation between the teacher and the taught is genuine, therefore, there is never a place in it for the authority of the know-it-all or the authoritative sway of the official. It is still an exalted matter, then, to become a teacher—which is something else entirely from becoming a famous professor. That nobody wants any longer to become a teacher today, when all things are downgraded and graded from below (for instance, from business), is presumably because the matter is exalted, because of its attitude. And presumably this disinclination is linked to that most thought-provoking matter which gives us to think. We must keep our eyes fixed firmly on the true relation between teacher and taught—if indeed learning is to arise in the course of these lectures. (15–16)

J. Glen Gray (1968, vi) helps to clarify the importance of learning and teaching to Heidegger by drawing attention to the fact that the lectures which constitute *What is Called Thinking?* were the first course of public lectures Heidegger was permitted to give by the French occupying powers since 1944, the point at which the Nazis drafted him into the people's militia. Gary (1968, vi) explains:

> What this long interruption in his teaching activity must have cost him is not difficult to guess, for Heidegger is above all else a teacher. It is no accident that nearly all his publications since *Being and Time* (1927) were first lectures or seminar discussions. For him the spoken word is greatly superior to the written, as it was for Plato. In his book he names Socrates, a teacher not an author, "the purest thinker of the West."

This collection of essays has the modest aim of introducing Heidegger's work to educationalists, to highlighting the educational content of his thinking, and to signaling aspects of his work that impinge on an analysis of "modern education." In this introductory chapter, first, I provide a brief picture of the reception of Heidegger in analytic philosophy and philosophy of education. Second, I introduce Heidegger's critique of modernity, and focus, on the one hand, upon Heidegger's politics and the relationship of his philosophy to Nazism, and, on the other hand upon the sources of his antimodernism. Third, I raise some questions of what it might mean, in Heideggerian terms, to go beyond modernity, and I briefly consider its relevance for education. Finally, I provide a brief introduction to the organization of the book and to each of the chapters that comprise it.

THE RECEPTION OF HEIDEGGER

Heidegger has been a neglected figure in the field of philosophy of education in the English-speaking world. Little has been written on him or about his work and its significance for educational thought and practice. This is, perhaps, surprising given the recent upsurge of interest in his work by philosophers in the English-speaking world and, in particular, the way his thought is a source of inspiration to contemporary French and German philosophy, especially those movements which we know as "poststructuralism" and hermeneutics. There are a number of possible reasons for this relative degree of neglect: first, his work is deemed to be too complex, and English-speaking philosophers of education, accordingly, have been discouraged from reading his notoriously neologized texts; second, ever since Carnap's attack upon Heidegger's metaphysics, analytic philosophers have been "taught" or conditioned to despise him for his "opacity" and "nonsense," even though Heidegger's professed aim is to move beyond metaphysics; and third, Heidegger's association with and support for the Nazis' cause during the year of his rectorship at Freiburg, and after, have rightly offended many scholars and had the consequence of making Heidegger both a risky and unappealing figure in which to intellectually invest, until very recently.

One could also tell a general story about the relative lack of engagement and interpenetration of two philosophical traditions—Anglo-American analytic and Continental—within which to understand the reception of Heidegger in philosophy of education. As Mark Wrathall and Jeff Malpas (2000, 3) comment:

> From the perspective of many Heideggerians, of course, analytic philosophy, with its emphasis on logical analysis as a basis for answering traditional

metaphysical questions regarding the nature of language, mind, and world, is part of the problem of modernity, which needs to be overcome. From an analytic perspective, on the other hand, continental philosophy in general, and Heidegger in particular, have often been viewed with extreme disdain . . .

This lack of engagement with Heidegger's thought by analytic philosophers prevailed up until the 1980s, yet we should also remember that Gilbert Ryle (1929, 370) was among the first to review Heidegger's *Being and Time*, and while Ryle was critical of aspects of his thought, at the same time he approved of Heidegger's general project, describing him as a "thinker of real importance" who with "immense subtlety" and "originality" "tries to think beyond the stock categories of orthodox philosophy and psychology."

After Ryle's early engagement we had to wait over fifty years in the English-speaking world before Heidegger became acceptable to read and the first commentaries began to appear. Charles Guignon (1993) records the recent upsurge of interest in the English-speaking world, especially in the influential writings of Richard Rorty (1991), Charles Taylor (1985), and Hubert Dreyfus (1991), who together have increased our appreciation of Heidegger as "one of the greatest thinkers of our time" (1)—a thinker who has contributed to the "hermeneutical turn" (David Hoy) in philosophy, humanities, and human sciences. Yet, in general, the importance of Heidegger's thinking has not been registered in the field of education.

In a survey of one humanities database (*Expanded Academic*) with over five million items or references, a general search turned up 781 bibliographic items on Heidegger going back to 1986.[1] The themes of these articles, in the main, were predictable: Heidegger's ontology, especially discussion of his opus *Being and Time*; Heidegger's appropriation by Derrida or Foucault; Heidegger's interpretation of early Greek philosophy, particularly, Heraclitus and Parmenides; Heidegger's flirtation with National Socialism; "enframing" and his philosophy of technology; Heidegger's poetics; Heidegger's critique of modernity. In several hundred references there is not a single reference to his educational thought or the educational significance of his philosophy.

Yet given this relative neglect, I think a convincing argument can be made for the centrality of his philosophy to education. Certainly, Heidegger's critique of the ontotheological tradition, his interpretation of Nietzsche's work, together with his overriding concern for the question of the meaning of Being, all point to issues that have obvious concern for the field of education. Heidegger's notion of "authenticity" and his influence upon French thinkers, especially Jean-Paul Sartre's existentialism, would make an interesting story if one was to adopt a phenomenological approach to the educational subject or to educational problems. Certainly,

Heidegger's influence on education might be traced indirectly through his impact on phenomenology, hermeneutics, and existentialism, as theoretical approaches in education considered as a social science, but also in terms of his subterranean influence upon the development of modern psychiatry, psychotherapy, and school counseling.[2] One also might argue that his understanding of "the question concerning technology" and modern science—his critique of forms of rationalism and instrumentalism—are essential to understanding modern and increasingly highly-technologized forms of education. Yet most obviously, Heidegger's critique of the "false anthropologism" of humanism—its inability in all the forms it has taken since Roman times to question its own status—is central to understanding humanistic education in the West, insofar as humanism has always been based upon an educational ideal (see Peters 2000). More directly, we should take account of Heidegger's specifically educational writings. I am thinking, in particular, of the notorious essay "The Self-Affirmation of the German University" (Heidegger 1985). There has been some reference to his work in the literature focusing upon Heidegger's analysis and understanding of humanism and the humanist ideal of education.

Within the tradition of philosophy of education in the United Kingdom, the works of David Cooper, Michael Bonnett, and Paul Standish are the exception to the rule (see Gur-Ze'ev, this volume, for a brief discussion of the U.S .literature). These authors, all contributors to this collection, have provided a positive engagement with Heidegger in relation to some of the educational themes mentioned above. Much of their work has focused upon a Heideggerian reading of the notion of "authenticity" (see Bonnett 1978, 1986; Cooper 1983) and the notion of "humility" as a virtue that goes beyond the self (Standish 1992).[3] Both Bonnett (1983) and Standish (1997) have examined aspects of the problem of education in the age of modern technology by reference to Heidegger's analysis. In addition, Bonnett (1995, 1996) has reconceptualized teaching in Heideggerian terms as a form of the poetic.[4] There have also been occasional essays that have provided a phenomenological account of learning based upon Heidegger's *Dasein* (Hoskins 1974), developed a hermeneutical account of Freire (Peters and Lankshear 1990), or compared Paul Hirst's and Heidegger's accounts of understanding (Okshesky 1992).[5] Of course, a case could be made for the direct relevance of Heidegger's thought to education on the basis of his contributions to understanding "knowledge," "thinking," science, and ethics. Furthermore, it could be said that many of his texts, especially those works that come to us as *lectures* he gave to specific audiences, are specifically and self-consciously *pedagogical*, and that Heidegger was explicitly concerned with pedagogical matters, as is well evidenced in his discussion of learning in *What is Called Thinking?*[6]

In one of the few educational engagements with Heidegger's thought, William Spanos' *The End of Education: Toward Posthumanism* argues that the crisis of higher education in the United States is related to Heidegger's thesis of "the end of philosophy":

> The basic claim of this book is that the crisis of contemporary higher education is a symptom of what Martin Heidegger has called "the end of philosophy." To be more historically specific, my argument holds that the events culminating in the Vietnam War revealed the essential contradiction inhering in the discourse and institutional practices of humanism: that its principle of disinterested inquiry is in fact an agency of disguised power. (1993, xiii)

Spanos argues that there is a strong connection between Heidegger's critique of the ontotheological tradition and Michel Foucault's critique of social institutions. He wants to demonstrate the complicity between liberal and conservative reforms in the U.S. after Vietnam and the state apparatus in constituting a strategy of incorporation that operates "to reduce the subversive threat of the emergent differential constituencies . . . by accommodating them to the humanist core or center; that is, the *anthropologos*" (xiv).

Spanos (1979) was instrumental in introducing Heidegger to the Anglo-American literary scene. He was closely associated with Charles Olson and other so-called Black Mountain poets who drew on Heidegger as a basis for an antimodernist cultural revolt. Olson, who staged an antimodernist improvisation with John Cage, Robert Rauschenberg, and Merce Cunningham in 1952, believed that Western culture closed itself off from experience through a relentless process of intellectualization, a process we inherited from the Greeks. Spanos, who started the Heideggerian journal *boundary 2, a journal of postmodern literature and culture*, sought to provide a way forward that ended the metaphysics of logocentrism by relying on the vitality of the spoken word. In the 1970s, Spanos tried to develop an "anti-humanist Heideggerian existentialism" based on Heidegger's existential analytic and the insistence on Heideggerian historicity and temporality, which he thought most U.S. academics in taking on French poststructuralism, especially Derrida's deconstructionism, had unknowingly bypassed (Bertens 1995, 46ff). He called for an understanding of distinction between the "destructive" and "deconstructive" Heidegger—the phenomenological and the poststructuralist—for a literary hermeneutics. He writes:

> Heidegger's *Destruktion* of what he called the Western onto-theo-logical tradition as it developed from his masterpiece *Being and Time* to his later meditations on poetic language as the saying of being was, despite the well-

known problematic "turn" (*Kehre*) after *Being and Time*, a continuing effort to overcome what Husserl, before him, called the "crisis of European thought," generated by the hardening of ontological inquiry. (Spanos 1979, xi)

Spanos locates Heidegger in relation to the critique of modernity, focusing on Heidegger's antihumanism. It is this critique that I have taken as central in understanding how his thought might apply to education.

HEIDEGGER'S CRITIQUE OF MODERNITY

In "The Age of the World Picture" Heidegger (1977) mentions five characteristics of the *modern* world. He mentions, first, "science" and, second, "machine technology," commenting that: "Machine technology remains up to now the most visible outgrowth of the essence of modern technology, which is identical with the essence of modern metaphysics" (116). He continues:

A third equally essential phenomenon of the modern period lies in the event of art's moving into the purview of aesthetics. That means that the art work becomes the object of mere subjective experience, and that consequently art is considered to be an expression of human life. (116)

This is a matter that he takes up at some length in the essay "The Origin of the Work of Art" (Heidegger 1971), where he suggests that the nature of art lies in the "truth of beings setting itself to work" (36) rather than in "beauty," and he explicates the conceptual and historical relations between the artwork and truth. Heidegger locates art and the artwork in terms of *techne* which he explains as a mode of knowing that consists in *aletheia*, a *bringing forth* of being out of concealment.

The fourth "modern phenomenon manifests itself in the fact that human activity is conceived and consummated as culture" which means that culture is "the realization of the highest values" and through such nurturance "becomes the politics of culture" (116). Finally, Heidegger refers to the "loss of the gods," a twofold process in which:

On the one hand, the world view is Christianized inasmuch as the cause of the world is posited as infinite, unconditional, absolute. On the other hand, Christendom transforms Christian doctrine into a world view (the Christian world view), and in that way makes itself modern and up to date. (117)

Heidegger maintains that "In the metaphysics of Descartes the existent was defined for the first time as objectivity of representation, and truth as certainty of representation" (9), and he suggests that the whole of metaphysics remains within this Cartesian conception. Heidegger suggests that the world becoming a "view" and man becoming a *subjectum* is part and parcel of the same metaphysical process, for, as he argues:

> The fundamental event of the modern age is the conquest of the world as picture. The word "picture" [*Bild*] now means the structured image [*Gebild*] that is the creature of man's producing which represents and sets before. In such producing, man contends for the position in which he can be that particular being who gives the measure and draws up the guidelines for everything that is. (134)

Heidegger traces the origin of modern subjectivity, and thus also modernity, to the Cartesian subject and the model of calculative thinking. As he says more directly elsewhere, modernity is founded upon "two mutually essential determinations" in Cartesian philosophy: "first, that man installs and secures himself as *subjectum*, as the nodal point for beings as a whole; and secondly, that the beingness of beings as a whole is grasped as the representedness of whatever can be produced and explained" (Nietzsche Vol. 3 1991, 178). Calculative thinking, while indispensable, is also dangerous when it is accompanied—as it is in modernity—by "homelessness," a kind of empty subjectivity that stands over and against objects, manipulating them and nature, in a ceaseless effort to affirm its own identity.

As Michael Zimmerman (1990) explains "modernity," for Heidegger, was not a final description of the contemporary situation but rather a symptom of a process of historical decline hidden from our view, a process that began with Plato's metaphysics—passing through the major historical epochs of Western history from the Greeks through the Enlightenment to the present technological era—and that signified the nihilistic culmination of the story of "productionist metaphysics" that represents an understanding of what it means "to be." Zimmerman rightly focuses upon "productionist metaphysics" and "modern technology", as the way to understand Heidegger's historical location of modernity:

> For Heidegger, "modern technology" had three interrelated meanings: first, the techniques, devices, systems, and production processes usually associated with *industrialism*; second, the rationalist, scientific, commercialist, utilitarian, anthropocentric, secular worldview usually associated with *modernity*; third, the *contemporary mode of understanding or disclosing things* which makes possible both industrial production processes and the modernist worldview. . . . Both industrialism and modernity are symptoms of the contemporary disclosure of things as raw materials to be used for expanding the scope of technological power for its own sake. This one-dimensional disclosure of things as raw material, in Heidegger's view, has resulted not from human decision, but instead from developments with "the history of being" itself. (1990, xiii)

Heidegger arrives at his clearest statement of modernity as a form of technological nihilism in *The Question Concerning Technology*: "Everything is ordered to stand by, to be immediately on hand, indeed to stand there just so that it may be on call for a further ordering. Whatever is ordered about in this way has its own standing. We call it standing reserve (*Bestand*)" (Heidegger 1977, 16–17).

It is this critique of modernity and "modern technology" that resonates for any study of "modern education," not just in relation to a theoretically informed approach to the increasing reliance upon new forms of technology—and, in particular, techno-pedagogical interventions in the formation of postmodern subjectivities—but also in relation to the associated question concerning the treatment of education itself as a "soft technology." Education as "soft technology" in the so-called knowledge economy, treats people as "human resources" or "human capital" and is designed to turn out flexible, multiskilled knowledge-workers for the twenty-first century.

We should remember that Heidegger grew up during an era that saw the massive industrialization and urbanization of Germany and the transformation of Germany from an agricultural country to one of the greatest industrial nations in a very short period of time. The reaction against the collapse of traditional culture and values led to a reaction against modernism which took the form of a conservative movement aiming at "recovering the essence of the *Volk* (people of folk)—the unique 'blood and soil' and ancient bonds of the German people—from the forces of Westernization" (Guignon 1993, 27).

Hubert Dreyfus (1993, 290) indicates that "Around 1930, Heidegger began to investigate the understanding of being peculiar to modern western culture" and "His early interest in the existential structure of the self had shifted to another Kierkegaardian concern—the lack of meaning and seriousness in the present age." Working on his Nietzsche lectures in the mid-1930s, Heidegger comes to diagnose the present age in terms of nihilism, a kind of undermining of commitment and loss of meaning or direction. Dreyfus (1993, 292) explains further:

> When everything that is material and social has become completely flat and drab, people retreat into their private experiences as the only remaining place to find significance. Heidegger sees this move to private experience as characteristic of the modern age. Art, religion, sex, education—all become varieties of experience. When all our concerns have been reduced to the common denominator of "experience," we will have reached the last stage of nihilism.

Dreyfus explains that Heidegge,r having accepted the Nietzschean dictum that "God is dead, and we have killed him," does not find it liberating like Nietzsche. Rather he traces the "terrible deed" and the loss of meaning to the very idea of values, advocated by Nietzsche. As Dreyfus (1993, 293) writes: "Heidegger claims that thinking about our deepest concerns as values *is* nihilism." By this Dreyfus means that Heidegger is criticizing the way in which values have become objective, something which we can choose or posit, and claims that they have power to provide direction only once we have adopted them in this rationalistic way. Yet this history of the concept of values, which only developed during the Enlightenment, in Heidegger's terms denigrates the notion of values and undermines the sense of commitment which flows from it by placing the emphasis on choice. For if values are simply a matter of choice and not part of the living force of tradition, then equally we can unchoose them, swap them, or change them at will when they don't suit us. Thus, they lose their meaning and authority, and fail to elicit our commitment.

On Heidegger's analysis, values, and the shared cultural practices of which they are a part, form the background against which people make sense of their world. Values, therefore, do not take the form of a kind of explicit moral knowledge—a knowledge that can be made manifest or known,—but rather are part of the cultural background—a knowing-how—which is presupposed in every attempt to articulate something. Thus, as Dreyfus comments:

> At the deepest level such knowing is embodied in our social skills rather than our concepts, beliefs, and values. Heidegger argues that our cultural practices can direct our activities and make our lives meaningful only insofar as they are and stay unarticulated, that is, as long as they stay in the soil out of which we live. (1993, 294)

Heidegger's analysis would seem to place in question an educational tradition that attempts to teach morality as we have come to teach science, and it would seem to raise some fundamental questions about the assumptions underlying most forms of modern, secular mass education. On Heidegger's analysis, modern education is part of the problem of nihilism.

HEIDEGGER, POLITICS, AND NAZISM

In the preface to his book *Heidegger's Crisis*, Hans Sluga (1993, vii) writes of the relations between philosophy and politics as follows:

> If philosophy is simply understood as a search for truth and politics as the pursuit of power, the two appear to have little in common. In reality, however, both are concerned with the production, use, and control of truth, with generating, channeling, and manipulating streams of power—though admittedly in different ways—and from this comes their closeness and their con-

flict. Philosophy and politics are, in fact, inextricably tied together, but their relationship is also precarious and unstable.

If the interaction between the two is to be successful or productive, Sluga suggests that two conditions must be met: first, that the complex relations between truth and power should be persistently scrutinized; and, second, that both philosophy and politics be treated as evolving "organic forms" so that we understand their relation as "historical in character, not as determined once and for all" (viii). This is the fundamental insight that drives Sluga's historicist study of Heidegger's fateful entry into German politics in 1933. Sluga situates Heidegger's personal crisis within a more general account of the crisis of German philosophy. His argument, I believe, is salutary. Having told the story of Heidegger's crisis he concludes by suggesting that we must reexamine the question of philosophy's relation to politics:

> Philosophers, in my view, are not qualified to lay down authoritarian standards of political action. Whenever they have tried their hand at this, they have either described useless utopias or given dangerous instructions. It might be more attractive to think of them as playing a critical role. But political critique is productive only if it is tempered by common sense and practical experience. Philosophical critics of politics, on the other hand, proceed all too often from supposedly absolute truths, and what they say then proves unhelpful and sometimes even destructive. Insofar as philosophy has any task to perform in politics, it is to map out new possibilities. By confronting actual political conditions with alternatives, it can help to undermine the belief that these conditions are inevitable. If the German philosophers of the 1930s had engaged in such reflection, they would not have surrendered so readily to the false certainties of Nazism. (ix–x)

Sluga suggests that the debate over the relation between Heidegger's philosophy and his political commitment can be understood in terms of factionalism. One group—his detractors, including Pierre Bourdieu (1991), Tom Rockmore (1992, 1995) and Richard Wolin (1990)—has argued that Heidegger's philosophy of being is inherently political and that his politics emerge naturally as a consequence of his philosophy. The other group—his defenders, unnamed by Sluga—has tended to minimize such links. Thus, the debate suffers from "factionalism," which "already knows the answers to the questions it asks" (Sluga 1993, 5). But the debate, in Sluga's view, involves two further difficulties: first, it is "marred by useless moralizing" directed at ascertaining Heidegger's moral guilt or culpability; and, the second is the "psychologizing" tendencies of much of the debate where Heidegger's politics has been framed solely as a matter of biography and character. As regards this tendency, Sluga's study offers a historical corrective to these psychologizing tendencies by locating Heidegger's politics within the broader spectrum of German philosophy and society. Heidegger's reluctance to speak of his support for the Nazi cause, his attempt to minimize his involvement with Nazi ideology, his omissions, denials and evasions of his complicity with Nazism, and his silence on the Holocaust, as Sluga (1993, 244) points out, were in fact characteristic of the whole of German society in the postwar years: "An entire society had devoted itself to the task of forgetting, and the philosophers were only too willing to participate in the communal act of erasure."

Sluga attempts to preserve the complexity of the connection between philosophy and politics, avoiding reductionist explanations characteristic of Marxist thinkers that treat consciousness as an epiphenomenon. By contrast, he adopts the view that there is "no single model for describing this manifold of relations" and suggests that "the relation between philosophy and politics cannot be described once and for all by means of any grand scheme, that their relation is intrinsically historical and understandable only in its narrative uniqueness" (253).

SOURCES OF HEIDEGGER'S ANTIMODERNISM

Martin Heidegger's antimodernism has at least three sources: his early Catholic training and Catholic theological antimodernism; the ideas of the *völkisch* movement; and finally, the influence of Nietzsche's works, especially the posthumous *The Will to Power*, exerted upon him from the mid-1930s on. The first two sources of influence are largely conservative, reactionary influences, while Nietzsche provides Heidegger with a means by which to think beyond modernity and our possible extrication from its nihilism.

Heidegger's antimodernism can be traced back to the first decade of the twentieth century. After his attendance at a Catholic seminary in Constance, Heidegger studied theology and philosophy at the University of Freiburg (1909–11), and during this period he began publishing antimodernist articles in Catholic journals. His antimodernism was to remain a significant part of his philosophy throughout his life. From his early antimodernist articles in Catholic journals in the year 1910, through his Nazi period of the early to mid-1930s, to his postwar philosophy, where the emphasis in his thinking fell upon the analysis of the essence of modernity as *Ge-stell* (enframing), an ethos of antimodernism prevailed.

Heidegger's early antimodernnism, his negative appraisal of modernity, was significantly influenced by prevailing views within Catholicism. In the first decade of the twentieth century the Church sought to combat the doctrine of modernism, understood as that radical transformation of thought, including Man's relationship to God, which began in its earliest forms with humanism, promoted by the French Revolution and further extended in significant ways by Kant's philosophy. Modernism, in this sense, contained the idea that the past was not to be revered over the present. Pope Pius X, in his "Pascendi" Encyclical of September 8, 1907, which bore the official title "De Modernistarum doctrinis," says that modernism embraces every heresy. He saw it as a perversion of dogma. The modernist remodelling of the Church sought a spirit of complete emancipation—of science, of the State, and of private conscience from conflict with the Church that was seen, among other things, to weaken ecclesiastical authority. In particular, the legitimacy of evolution was seen to lead to the corruption of dogma.

In 1910, the year Heidegger wrote his antimodernist articles, the Church moved against modernism, requiring every cleric to take a personal oath against it. Heidegger was to side with Catholic tradition and authority, against modernism per se, and even in the 1930s, when Heidegger talked of the "death of God," he did so not as the end of the Church as an institution or the Catholic religion but simply as the end of its power to fundamentally shape world history.

A number of authors such as Michael Zimmerman (1990) and Julian Young (1997) also point to the influence of the *völkisch* movement on Heidegger's antimodernism—an ideology that asserted the concern for "folk" and "folk-values" against the values of modern culture and the dislocating and alienating process of industrialization that accompanied it. As Zimmerman (1990, 9) explains:

> Believing that spiritual strength came from rootedness in the natural soil of their homelands, *völkisch* thinkers called for a reconciliation with nature, not for the technological domination of it. . . . *Völkisch* ideologues maintained that scientific rationalism, economic and political individualism, and industrial technology were behind such rootlessness.

While Zimmerman emphasizes the way in which *völkisch* claims lent themselves to racist doctrines and especially to anti-Semitic notions, Young (1997) argues for the "de-Nazification" of Heidegger—where "Heidegger" serves as the name of a body of philosophy—at least partly on the grounds that Heidegger's political ideology in 1933 is to be understood in terms of the historical tradition of *völkisch*. His thesis is that Heidegger's 1933 ideology is a repetition of the "ideas of 1914," meaning the sentiments expressed by a group of nationalistic, antidemocratic thinkers, including Ernst Troeltsch, Max Scheler, Max Wundt, and Werner Sombart. Young alleges that these thinkers were wedded to a *spiritual* rather than naturalistic conception of *Volk* that emphasized the uniqueness of German *innerlichkeit* (inwardness) and looked to Germany, through its spiritual leadership, to restore *Kultur* to the world. Young (1997, 16) argues:

> As with the thinkers of 1914, Heidegger derives from the uniqueness of German inwardness a uniquely German mission to take over the spiritual leadership of the world. Once again the world is in crisis: Heidegger simply transfers the crisis from 1914 to 1933. The world, that is, is "darkening," afflicted by the "flight of the gods" (*IM*, 38) by an "emasculation (*Entmachtung*) of the spirit" (*IM*, 45), so much so that Europe is "on the point of cutting its own throat" (*IM*, 37).

Analyzing the language of Heidegger's Rectoral Address, Young suggests that Heidegger appeals to the renewal of *Volk* as the means by which Germany can take on its spiritual role of steering a course between the "pincers" of Russia and America—both characterized by the same technological nihilism and empty materialism—to rediscover its historical essence and its world-historical purpose of leading the West back into "the primordial realm of the powers of Being."

Volk is the foundational concept for Heidegger, Young maintains, in that as the supreme value it has priority over both the state and the individual. The state is merely a vehicle of the German *Volk* in that the *Volk* creates the state rather than vice versa. More importantly, perhaps, the priority of the *Volk* over the individual, which found its articulation in the contrast between the new Germany and Western democracies, involved an explicit rejection of representative democracy. Heidegger expressed doubts that democracy as a political system was able to accommodate itself to the technological age and, by contrast, favored the "*Führer*-principle" or a form of authoritarianism or dictatorship. The primacy of the *Volk* became an endorsement of National Socialism where the will of the collective whole meant a form of national cooperation focused on the fulfilment of the needs of the state. This form of national socialism differed from Marxist socialism in that it was "hierarchical rather than egalitarian," and it rejected both "the Marxist dogma of the inevitability of class warfare" and "Marxist internationalism" (Young 1997, 24). Young (1997, 35ff) argues that racism and anti-Semitism was not an essential part of either the "ideas of 1914" or, therefore, of Heidegger's political ideology of 1933, although totalitarianism was a central feature and that briefly for a period during 1933 Heidegger embraced a form of "criminal" totalitarianism.

The third source of Heidegger's antimodernism is Nietzsche. In Nietzsche Heidegger finds not only a fully articulated confirmation of the idea of modernity as a form of nihilism and decadence, but also modernity as the condition of possibility for overcoming nihilism and for expressing a counter-ideal to asceticism, expressed as the "revaluation of all values."[7] The limitations of space do not permit me to investigate this theme in any detail, for such an investigation would require a full examination of Heidegger's *Nietzsche* (1991, orig. 1961), based on four lecture courses delivered during the period 1936–40 and individual lectures given and essays written thereafter through to the early 1950s.[8] (The first English version of Heidegger's *Nietzsche*, published in four volumes, appeared during 1979–87.)

BEYOND MODERNITY?

> It is one thing just to use the earth, another to receive the blessing of the earth and to become at home in the law of this reception in order to shepherd the mystery of Being and watch over the inviolability of the possible. (Heidegger 1973, 109)

Heidegger (1973, 84) notes in "Overcoming Metaphysics" that this rubric, in the thinking of the history of Being, is simply an aid to make the possibility of thinking in this sense to be comprehensible at all because "metaphysics cannot be abolished like an opinion" (85). Modernity as the final stage of technological nihilism, and a productionist metaphysics inherited from the Greeks, also cannot be simply abolished or escaped from, although we can learn to see things differently and, indeed, to keep some aspects at a distance.[9] Heidegger suggests that "the epoch of completed metaphysics stands before its beginning" (93) yet "the ending lasts longer than the previous history of metaphysics" (85). While we cannot escape from modernity, we can better appreciate its historical nature and also we can become aware that modern subjectivity is only one way of being in history. We can exist other than as "producer" or "resource" and, in this respect, thinking (*Denken*) replaces philosophy (which has become anthropology) for inquiring into being and for liberating man's essence. This is nothing less than the task that Heidegger (1999) sets before himself in *Contributions to Philosophy (From Enowning)*, a kind of thinking that helps us to move beyond metaphysics and humanism, beyond the form of modern subjectivity with its associated mode of calculative thinking, indeed, beyond representational thinking and will power. Richard Palmer tentatively indicates what such a move "beyond" modernity might entail for Heidegger:

> The "postmodernity" of Heidegger is of a special kind, for his is a thought and path that resists categories, so that he himself wishes to leave it in the nameless. Yet he has left some suggestive articulations of that path of

thought: the step back from metaphysical thinking, the search for the unthought within thought, the inbetween-character of man's existence, the importance of co-responding to the Saying of language, and so on. . . . When
one has explored in some detail the way in which Heidegger's thinking
moves beyond objectivity, beyond "humanism," beyond technological rationality, beyond traditional concepts of language, truth, and thinking as
such, one cannot escape the sense that this is a path resolutely outside and
beyond the general horizons of modern thought. (1979, 88–89)

What might an education look like in these terms?

The answer to this question may well involve a critique of modernity
and the nihilism of modernity and modernization that levels everything
and reduces human beings to flexible raw materials in the service of the
world technological system. Exactly what can Heidegger contribute to an
education that starts from this premise, rather than from the very opposite or opposing premise—one based on principles of the modernization
of education, that seeks to enhance education's maximum contribution to
national competitive advantage in the world techno-economic system?
Hubert Dreyfus poses this question nicely both in a paper with Charles
Spinosa (Dreyfus and Spinosa 1997) and in response to Michael Zimmerman's (2000) attack upon their position. The question is: "how can one
have a positive relation to technology and still live a life that manifests
what is essential to human being?" And the related scholastic question explicitly concerning technology is: "does late Heidegger's response to nihilism in the name of world and thing save enough of early Heidegger's
resolutely authentic strong identities to save us from becoming postmodern technological resources?" (Dreyfus 2000, 323–24). He summarizes the
position in the paper with Spinosa, thus:

> The technological understanding of ourselves as flexible resources, as man-
> ifest, for example, in the growing amount of time that we spend on the
> World Wide Web, has already begun to undermine all our identities. We sug-
> gest in our paper that one can only resist this postmodern way of life in the
> name of what Heidegger calls the saving power of the humbler things. More
> specifically, we propose that we can cultivate those skills and sensitivities
> that enable us to be attuned to this technological world when that is appro-
> priate, without losing our capacity to disclose other worlds too. Being able
> to open and dwell in a number of worlds, we argue, is as much integrity as
> a human being needs in order to resist becoming a flexible resource. (2000,
> 324)[10]

Perhaps, this is the best we can expect of an education that teaches us
to dwell in a number of worlds as a basis for resisting the drilling and
training that passes for education, especially in relation to its technologization.

ORGANIZATION OF THE BOOK

In the opening chapter Valerie Allen and Ares D. Axiotis provide an edited and excerpted English translation from the original transcript of the deposition of Martin Heidegger that he submitted to the Committee on De-Nazification of Freiburg University on July 23, 1945. As the editors explain, this is the first time that the text of Heidegger's deposition has been translated into English. They also explain that the Committee's inquiry into whether Heidegger should be debarred as a faculty member focused on two related charges: that he violated "academic freedom by turning the University into an instrument of Nazi propaganda" and that he was "an ideologically corrupting influence on students." Heidegger himself describes these charges as allegations "cast in terms of subversion of identities, of crossing the line between education and politics, university and state; of exceeding the limit beyond which philosophy becomes ideology and teaching turns into propaganda; of overstepping the bounds between advocacy and action." As a result of the inquiry Heidegger was suspended from university teaching until 1951. Allen and Axiotis remark: "Apart from its historical merit, the deposition is of interest for its exposition of Heidegger's views on higher education and pedagogy in general, which are not found elsewhere in any of his philosophical works, at least in such a sustained manner." It is, indeed, a remarkable document and one that clearly illustrates the central importance of teaching and pedagogy to Heidegger's life.

David Cooper begins chapter 2 with the assertion that "The contributions of great philosophers to educational thinking are not confined to remarks that they explicitly address to educational matters." The remark is, of course, directly applicable to Heidegger, and Cooper develops an exposition and interpretation that demonstrates this by reference to the corpus of Heidegger's writings. To begin with he focuses on Heidegger's writing on the state of university education, outlining the three threats that Heidegger saw facing "the essence of the university" and drawing the connection between the atrophy of the university and what Heidegger perceived as the growing dominance of "the new science of modern times." By emphasizing the link between the questions concerning the essence of both the university and science, Cooper locates Heidegger's remarks on education in the neighborhood of a set of wider reflections by Heidegger on the nature of philosophy, the nature of truth, and the "distress" of the human condition in the modern era. Cooper provides a reading of Heidegger on the essence and centrality of truth which indicates the way in which the dominant mode of inquiry has become "research" embodying a notion of truth as certainty of representation (rather than as aletheia). Thus, as Cooper quotes from Heidegger, "science does not think" unlike philosophy, at least as in the *Beiträge*, where Heidegger talks of "thinking-mindfulness of the truth" (distinguished from philosophy as metaphysics), which is occupied with fundamental ontology. Any notion of education based on the dominant mode of inquiry and its underlying notion of truth in terms of measurable representations, therefore, will be stunted and unable to approach the disclosure of Being.

In chapter 3 Ilan Gur-Ze'ev investigates the philosophy of Heidegger in relation to the question of transcendence and the possibility of counter-education which he contrasts with normalizing education. Gur-Ze'ev surveys the reception of Heidegger's work in education, including various attempts to implement and domesticate his philosoph, making it "relevant" to teaching in schools. These attempts tend to consider Heidegger only in relation to normalizing education, yet as Gur-Ze'ev argues, "counter education can find in Heidegger's philosophy a different kind of concept of transcendence"—one "conditioned by overcoming authority, any authority, especially that of the one who 'knows' or sets standards, quests or telos." In such a notion it is "impossible to differentiate between self-overcoming as 'lets-learn' and unconcealment as let-things-be that already are in their essence." It is in both, Gur-Ze'ev maintains, that "thinking manifests itself."

Can education be understood as a work of art whose essence is concerned with being and truth? This is the central question that Paul Smeyers pursues in chapter 4. He argues that the obsession with performativity in education today must be understood as *Seingeschick*, a term which expresses that "the human being is at the mercy of the manner Being reveals itself in an epoch in a particular mode." Heidegger's philosophy, thus understands the materiality of education in the teacher who cannot but help to engage in certain activities. The saving power is that the educator "has to be made aware of the fact that she represents a particular mode of the openness of Being." Smeyers provides an excursus on Heidegger's *The Origin of the Work of Art*, before commenting upon the context of contemporary education and its origins in the Enlightenment. Finally, he entertains the notion of education as a work of art, as a pathway beyond the performative.

In chapter 5 Bert Lambeir pursues the Heideggerian questioning of technology, extending this questioning into the related realms of information and communication technology. He suggests that such questioning undermines "the illusion that man stands deliberately above the machine, as an autonomous creator." More than ever before, in digitally mediated reality, man "has become standing-reserve," yet as Lambeir argues, Heidegger's philosophy provides a space for an alternative understanding of computers and for altering educational practice. His discussion of the question of the condition of language in relation to new communication technologies and their programming languages is particularly pertinent to the question of the space left for *Dictung* in a technocentric universe. As he concludes: "That human beings are present as human bodies in social contexts tells us that teachers and students might still want to walk through the classroom door to encounter each other as *Gegenstand*."

"Heidegger sought to deconstruct education," Iain Thomson argues in chapter 6, "not to *destroy* our traditional Western educational institutions but to 'loosen up' this 'hardened tradition and dissolve the concealments it has engendered' in order to 'recover' from the . . . tradition those 'primordial experiences' which have fundamentally shaped its subsequent historical development." Thus, as Thomson explains, Heidegger's "deconstruction" has both a negative and a positive element—a clearing away of debris, of the accumulated layers of distorted understanding and the recovery of that which has been long concealed. Applying this general analysis Thomson follows Heidegger in tracing back the technologization of education to Plato's founding pedagogy, whilst at the same time seeking "to recover the ontological core of Platonic *paideia*." Thomson follows his analysis of Heidegger's deconstruction with a discussion of the history of being as the ground of education, education as enframing, and ontological education as the essence of paideia, before envisioning a university of teachers no longer wedded to the empty notion of "excellence."

In chapter 7 Paul Standish begins by examining Thomson's discussion of Heidegger's allegory of the cave and Heidegger's insistence that "the essence of paideia must be understood in terms of the constant overcoming of the lack of education." He considers the problem of the university, comparing Heidegger's account (in terms of the passage towards aletheia) with the more dystopian account given by Bill Readings in *The University in Ruins*. Standish focuses on "the kinds of resources that the enlightened teacher might be thought to bring back to the cave" which he discusses in terms of Heidegger's turn to the poetic and the ways that the poetic offers resistance to the logic of enframing. Standish maintains, following Heidegger, that the poetic as *poiesis* and language as apophantic, "is critical not only for the kind of world and education that there is to be but for a necessary and integrally related ontological reflection on the very possibilities of that *poiesis*." Standish proceeds to examine Heidegger's notion of the poetic, before returning to the question of Heidegger's significance for education.

"*Enframing* Education" is Patrick Fitzsimons' succinct title for chapter 8. Like Lambeir, Fitzsimons turns to Heidegger's thinking on the essence of technology as one of the issues that is germane not only to education but an issue on which species survival rests. He examines Heidegger's notion of *enframing* as the current technological understanding of the world and our present mode of being, distinguishing between the essence of ancient and modern technology. He discusses the dangers of modern technology, what we can do, and the question for education, before alerting us to other possibilities and what we can hope for. Like other contributors, Fitzsimons emphasizes the alternatives inherent in *poiesis*, and, in turning to the recent work of Dreyfus and Spinosa, follows them by abandoning the notion of a single understanding of being and one unified world, emphasizing, by contrast, the openness to dwelling in several worlds with the capacity to move among them.

In chapter 9 F. Ruth Irwin emphasizes the relation of Heidegger to Nietzsche in her investigation of nihilism and the question of value in education. In the first part of her essay, Irwin focuses on Heidegger basing her discussion on an account of a series of related notions: lifeworld, Being, nothingness, *Das Dasein*, Being and becoming as struggle, Being and appearance. In the second half of the essay, she turns to Nietzsche and the differences Heidegger's thought exhibits, especially in relation to the notions of Being and nothingness. Irwin's chapter provides an account of Heidegger's and Nietzsche's approach to metaphysics and the associated problem of nihilism on the understanding that education must entertain these questions in its positioning as a wellspring of values in society.

Pádraig Hogan in chapter 10 uses "leavetaking" and "homecoming" as metaphors for learning in his discussion of the educational significance of Heidegger's philosophy. Hogan explores the ways in which Heidegger's thought confronts the prevalent conceptions of Western education: a series of insights that confronts the classical metaphysics of Plato's *Republic*, the metaphysical theology of the Middle Ages, scholastic philosophy, and various forms of epistemology. Hogan describes Heidegger's break with Catholicism as one such leavetaking—as he says, "a departure not just from traditional metaphysics and epistemology but from an entire assemblage of education assumptions, traditions and practices." He also points to "estrangements," meaning, in particular, Heidegger's engagement with Nietzsche, and, finally, "homecomings," by which Hogan means the openness to the truth of Being that Heidegger discusses in his later work. Thinking and teaching (as active thinking), thus, are among the first of our responsibilities.

Michael Bonnett, in the final chapter (chapter 11), argues that a Heideggerian approach to learning and the teacher-pupil relationship conceives of education as a form of the poetic. Bonnett draws on the philosophical anthropology of the early Heidegger and the late Heidegger, who makes the distinction between calculative, meditative, and poetic thinking to develop an account of the full *educational* relationship between learner and teacher. In doing so he indexes a series of questions against

Heidegger's notion of personal authenticity: "What is the role of education in initiating individual into the nature and truth of their own freedom and their own mortality? How is 'real' learning from others . . . possible? How should we conceive of knowledge and truth in education and how are they acquired? What implications do these issues have for the teacher-pupil relationship whose prime concern is with authentic learning?" Bonnett then focuses upon "poetic thinking," authentic learning, and a Heideggerian reworking of the teacher-pupil relationship.

This collection of essays on Heidegger's thought, the first of its kind devoted to education, reveals only that we are at the beginning of understanding Heidegger, whose own comment about Nietzsche might summarize our present relation to Heidegger:

> The confrontation with Nietzsche has not yet begun, nor have the prerequisites for it been established. For a long time Nietzsche has been either celebrated and imitated or reviled and exploited. Nietzsche's thought and speech are still too contemporary for us. He and we have not yet been sufficiently separated in history; we lack the distance necessary for a sound appreciation of the thinker's strength. (Heidegger 1991, 1: 4)

Heidegger is not only too close to us, but much of his work has not yet been published or translated into English. I can think of no better place to end this introduction than with a quotation from the Preview of his *Contributions to Philosophy (From Enowning)*, especially in light of the intimate connections between being and education:

> The time of "systems" is over. The time of re-building the essential shaping of beings according to the truth of be-ing has not yet arrived. In the meantime, in crossing to an other beginning, philosophy has to have achieved one crucial thing: projecting-open, that is, the grounding enopening of the free-play of the time-space of the truth of be-ing. How is this one thing to be accomplished? (Heidegger, 1999, 4)

NOTES

1. A search of the *Philosopher's Index* turned up similar results. I made these computer searches in August 2000.

2. See, for instance, Charles Guignon's (1993) "Authenticity, Moral Values and Psychotherapy" and Michael Bonnett's (2001) "Education as a Form of the Poetic: A Heideggerian Approach to Learning and the Teacher Pupil Relationship" in this volume.

3. I would like to thank both Michael Bonnett and Paul Standish who provided useful criticisms of an earlier version of this paper and guidance on Heideggerian strains within philosophy of education.

4. Bonnett's project in understanding teaching as a form of the poetic is, I think, much more successful than Haim Gordon's (2000) more limited perspective which seems preoccupied with the benefits of a Heideggerian approach to teaching poetry. Gordon's (2000, 6) project is summarised as in the following: "No scholar has viewed Heidegger's writing on the gifts of poetry. . . . as indicating a realm from which we simple people may learn much about our everyday life . . . No educator has undertaken to suggest how you may teach students to relate to poetry in accordance with Heidegger's insights. No student of Heidegger has suggested how to act so as to dwell poetically."

5. Neither Peters and Lankshear (1990) nor Okshesky (1992) are concerned to treat Heidegger's work primarily in educational terms. In the former, Heidegger's understanding of 'being' and 'time' (i.e., the early Heidegger) is used to explicate hermeneutics, as a preliminary to providing a hermeneutical account of Paulo Freire's work; in the latter case, Heidegger's notion of understanding, construed as a praxeological competence, is a basis for assessing Paul Hirst's theory. See also Vandenberg (1979).

6. It could be argued, given Heidegger's preference for the lecture and seminar, that his thought has an essential pedagogical form.

7. I provide an analysis of Nietzsche's critique of modernity and its influence on contemporary thinkers such as Foucault and Habermas, in Peters (2001). See also my essay in Peters (2000). For an original account of Nietzsche's critique of liberal reason see David Owen's (1995, 105) *Nietzsche, Politics and Modernity*, where he argues "that through the contrasting figures of the *Last Man* (as the completion of modernity) and the *Overman* (as the overcoming of modernity) Nietzsche attempts to seduce his readers into adopting his perspective by providing a counter-ideal to the ascetic ideal in which the will to nothingness is displaced by the will to *amor fati*."

8. See especially vol 4: *Nihilism*, and also the essay "The Word of Nietzsche: God is Dead" [in Heidegger (1977)] where he provides a sustained exposition of the famous section 125 "The Madman" in *The Gay Science*.

9. I am indebted to Michael Bonnett for a clarification of this point. He suggested to me "we can learn to keep some aspects [of modernity] at a distance (*Discourse on Thinking*) see things otherwise, and thus begin to extricate ourselves from it" (conversation with author). I am unclear and still have doubts about what Heidegger means by "overcoming" modernity and whether, indeed, and in what forms, it is possible to overcome modernity.

10. See also Dreyfus' discussion of Zimmerman's criticisms and his recent book (Dreyfus 2001) *On the Internet*.

REFERENCES

Berten, Hans. 1995. *The Idea of the Postmodern: A History* London: Routledge.
Bonnett, Michael. 1978. "Authenticity and Education." *Journal of Philosophy of Education* 12.

Bonnett, Michael. 1983. "Education in a Destitute Time: A Heideggerian Approach to the Problem of Education in the Age of Modern Technology." *Journal of Philosophy of Education* 17 (1). Reprinted in *Major Themes in Philosophy of Education*, eds. P. Hirst and P. White. London: Routledge, 1998.

Bonnett, Michael. 1986. "Personal Authenticity and Public sSandards: Towards the Transcendence of a Dualism." In *Education, Values and Mind*, ed. D. Cooper London: Routledge & Kegan Paul.

Bonnett, Michael. 1995. "Teaching Thinking, and the Sanctity of Content." *Journal of Philosophy of Education* 29 (3).

Bonnett, Michael. 1996. "'New' Era Values and Teaching as a Form of the Poetic." *British Journal of Educational Studies* 44 (1).

Bourdieu, Pierre. 1991. *The Political Ontology of Martin Heidegger*. Stanford: Stanford University Press.

Cooper, David. 1983. *Authenticity and Learning: Nietzsche's Educational Philosophy*. London: Routledge & Kegan Paul.

David, Pascal. 1997. "New Crusades Against Heidegger: Riding Roughshod over Philosophical Texts (Part One)." *Heidegger Studies* 13: 69–92.

David, Pascal. 1998. "New Crusades Against Heidegger: Riding Roughshod over Philosophical Texts (Part Two) The Genealogy of a Mystification." *Heidegger Studies* 14: 45–64.

Dreyfus, Hubert. 1991. *Being-in-the-World: A Commentary on Heidegger's Being and Time, Division I*. Cambridge,: MIT Press.

Dreyfus, Hubert. 1993. "Heidegger on the Connection Between Nihilism, Art, Technology and Politics." In *The Cambridge Companion to Heidegger*, ed. Charles Guignon Cambridge: Cambridge University Press.

Dreyfus, Hubert. 2000. "Responses." In *Heidegger, Authenticity, and Modernity: Essays in Honor of Hubert L. Dreyfus, Volume 1*, ed. Wrathall, Mark & Malpas, Jeff Cambridge, MIT Press.

Dreyfus, Hubert. 2001. *On the Internet (Thinking in Action)*. New York: Routledge.

Dreyfus, Hubert and Charles Spinosa. 1997. "Highway Bridges and Feasts: Heidegger and Borgmann on How to Affirm Technology." *Man and World* 30: 159–177.

Gordon, Haim. 2000. *Dwelling Poetically: Educational Challenges in Heidegger's Thinking on Poetry*. Amsterdam: Rodopi.

Gray, J. G. 1968. "Introduction" to M. Heidegger, *What is Called Thinking?* Trans. J. G. Gray, New York, Harper & Row.

Guignon, Charles. 1993. "Introduction." in *The Cambridge Companion to Heidegger*, ed. Charles Guignon Cambridge: Cambridge University Press:.

Heidegger, Martin. 1968. *What is Called Thinking?* New York: Harper & Row.

Heidegger, Martin. 1971. "The Origin of the Work of Art." In *Poetry, Language, Thought*, trans. Albert Hofstadter, New York, Harper & Row.

Heidegger, Martin. 1973. *The End of Philosophy*. Trans. Joan Stambaugh. New York: Harper & Row.

Heidegger, Martin. 1976. "The Age of the World View." In *Martin Heidegger and the Question of Literature: Toward a Postmodern Literary Hermeneutics*, ed. William Spanos, trans. Marjorie Grene. Bloomington: Indiana University Press.

Heidegger, Martin. 1977. *The Question Concerning Technology, And Other Essays.* Trans. William Lovitt. New York: Garland.

Heidegger, Martin, and Eugen Fink. 1979. *Heraclitus Seminar, 1966/67*, Martin Heidegger and Eugen Fink. Trans. Charles H. Seibert. Tuscaloosa: University of Alabama Press.

Heidegger, Martin. 1985. "The Self-Affirmation of the German University," together with "The Rectorate 1933/34: Facts and Thoughts." *Review of Metaphysics* 38 (March): 467–502.

Heidegger, Martin. 1991. *Nietzsche.* Vols. 1–4. Trans. David Farrell Krell. San Francisco: Harper & Row.

Heidegger, Martin. 1999. *Contributions to Philosophy (From Enowning).* Trans. Parvis Emad and Kenneth Maly. Bloomington: Indiana University Press.

Kolb, David. 1988. *The Critique of Pure Modernity: Hegel, Heidegger and After.* Chicago: Chicago University Press.

Macquarie, John. 1994 *Heidegger and Christianity.* The Hensley Henson Lectures 1993–94. London: SCM Press.

Okshevsky, W. C. 1992. "Epistemological and Hermeneutic Conceptions of the Nature of Understanding: The Cases of Paul H. Hirst and Martin Heidegger." *Educational Theory* 42: 5-23.

Owen, D. 1995 *Nietzsche, Politics, and Modernity.* London: Routledge

Palmer, Richard. 1979. "The Postmodernity of Heidegger." In *Martin Heidegger and the Question of Literature: Toward a Postmodern Literary Hermeneutics*, ed. William Spanos. Bloomington: Indiana University Press: 71–92.

Peters, M.A. 2000. "Heidegger, Derrida, and the New Humanities." In *Derrida and Education*, ed. G. Biesta and D. Egea-Kuehne London: Routledge.

Peters, M.A. 2001 "The Analytic/Continental Divide: Nietzsche and the Critique of Modernity" in *Nietzsche's Legacy for Education: Past and Present Values*, eds. M.A. Peters, J.D. Marshall, and P. Smeyers. Westport, Conn.: Bergen and Garvey.

Peters, M. A. and C. Lankshear. 1990. "Education and Hermeneutics: A Freirean Interpretation." In *Politics of Liberation: Paths from Freire*, eds. P. McLaren and C. Lankshear. London: Routledge: 173-192.

Rockmore, Tom. 1992. *On Heidegger's Nazism and Philosophy.* London: Harvester Wheatsheaf.

Rockmore, Tom. 1995. *Heidegger and French Philosophy: Humanism, Antihumanism and Being.* London: Routledge.

Rorty, Richard. 1991. *Essays on Heidegger and Others.* Cambridge: Cambridge University Press.

Sluga, Hans. 1993. *Heidegger's Crisis: Philosophy and Politics in Nazi Germany.* Cambridge, Mass.: Harvard University Press.

Spanos, W. 1993. *The End of Education: Towards Posthumanism.* Minnesota: University of Minneapolis Press.

Standish, Paul. 1992. *Beyond the Self: Wittgenstein, Heidegger and the Limits of Language.* Aldershot: Avebury.

Standish, Paul. 1997. "Heidegger and the Technology of Further Education." *Journal of Philosophy of Education* 31 (3): 439–460.

Thiele, Leslie Paul. 1995. *Timely Meditations: Martin Heidegger and Postmodern Politics*. Princeton, N.J.: Princeton University Press.

Vandenberg, D. 1979. "Existential and Phenomenological Influences in Educational Philosophy." *Teachers College Record* 81: 166-191.

Ward, James E. 1995. *Heidegger's Political Thinking*. Amherst: University of Massachusetts Press.

Wolin, Richard, ed. 1993. *The Heidegger Controversy: A Critical Reader*. Cambridge, Mass.: MIT Press.

Wrathall, Mark and Jeff Malpas, eds. 2000. *Heidegger, Authenticity, and Modernity: Essays in Honor of Hubert L. Dreyfus, Volume 1*. Cambridge Mass.: MIT Press.

Young, Julian. 1997. *Heidegger, Philosophy, Nazism*. Cambridge, Mass.: Cambridge University Press.

Zimmerman, Michael E. 1990. *Heidegger's Confrontation with Modernity: Technology, Politics and Art*. Bloomington: Indiana University Press.

Zimmerman, Michael E. 2000. "The End of Authentic Selfhood in the Postmodern Age?" In: *Heidegger, Authenticity, and Modernity: Essays in Honor of Hubert L. Dreyfus, Volume 1*. Ed. Mark Wrathall and Jeff Malpas. Cambridge, Mass.: MIT Press: 123–148.

1

Heidegger on the
Art of Teaching

*Edited and Translated from German
by Valerie Allen and Ares D. Axiotis*

**EXCERPTED FROM THE TRANSCRIPT OF THE DEPOSITION[1] OF
PROFESSOR DR. MARTIN HEIDEGGER, SUBMITTED BEFORE
THE COMMITTEE ON DE-NAZIFICATION OF THE ALBERT
LUDWIG UNIVERSITY, FREIBURG IM BREISGAU, JULY 23, 1945.**

PRESIDING: Constantin von Dietze, President
                      Artur Allgeier, Adolf Lampe, Friedrich Oehlkers, Gerhard
                      Ritter, Members
APPEARING: Martin Heidegger

The undersigned deponent, Professor Dr. Martin Heidegger, having been duly sworn by a Notary Public in and for the State of Baden, deposes and states to this session of the Committee on De-Nazification of the Albert Ludwig University, under penalties of perjury, as follows:

Esteemed President and distinguished Members of the Committee, appointed under the auspices of the Academic Senate of Freiburg University by commission of the Provisional Allied Military Administration for the City of Freiburg, your fellow colleague, Martin Heidegger, hereby respectfully appears before you at your behest to be heard in his own behalf to answer the charges preferred against him. Before you is the issue of whether I shall be allowed to resume the tenure of office of ordinary professor in this learned university or whether I shall be debarred therefrom by reason of unfitness to hold such office and to discharge its duties faithfully and responsibly in a manner consistent with the values and ideals intrinsic to higher education. The gravity of the matter committed to your collective charge for exercise of judgment is of such magnitude, especially to anyone who has dedicated an entire life to higher education, that it must unavoidably be daunting to whomever it befalls to take the stand so untutored in the arts of advocacy. I am sensible how much hangs upon not only the cogency, but also the manner of my speech itself, which has generally been reputed of obscure and impenetrable idiom. I cannot but reflect that if either my pleading be injudicious or its defenses lame, it will cast such damp upon the goodwill you have exhibited toward me as to prejudice my cause. This prospect is even more daunting as I am overwhelmed by how unequal I am to the task at hand, since it is clear that all explanations I have hitherto rendered have fallen short of the mark of persuasion. You will bear with me, therefore, if I abjure the sophistication of the advocate for the halting speech of the beginner from Messkirch.

The bill of indictment, which you have afforded me a reasonable opportunity to examine and to answer, contains two main counts. As and for the first count, it is alleged that during the term of my rectorate I sought willfully to place the University in the service of [*Gleichschaltung*] the state-regime of the National Socialist German Workers Party by conforming the institution of the University to the rule of the National Socialist leader-cult [*Führerprinzip*]. As for the second count, it is alleged that in and through my teaching and research as a member of the philosophy faculty of the University, I willfully propagated the ideas of the National Socialist German Workers Party with a view to indoctrinating students and inciting them to engage in action in conformity therewith.

These allegations are cast in terms of subversion of identities, of crossing the line between education and politics, university and state; of exceeding the limit beyond which philosophy becomes ideology [*Weltanschauung*] and teaching turns into propaganda; of overstepping the bounds between advocacy and action. The delict complained of is, in essence, none other than the vice of intemperance, an unfitness in the direction of excess in respect of the right measure or proper degree. What is adverted to is a deficiency in the mode of rational deliberation that issues in the propensity for immoderation in all things, conduct and thought utterly lacking in self-restraint. Where the intemperate is said to go wrong is precisely in the unwillingness to abide the rule or limit of reason. In the instant case, the accusations impute irreverence toward academe: the province of reason itself, staked in metes and bounds by calls and distances, has been adversely possessed by other than the rightful title-holder. Possession having now been recovered by right reason, an action for ejectment ensues to restore the proper boundaries by summoning the encroachers to renounce any competing claims to the estate.

I am admonished by earnest supporters to seize this occasion publicly to recant any offending words and deeds from the past and to promise to do the same in future lectures and publications in order [*wieder*] to rehabilitate [*habilitieren*] myself. Convincingly reformed in word and work, such a teacher could without risk be placed before the impressionable young minds of today. If anything, an academic of acknowledged renown, it is argued, is more likely to be readmitted into the fold of the postwar university as an exemplar of self-criticism than to be rejected altogether in retribution for alleged past misdeeds. To pray for your clemency by an admission of fault, however expedient, would nevertheless be to perpetrate a fraud upon this tribunal and the institution to which I have devoted myself, if the motive were simply what is good in the way of consequences. So reprehensible would it be to retain one's academic status under such pretenses, irrespective of the question of responsibility, that I am loath to give even the appearance of implementing such a tactic.

Still other well-meaning supporters advise taking an altogether different tack: to defend on procedural grounds that point to the extraordinary nature of this academic disciplinary proceeding, which has no basis in the statutes and ordinances of the University. A proper action [*Prozess*] to discipline a member of the faculty, it is argued, presupposes the distinction between law and fact and involves the application of rule to fact, which issues in a reasoned verdict. As distinguished from an ordinary action, the instant matter, it is held, is a controversy undecidable in principle, because judgment cannot be rendered by appeal to controlling rules, and, therefore, justice cannot be done. Here perhaps only politics prevails. Where the validity of one side's cause does not entail the invalidity of the other's, to submit the dispute to the jurisdiction of an abstract measure, hoisted *ex post facto*, as if it were common to both, commits an injustice of an order equal to the wrong originally complained of. I am told that it is of the nature of this controversy to confound the statutes and ordinances of the University: the cause of action defies being put into legal idiom at the same time as it gains its sense from the very idiom of law. One might therefore say: "I cannot find words to answer charges that institute an idiom that does not yet exist." Here a cause of action demands to be expressed in the law, yet is prejudiced by the inability of the law to give it voice. Silence therefore corresponds [*entspricht*] intrinsically to the nature of the facts as charged. It does not necessarily bear witness to guilt.

There is, however, too much at stake, is there not, to take refuge in what may appear to many to be self-serving distinctions. One cannot but ruminate on the duty of giving utterance to the unspeakable. What is required is to bear witness to the tragedy of our time for posterity, not to testify in favor of one side or the other, *for* or *against*, but to bear witness as such. It is a matter not of giving *testimony*, but of making a *testament*. A testament is by its nature an ambulatory instrument, speaking of the present to the future, binding one to the other in a future past: as an execution of one's purpose, the meaning of the testament is always deferred to some uncertain future date. If I commit these words to you today, it is with such testamentary, rather than apologetic, spirit that I speak, not in order to be exonerated, but to be acknowledged by you and to have my declaration and intent attested for the future by your authority. Indeed, what has to be said, what demands to be asserted, is an *extraordinary* pronouncement of the order of a will. A testament may be oriented to the future, but it also always arises out of and is motivated by the experience of the present as the decisive moment of dispensation in one's life, whether brought about by a shattering crisis or simply a calmer moment of transcendence of the everyday. As I have been immersed in the business of university teaching for so many years, it strikes me now that, in addressing this tribunal, it would be especially fitting that any declaration I should make be in the way of a testament to the postwar university: *Testament*, that is, taken in its original derivation from the Latin rendering of the Greek legal term *diatheke*, meaning "covenant": a compact with the next generation who shall follow in our footsteps, inheritors of the legacy of our words and deeds.

To the postwar German university, I bequeath the principal task [*Aufgabe*] that I set myself many years ago and that has exercised me ceaselessly ever since to one degree or another. It is the task of understanding in ever more radical ways the notion of intentionality. This is what we venture the task of education to be all about, as first articulated by the Greeks with the concept of paideia. Viewed in this general way, the learning process extends without limit before an open horizon of radicalization, as each succeeding generation brings its own fund of experience to bear on interpreting such notions of fundamental import to the leading of a life. The function of the university, as the pinnacle of our educational system, is to assume and to remain faithful to just such a role, regardless of consequence, because, according to the nature of its task, the university finds itself under a categorical imperative to advance the understanding of intentionality before all other service to society, whether in the interest of church, state, or civil society. Pedagogy, insofar as it remains in touch with and perseveres in its original Greek spirit, eschews the rational imperative of relevance in all the forms that fitness for purpose may take, such as utility and expediency, on the one hand, or conformity to convention and custom, on the other. To grasp the task of education is thus already to know something essential about the structure of the university, that it cannot be an instrument of social engineering or, more generally, simply a *means* to an end, without ceasing to *educate*. Professional training and liberal education, though differing in orientation, both miss the mark in the same respect in that they both seek to perfect the pupil, each after its own fashion, as effective *bourgeois* or universal *citoyen* [sic]. Elsewhere,[2] I have, at risk to my reputation, laid great emphasis upon this cardinal point: that the defining trait of the university lies in its *self-assertion* [*Selbstbehauptung*] from the social powers that are bent upon bringing it to heel, insofar as they are ultimately threatened by the institutionalizing of the practice of interpreting intentionality and transcendence in a free and unfettered way.

The youth of tomorrow, born of today's devastation, will one day demand of us an answer to a simple, but profound, question: why attend university? What they are after will be nothing less than an insight into the meaning of education appropriate to the needs of their postwar era, in the same way as the Humboldt-university idea arose out of the national ferment generated in the aftermath of the Napoleonic Wars to dominate higher education for the next century. It will not do then to serve up warmed-over platitudes from the bygone tradition of German Idealism. The way of education leads today to a crossroads [*Scheideweg*]. In my time, I came to realize that the first, faltering step forward must be to release the stranglehold that reason in the form of theory has exercised over higher education since the founding of the Academy by Plato. The idea of the university as it has come down to us has essentially been defined by two moments: an abstraction and a generalization. The abstraction has been to reduce education to theoretical understanding alone, to seeing the world in a contemplative way in order to bring into view general principles that govern the manifold of phenomena. This marks the transition from traditional education as mere socialization into the customs of the tribe to rational education as ascending from the concrete particular to the abstract universal and back again. The generalization has been to hold that theoretical understanding—this way of seeing things *sub specie aeternitatis*—can be had of anything and everything, without exception, including ourselves as human beings. Rational education, insofar as it elevates us to the god's eye view of the world, comes thus to define our highest aspiration—the true good of human life, when we are *kata physin* in our most human relation, means living according to theory. From its very beginning, then, the university got off on the wrong foot by instituting itself as the privileged site of access to what is real, where all things submit to the theoretical gaze. The thought that I have sought to phrase in my writings with varying degrees of success is the recognition of the inherent limitations of the university, imposed by the monopoly of theory over education, which gives primacy to the theoretical relation to the world over other, concrete ways of relating to things. A university cannot truly profess to have its beginning in theory. Its beginning originates in mood [*Stimmung*], springing from the *thaumazein* or astonishment of which Aristotle spoke as the concrete bond between life and thought.

I am acutely aware that I stand at a crossroads [*Scheideweg*] in my career and in my life, just as the German University does. I do not use the metaphor lightly, for the path, the way [*Weg*], has all along been the guiding principle of my thought, not to mention, of education itself. After all, the crossroads [*Kreuzung*] of the trivium (grammar, rhetoric, and dialectic) was precisely the turning-point [*Scheideweg*] where our medieval students in Freiburg began their education.[3] Yet we have repressed the memory that the university is but a chance meeting-place of roads in the open. What is more, today's university has lost the sense in which the threefold divergent way was originally an ominous place, one where all is put at risk. It was where three fatal roads met that Oedipus unwittingly fulfilled the Delphic oracle's prophecy and, at Jocasta's subsequent description of the place, recognized his horrible destiny; it was the place sacred to Hekate, Daughter of Night.[4] But it also bore the meaning of a common place of ill repute, of the gutter.[5] We retain a faint resonance of this derogation in the term "triviality" [*Trivialität*]. However, the university bears acknowledging its bastard pedigree on its escutcheon of pure reason. By the heyday of scholasticism, the three paths had already been cleaned up, their inherent dangers tamed, their mystery withdrawn. Nevertheless, the way of education ineluctably returns us from the soaring heights of theory to the lowly gutter of our finitude. The way of education constitutes the passage into thought, but not a lifeless conduit connecting us as subject to an object by way of representation. No, where it leads only discloses itself as we venture onto it with the weight of our entire being.

Our professors have forgotten that the three subjects of the trivium were pursued singly, not simultaneously, on the assumption that one "graduated" [*graduiert*] along the path from one to the other: first from grammar, which teaches us to speak aright, then to dialectic, which teaches us to reason aright, and finally to rhetoric, which teaches us to speak and reason well. Trivium, although a singular word, already points to the multiplicity within–*tri-via-ium*, three roads made into one. To translate this as "cross-roads" [*Kreuzung*], as one does and ought to, properly implies that one is *standing* between paths, *inter vias*, looking down each road and debating which to take, for actually to traverse the way requires that one has already moved beyond the cross-roads and committed to a single path. To walk the tri-vium is in one sense an impossibility, obliging us to recognize that our forward motion comes from standing and deliberating—being undecided or even lost. It is a strange kind of perambulatory progress that requires perpetual hesitation at a turning point. Each step forward is simultaneously a *faux pas* [*sic*] that must be retracted to return us to our crossroads [*Kreuzung*]. Hesitation before possibilities both visible and concealed, itself a kind of unknowing, is how we progress into knowledge. As one is called to account for oneself, one hesitates and does not suppose to know.

Who among the linguists and philologists remembers that grammar, the first way trodden in the liberal curriculum, employed a terminology taken from quotidian life and hence was already dense with pun and metaphor, making apparent the familiarity and strangeness of language? Just as in German, the Latin grammatical term "case" [*casus*] denoted a falling away from the uprightness of the *nomen* into an oblique relation; indeed, the "nominative" is not, strictly speaking, a "case" [*Fall*] at all, and *casus rectus*, literally meaning "the straight obliqueness," is a contradiction. Lucillius makes the innuendo in an epigram that Menander the grammar teacher keeps his pupil's mother Zenonis up all night practicing her declensions. With Christianity, the theological association between Adam's *lapsus* and grammatical declension came to the fore. Labored and arcane as these puns must have appeared, they nonetheless convey a renewed wonder at the abundance of language. The fixed case-options of genitive, dative, accusative and so on that we employ countless times a day in the service of idle chatter assume in these puns a certain unfamiliarity, which obliges us to consider that our relation to the world must always remain, in some larger sense of the word, ethical. As prior, this relation cannot be theorized in the puritan language of science without already begging the question of value [*Wertfrage*]. Now, this ethical aspect of the grammatical art has been quite lost from the modern university. Language occurs as a result of chosen words, and thus grammar is the art of choosing aright; it is, as Boethius declares, the art of right speaking [*recte loquendi*] and any violation of its rules is a deviation of the rectitude of speech, a verbal *vitium*. Properly grounded, the university is home to an indivisible inquiry in which the question of being [*Seinsfrage*], the Parmenidean *ti to on*, and the question of value [*Wertfrage*], the Socratic *ti bioteon*, are brought together again under one roof.

In the grammar of *Dasein*, the declining [*Verfall*] is perpetual value-motion, never coming to rest at any fixed point of case-relation; nor is there any formerly erect, pre-lapsarian subject-position from which it falls in declining relation with objects. Fallenness, relatedness to the everyday things of here and now, is our first condition. That prepositional bridge, that *pons asinorum* we construct between nominative subject and the object, collapses. As I explained in *Being and Time*: "In falling, nothing other than our potentiality-for-Being-in-the-world is the issue, even if in the mode of inauthenticity. *Dasein can* fall only *because* Being-in-the-world understandingly with a state-of-mind is an issue for it. On the other hand, *authentic* existence is not something which floats above falling everydayness;

existentially, it is only a modified way in which such everydayness is seized upon."[6] The self-containment expressed in Descartes's postulate *ego cogito ergo sum* asserts both the primacy of the transcendental ego as absolute consciousness intact from the taint of involvement with external objects and existence as prior to all such involvement; but the fallenness of *Dasein* denotes its fundamental condition of being alongside the world and its concern with the here and now, with the ready-to-hand matters that inevitably distract us from asking ourselves where the path we tread is leading. More ominously, it can also take us along the path of the They [*Man*], the public highway of mediocrity where right speaking is mere chatter [*Gerede*] and beautiful writing mere scribbling [*Geschreibe*].

Logic, the art and science of right reasoning, teaches us the proper sense of words, gives us the tools to form concepts and to put them together in a proposition. Philosophical tradition ascribes logic's "birth" to Aristotle, who articulated the syllogistic figures of reasoning and the primary categories under which all entities can be classified. Among these, that of the relation between subject and predicate stands preeminent. The term, in Greek *hypokeimenon* and in Latin *subiectum*, literally means "lying beneath" [*darunter liegende*]. In German, we retain the Latinate term *Subjekt* for application to logic and linguistics, but we transliterate the sense of throwing under into Germanic terminology to achieve a different sense: subjection [*Unterwerfung*]. The meanings point in contrary directions. In its political sense, one is subjugated [*unterworfen*] by a sovereign authority: the word suggests obligation.[7] Aristotle, however, uses it in the sense of sub-stance, that which stands beneath, that of which properties, accidents, and relations are predicated.[8] Here, in the Aristotelian use of the term, *hypokeimenon* or *subiectum* constitutes the very center of one's identity; sub-stantiality is essential, coterminous with and forever present unto the self. The violent sense of throwing [*werfen*] has receded into the background. The original sense of Latin *subicere*, "to place beneath," was applied in the most basic of senses, as in placing a mare beneath a stallion, while *adicere* (from which we get the grammatical *adiectum*) meant "to insert," "to hurl (oneself) on top of."[9] In a curious reversal of fortune from inferior to superior position, the theoretical subject [*Subjekt*], now sovereign, seizes upon the object [*Objekt*], thrown before the mind, to re-present it in the abstraction of thought. Likewise, in the university, where logic and argument prevail, the pedagogical relation between teacher and student is understood in homologous terms as a practical instance of the more general relation of subject to object. The teacher gives *eidos*, form and finality, to the student as spiritual material presented for shaping and forming *kata ton logon*, in accordance with an abstract model. The Greek metaphors of formation that provide the basis for our concept of education [*Bildung*] bear out this connection. In the word *morphe*, there is still to be found the potter's poietical [*sic*] hand at work on malleable clay. The teacher stands as *typos*, the mold, from which students will emerge as exemplars. As a verb, *typto* reminds us of the violence of education in subject-object terms, for it has the meaning "to beat" or "to pound," as when combating an adversary or, more to the point, pressing a coin. The student is to be beaten into an image, fashioned [*plattein*] as if he were a drachma coin to be put into circulation. What becomes clear is that the university as pedagogical community is constructed to be hierarchical and authoritarian: the student is subjected to the discipline of the teacher. Implicit in all of this, of course, is that the representation of the teacher is borrowed from *techne* and its relations of production. It is precisely this reduction of education to the instrumental, by analogy with *techne*, that is the source of everything awry with the university today. In truth, Aristotle also points out where one is to look for the solution: pedagogy understood by analogy with *physis*. In this regard, *morphe* is to be paired with self-creating and self-emerging *physis* rather than with technical *hyle*, the raw matter of production. As a mustering into appearance, the essence of education is thus inextricably bound to the meaning of being [*Sinn des Seins*] with the result that the university emerges as a clearing [*Lichtung*] in which the relation between teacher and student takes on different shapes and forms. In a movement of transcendence, *Dasein* is torn and dislocated from its world by entry into the clearing of the university. It loses its substance, which stands constant and sturdy beneath the daily flux of moods and petty duties that preoccupy. The soul, according to custom, is a self-moving principle; by definition, it cannot be moved or thrown. But, within the walls of academe, strange is the self-government [*Selbst-Gouvernement*][10] of the subject whose ship only reaches its harbor when thrown off course.

Although insisting that the category of substance cannot also be a category of relation, Aristotle raises the possibility that "being is the same as being somehow related to something,"[11] only to deny it at once. Yet here precisely is the unthought of the university: that theory is ever only an abstraction from life and must always be referred back to it for meaning. For Aristotle, the category of substance alone escapes the touch of the category of relation; only the subject can be thought of as a self-standing entity. The category of relation, denoted by the Greek accusative *pros ti* or genitive *tinos* (Latin *ad aliquid* and *cuius*), subsumes all oblique positions, all declining and, hence, all relation with the other. But the relatedness of *Dasein* and world, misconstrued by theory, is of an order of relation that can neither be captured by any single preposition of choice nor frozen into any one grammatical *casus*.

Lastly, to rhetoric, to the task of persuasion as the end of speaking and reasoning well. Although it was traditionally to the lot of grammar that the business of reading poetry and appreciating tropes fell, nonetheless it is rhetoric that I here identify as the bastard son of academe, who deserves legitimation. Today, under oath, I am required to speak the truth [*Wahrheit*] before you. In *Being and Time*, I began to rethink the traditional correspondence theory of truth in terms of the rhetorical notion of figuration. I came to see that the idea of truth as adequation of exchange between two things, representation and what is represented, was itself but an instance of figurative disclosure [*Erschlossenheit*] that had become fixed in our imagination. Since Plato there has been a fatal relocation of truth away from concrete things themselves as they naturally show and reveal themselves in the richness of our vernaculars toward the idea of the exchange of equivalents. To be established, however, equivalence, as the word implies, requires a general notion of value, a common denominator by which the equality of the exchange is to be measured. In exchange, formal identity is preserved over material change. Something remains the same and self-identical, while in all other respects it is replaced by something entirely different from itself. Now, this commensuration can only take place by means of abstraction, generalization, and reduction to what is held in common. To advert to Aristotle again, exchange, whether in commerce or in theoretical representation, implies the notion of a general equivalent, a standard measure "which by making things commensurable, renders it possible to make them equal."[12] The truth of theory, being truth as adequation, is thus the abstract, one-sided, and fragmented truth of general equivalence. The genesis of the general equivalent is no more than the invention by the Greeks of conceptual thinking, in which thought sloughs off what is fortuitous, separating essential from inessential in the phenomenon, thereby creating an abstract representation of it. Whereas in intuition we stand in immediate relation to the whole, rich but undifferentiated, thought sunders, allowing us to mediate between many different things, thus bringing them into relation with one another by means of universal representations. The development of the concept is a rising movement from the singular to the particular and, thence, from the particular to the universal as general equivalent. In the process of rising to the concept, theory exiles thought from its prior status, inscribed with a truth more integral than that of the law of exchange, which results only in more and more complex substitutions of equivalents. What I designated by truth as aletheia is this primordial, concrete truth as world disclosure, which does not efface difference and accentuate identity in order to prevail. Against the communism of the concept, to which our universities had succumbed wholesale, I erected a bulwark to the erosion of distinction in life and the flattening out of relief in the world. My interest in the Greek beginnings of education represents a glimpse of the possibility of the Academy on the basis of aletheia, as one of the ways in which truth essences. In the early thirties, I conceived the institution of the university as a possibility of a similar occurrence of truth. Now, my disagreements with the official tenets of National Socialism are a matter of record before you. Any afterthought I might have to add is this: National Socialism has more to do with the replacement of the propositional truth of theory by an equally abstract, voluntarist view of truth than with any affinity to the concrete truth of the Greeks as world disclosure. To think otherwise is to conflate the very real difference in kind between, on the one hand, communism, whether of the concept under reason or of the will under the *Führer* [*sic*], and on the other, the anarchism of the rhetorical trope.

Great thinking has rarely been a matter of pronouncing upon the pros and cons of a thesis. It is a struggle [*Kampf*] between an entrenched vernacular and one better expressing the demands of the age. The unit of persuasion is the vernacular as a whole rather than this or that compelling enthymeme; the method, translation rather than inference; logic is ancillary to this process. *Elocutio* or *lexis*, the stage of rhetoric in which one chooses the colors to deck out the arguments of invention, has no purchase here, for vernaculars break completely with the notion of an ideal language against which all others are measured for clarity and refinement.

To think of rhetoric's turns [*Wenden*][13] as forerunners of new ways of world disclosure is to consider the trope on a cognitive par with intuition and inference, rather than considering it to be either instrumental or ornamental in function. Theory has aimed to forget its history and to fashion thought as pure presence by freeing us from the language we have inherited from past thinkers; but those thinkers are the rhetors of being. Our relation to tradition must be a hearing, or rather, a rehearing of thought's oration. To me, the business of philosophy is to preserve the force of the most elemental tropes in which *Dasein* expresses itself. We need to hear the words, hear their oratory, hear their metaphors as if for the first time. The relatedness between *Dasein* and the world is not only a question of grammatical preposition; it is also exactly that—a question, a calling [*Anruf*], a response. As subjects, we are in the vocative [*Vokativ*], in the condition of being called. The language of *Dasein* is no *lingua franca* but a vernacular whose words are a matter of sounds altogether untranslatable in the same sense in which poetry and its metaphors are untranslatable. My own "metaphors" have earned me some reproach, for it is as the so-called "philosopher of the Black Forest," with all the figurative baggage that goes with it—the way, foothills, and sublime landscapes—that I am accused of reactionary romanticism in the service of irrational nationalism.

I do tend to eschew the ocular metaphor, whose use is largely due to Platonic idealism. It is the metaphor par excellence of theory, if "metaphor" is even permissible here; call it rather a momentary lapse [*Lapsus*] from abstraction into the material, a metaphor that denies its figuration. It exhorts us to ascend to a point of view from which everything can be seen steadily and whole; it is *theoria*, which sweeps our feet off the ground (dare we call it groundless [*grundlos*]?), takes the long view, maps out all logical space, and stands ready with a pigeonhole for every occurrence. Rhetoric, on the other hand, keeps one's feet on the ground [*Grund*] but also turns [*wenden*] it, such that our falling precludes any safe return to undeclined ideation. No long view here, but myopia [*Myopie*],[14] narrowing the eye to a pinpoint [*Nadelspitze*] in the glare of theory. The metaphor of the way, as ubiquitous in my work as that of the eye in Plato's, differs in that its figurativeness cannot be forgotten. Rhetoric's metaphors get in the way [*den Weg versperren*] of abstract thought.

We think of error [*Irrnis*] as wandering [*verirren*], implying that truth is a matter of traversing most directly the distance between the two termini of idea and thing. It is with our feet that we either stumble or make progress. The foot has long been an important register of the exotic— think of the Queen of Sheba[15] and the Sciapods.[16] But since two-footedness is the common lot of the rational animal, our understanding of mental progress has generally developed around a binarity of some sort. We think not in sciapodal hops but through the interconnected lurches of ambulation. Rational thought is all about taking a walk, for "division," in its arithmetical sense, underlies the meaning of *ratio* as the *differentia* of our species. Where pure reason represents a grasping of the thing in its entirety, the rational animal, as Plato teaches us, first gathers thought into its genus and then "divides" it into its species. Just as we cannot grasp the whole without apprehension of its parts, so our whole body cannot propel itself without the separate motion of its discrete parts, right, left, *sic et non*, thesis, antithesis. Thus, *ratio* thrusts us forward in hopscotch fashion from privation to possession. Dialectic is the name we give to thought's ambulation, and it is a gait that holds its destination in full view before it starts, that cannot stray [*verirren*]. But to ask a question that itself opens up the way by virtue of the asking is to position our feet in a new way.

Philosophy's early form, the Socratic dialogue, is even then resistant to a totally logical mapping, for it meanders around, tells myths, takes detours. Purest of thinkers for writing nothing down, Socrates, shoeless as tradition has it, roved the *agora*, the meeting place of riffraff and of roads. Iconoclastic and impious, he nonetheless went barefoot in perpetual presence of the holy. Refusing to abandon his homeland of Athens, he nonetheless roamed perpetually within the city. A native citizen, Socrates yet was a stranger in his own land, while his student's student, Aristotle the Stagyrite, was a metic, a settled outsider who made foreign Athens his home. Where Socrates would ostracize foreign poetry (and rhetoric) from his Republic, Aristotle, tutor to Alexander the builder of empires, maps a mighty domain in which all human knowledge [*Wissen*] is parceled out to its inhabitants. The inclusive empire, which claims all known terrain for itself, leaves no one out, not even barbarian rhetoric or poetry, which now is civilized and made subject to the higher *scientiae* of dialectic and politics. Socrates' sense of place, whether inside the city-state or outside it, fades in the Aristotelian empire of knowledge, for all places are now within, and the totality of space must become all the space that is. Ironically, it is at this loss of fundamental distinction for Aristotle that smaller distinctions proliferate: here rhetoric must be distinguished from politics, there politics from ethics, this faculty from that; each special *techne* now needs another by which to identify what it is not. In the erasure of fundamental difference, the need to tell each other apart overrides all other concerns. More vehement in his denigration of rhetoric than Aristotle ever was, Socrates nonetheless came closer to its spirit, recognizing the threat it posed to the business of philosophy.

As early as 1919, I alone among academic reformers focused on the presence of theoretical abstraction as a totality within the very idea of the university. By making theory into its principle, the university inevitably conditions the quality of the pedagogic relation. The result is an encounter between teacher and student, mediated by the theoretical abstraction, which regards the terms of this relation as a matter of minds meeting together in an act of speculation. Instead of starting with a conception of the teacher/student relation at once inflected by both head and hand, the university conceives the pedagogic process in conformity with the model of abstract exchange derived from theory, according to which the fundamental relation is that of mind to the world, regarded as a relation of subject to object by way of representation. The exchange abstraction is thus imparted to the learning experience from without to give it the form and substance of a *quid pro quo*, a relation in which the teacher offers something of value in return for something else of value from the student, the result being that pedagogy now becomes regulated by the logic of contract. Teacher and student always stand to each other, first and foremost, as parties to a contract. The contractualizing of pedagogy has, in fact, achieved such an axiomatic status within the university tradition that discussions of educational reform, even supposed radical ones, simply take it for granted, ignoring ways of conceiving pedagogy innocent of contract as counterintuitive. Indeed, one must go back to the figure of Socrates in order to find an example of teaching and learning at odds with the law of exchange.

In a system of higher education in the thrall of theory, we find pedagogy confined within the coordinates set by certain fundamental distinctions, among them the distinction between teacher and student, head and hand, knowledge and opinion, disinterest and interest, earnest and game [*Ernst und Spiel*], and the liberal and the vocational. Through these and other derivative distinctions, the set of priorities definitive of the life of the mind are affirmed, while the values associated with more concrete and integral modes of human expression are denied. The language of the distinctions itself already entails that the first of the terms takes privilege over what it is contrasted with. To the contrary, I have long endeavored to develop concepts and distinctions more nuanced than any such set of stark dichotomies might indicate in order to express the essence of paideia. In particular, what is to be avoided is negative determination: for example, the student defined only in relation to the prior notion of the teacher as what the teacher is not. For such an approach implicitly makes use of the metaphysical distinction between being and becoming by defining the student as on the way to becoming *like* the teacher, as aiming to be that which the teacher *is*. Early on, this seemed to me to be utterly misguided. Once again, the figure of Socrates points the way forward. In the *Symposium*, Socrates purports to show how head and heart are not to be radically separated, but belong together as integral moments of education. Likewise, Socrates' self-referential paradox "I know that I know nothing"[17] gestures towards a pedagogy in which ignorance lies at the foot of knowledge and contradiction at the font of truth. In a similar vein, it occurred to me unexpectedly as a result of the decisive turn in our history that there were vital prescriptions for the future of the university to be gleaned by going against the grain of our idealist Humboldtian heritage of higher education. At a stroke, the hackneyed representations of teaching and learning fell by the wayside, opening a new horizon to be charted with the compass of Greek paideia to hand.

Characteristic of paideia, as it has come down to us from antiquity, has always been the Socratic injunction against receiving payment for one's teaching. That this is original to the concept, and not simply some Socratic innovation, can be surmised from Socrates' telling anachronism that the Seven Sages, unlike the sophists of his day, never charged their pupils fees for tuition.[18] What Socrates decries as inimical to paideia is the reduction of education by the logic of contract to the status of commodity to be exchanged for consideration according to the law of equivalence. There is an internal connection to be drawn between centralization in the life of the university and theory's rise to the level of the general equivalent. What becomes apparent in the lecture and the seminar is the division between the many, the particular manifold, and the one, the general equivalent that dominates and governs it. The teacher's role in the pedagogic exchange is to represent the general equivalent, administering equivalences among the students, who participate in his unity by subsuming themselves under his generality. Before the teacher, there is formal equality within the collective of students. Instruction is thus modeled on exchange: to teach, the teacher disregards the differences and distinctions within the concrete student manifold and addresses himself to the faceless, abstract student that is his counterpart. Likewise, to learn, the student abandons the idiosyncratic expressions of his life for a generic way of thinking that raises him to the level of the teacher.

As a teacher, I have strived to confound commodity exchange in the classroom. For this reason, my lectures and seminars have appeared odd to many, who are accustomed to the norm of generic education. My paradigm of teaching and learning is the Socratic conversation, the question and answer between individuals who embody the pedagogical scene concretely in ever shifting and undefined ways, such that their respective identities may be thrown into doubt. The desire to know does not arise from lack *per se*, but is engendered upon the realization that one lacks what is good. One utterly ignorant cannot desire to become wise, as his condition prevents him from recognizing his deficiency. Ignorance is thus never simple and unqualified, and the knowledge of one's ignorance results in *eros* or the desire to know. The philosopher, lover of wisdom, is neither actually wise nor entirely ignorant. Ignorance is a condition of knowledge and wisdom. The claim then to know that one does not know is not so much a self-contradiction as it is a sense of what conceals itself in the revealing.

The Socratic encounter employs various techniques of discourse in the service of concrete pedagogy. With his needling remarks [*Nadelstiche*], Socrates questions his interlocutors into contradiction and confusion, reducing them to *aporia*, lack of resource. *Aporia* is a specific kind of lack or want, a perplexity achieved by encounter with the previously unthought, an uncertainty about where to go next driven by a desire to progress. The institution of the university as such confers upon the teacher a recognition of status, an authority that can impede communication. A pedagogy that regards the teacher as the authoritative repository and dispenser of knowledge and wisdom inevitably averts desire. Tyranny in the pedagogical scenario is counterproductive. If the pose of teacherly omniscience and the authority that this pose articulates are disincentives to learn, then the question of education is the question not of how to transmit knowledge but of how to suspend it. The concrete teacher is one who temporarily stages the scene of resourcelessness. Education is not a passing on of knowledge and skills either in the medieval paradigm of master/apprentice or in the modern of seller/consumer. Rather call it a withholding, a delaying of articulation, in order that the student may attain an answer. Ignorance as a mode of suspension interrogates the role of the teacher as the one who knows and of the student as the one who does not. The teacher's silence is finally what has to be heard. Yet it is precisely as teacher that I here must speak.

The university has always focused on the theoretical over the practical, implying that the detached, contemplative point of view is prior to and independent of the background practices of involvement and concern with people and things. Human actions—excluding our involuntary actions, such as blinking and the beating of the heart—cannot count as the stuff of practical virtue unless at every step they apply and are informed by consciousness and intention. Hitherto, intention and intentionality have been understood as aspects of consciousness, as a subject to be studied in epistemology. Medieval philosophy left us with the distinction between an object in its unobserved, natural being (*in esse naturali*) and that same object in its significant being (*in esse intentionali*) as apprehended by the individual knower. It is through the concept, the that-by-which or *medium quo*, that brute matter, which itself has no intelligence, can be rendered intelligible. By positing a concept to be always a concept *of* something, the theory of the intentional existence of forms bridged the gap for the medieval world between the knowing subject and the external world, and as such, it remained within the domain of cognition. Likewise for Brentano and Husserl, intentionality formed the backdrop which conditioned and relativized the gap between subject and object. As a psychical phenomenon, intentionality is attributed to consciousness [*Bewußtsein*], and, in accord with the tradition of Western philosophy, privileges theoretical directedness over the practical. To break the tradition entails surpassing the subject/object distinction in all its domains, including action. The task is not to decide which kind of intentionality, practical or theoretical, is prior, but to get beyond the terms altogether. Displacing the priority of *theoria* is not achieved by simply inverting its relation with *praxis*. The traditional account of both these ways of relating, knowing and doing, contemplation and action, the head and the hand, presupposes a more fundamental sort of intentionality. I do not deny Husserl's great insight that intentional directedness is essential, but I question that it is to be understood primarily in mental terms. Intentionality is first and foremost to be attributed to *Dasein*, not to consciousness [*Bewußtsein*]. Echoing its immediate Latin source *intendere* and the more distant Greek *teino*, intentionality has more to do with an initial act of stretching out, with a hand reaching for something, with tendons tautening purposefully. Intentionality involves doing something for a purpose, rather than being conscious of something, and hence its meaning as mental directedness is derivative and abstracted from a more concrete, nonrepresentational relatedness to things. The bare object of pure, disinterested contemplation, instead of being that which is, is an impoverished residue of what we already handle, what already is of significance and concern to us in a world organized in terms of purposes. The way we relate to things is by comportment [*Verhalten*]. Comportment is nondeliberate, concrete involvement with people and things, practices and institutions, economy and nation.

Intentionality as comportment and truth as world disclosure go hand in hand. Without radically rethinking intentionality, the university's attempts to lay claim to its much vaunted neutrality, to evade being the organ of the nation-state and of the market, is quite futile. The religious particularity of the premodern university was eroded from two sides: nascent nationalism and economic utility. Despite the university's efforts to maintain a theoretical detachment from state and market interest, secularization does not result in independence from values [*Wertfreiheit*] but in replacement of one set of religious values with other, more abstract ones.

How then have I comported myself as I stand here before you, a legal subject asked to render account of my philosophical concepts, my political opinions, my actions, and my relatedness to the students and teachers of this university—experiences that were at no point not already cancelled [*durchkreuzt*] even as they were asserted [*behauptet*]?[19] Those who sought herein for the entry of a plea of guilty or not guilty will have been disappointed by what they found. Under seal of this tribunal, mine have been rather words of bequeathal, however untimely, by a tragic educator, divided between a *not-yet* and a *no-longer*.

EDITORS' AFTERWORD

What do we do when we expound a sustained theme in someone's writing? We speak, as it were, on their behalf, staying faithful to the testimony of their words, but representing them systematically and in the language of the court of philosophy. We attorn for them. What do we do when we expound a theme in someone's writing that is present only in an *ad hoc* and unsustained manner? We do exactly the same thing.

As early as summer semester 1919, Heidegger was thinking about education in his lectures "On the Essence of the University and Academic Study." It is no accident that almost all his publications since *Being and Time* were first lectures or seminars. Winter 1929–30, and Heidegger once again linked the possibility of philosophy to the question of the role of the university, in the Freiburg Inaugural Lecture and in the lecture course "Introduction to Academic Study." Heidegger's understanding of the role of the philosopher changed, in that he came to make a conscious break with strictly academic philosophy in order henceforth to philosophize in another, nonprofessional way, in immediate confrontation with problems of the time perceived as urgent. His Rectoral Address to the University in 1933 epitomizes this gesture. His consciousness of crisis of the present moment, his interpretation of the German situation at the beginning of the thirties, must always be balanced against his fascination with the past, against an apparent disregard for *Historie*, which refers to undisputed "factual" events, in favor of *Geschichte*, which designates an authentic relation with the past. His search was for a third way irreducible to either of the two then predominant educational alternatives—liberal education and vocational training.

In view of the absence of some definitive text on education written by Heidegger, and in the spirit of improvisation and of imitation, we wrote one for him. We present here Heidegger's apology. Apologetic writing was itself a renowned literary genre in antiquity. An aspiring rhetor was put through his paces by inventing his own defense of Helen of Troy or of Socrates at his trial. The apology presented itself as a formidable test of rhetorical virtuosity. Numerous Socratic apologies existed, of which only three survive, by Xenophon, Plato, and Libanius in the fourth century A.D.

NOTES

1. [Ed.] This abridged text of Martin Heidegger's deposition before the Committee on De-Nazification of Freiburg University, translated for the first time into English, has been rendered from the official typewritten transcript of the record of the Committee's proceedings, preserved in the archives of the University. Heidegger read from a handwritten draft, no longer extant, composed specifically for the occasion. The charge of the Committee was to conduct an inquiry into whether Heidegger should be debarred as a faculty member from the University for the nature and manner of his teaching, research, and administration during the Nazi period. The investigation came to focus on the twin issues of violating academic freedom by turning the University into an instrument of Nazi propaganda, and of being an ideologically corrupting influence on students. Although the Committee's predilection was to allow Heidegger to continue in the University in some faculty capacity, upon the insistence of the Allied military government, which saw the internationally renowned philosopher's case as exemplary, the Committee came out in favor of a compromise: suspension. The suspension was only rescinded when Heidegger was allowed to resume university teaching again in 1951.

Apart from its historical merit, the deposition is of interest for its exposition of Heidegger's views on higher education and pedagogy in general, which are not to be found elsewhere in any of his philosophical works, at least in such a sustained manner. Purposely departing from his signature style, Heidegger adopts a plainer idiom, less immersed in the characteristic philosophical jargon, and provides a unique glimpse into the man himself *in extremis*.

2. [Ed.] See Heidegger's 1933 Rectoral Address, "The Self-Assertion of the German University." In *Review of Metaphysics*, 38 (March): 467–502.

3. [Ed.] The University of Freiburg was founded in 1457.

4. [Ed.] See Virgil, *Aeneid*, trans. R. Fitzgerald, New York: Random House (1983), IV, 609.

5. [Ed.] See Horace, *Ars Poetica*, edited by E. H. Blakeney, Freeport, N.Y.: Books for Libraries Press, (1970), 245. As Phaedrus says in his *Fabulae*, "conceived in the gutter [*trivio*], educated in dung" (1.27.11).

6. [Ed.] Martin Heidegger, *Being and Time*, trans. J. Macquarrie and E. Robinson, London: SCM Press, (1962), 179.

7. [Ed.] Plato uses *hypokeisthai*, "to underlie," in this political sense (*Gorgias* 510c).

8. [Ed.] See Aristotle, *Metaphysics*, Oxford: Clarendon, (1980), 1017b, 13.

9. [Ed.] The *double entendre* in "subject" meaning "placed under" and "adjective" meaning "inserted" is part of an array of grammatical puns in the Middle Ages. See Alan of Lille's *Complaint of Nature*, trans. J. Sheridan, Toronto: Pontifical Institute of Mediaeval Studies, (1980), Pr.v.

10. [Trans.] Latin *gubernare* means originally to "steer a ship" and then, by extension, "to govern."

11. [Ed.] Aristotle, *Categories*, trans. J. Dillon, London: Duckworth, (1990), 8a.

12. [Ed.] Aristotle, *The Nicomachean Ethics*, trans. and introduction by D. Ross, revised by J. A. Ackrill and J. O. Urmson, Oxford, Oxford University Press, (1980), V, 5.

13. [Trans.] In "turns" [*Wenden*], Heidegger brings together the ideas of rhetorical trope, the "fall" of grammatical case, and the "lapse" of philosophy into metaphor.

14. [Trans.] Heidegger here chooses the word with the Greek root, *Myopie*, rather than the Germanic word for shortsightedness, *Kurzsichtigkeit*. This is not casually done, as is made clear by its juxtaposition with "pinpoint" [*Nadelspitze*] and by a subsequent reference to Socrates goading the Athenians with "needling comments" [*Nadelstiche*]. Plato describes Socrates as a sharp stinging insect (*muops*), the same word for shortsightedness, the condition of myopia.

15. [Ed.] The Queen of Sheba is traditionally depicted with webbed feet. See *The Book of Hours of Catherine of Cleves*, ed. John Plummer (New York: Pierpoint Morgan Library, 1964), plate 21, p. 49.

16. [Ed.] Mentioned in Pliny and numerous later writings, the Sciapods were alleged to have one huge foot, and they are depicted lying on their back with their foot shielding them from the sun's rays.

17. [Ed.] Plato's *Apology of Socrates*, trans. T. G. West, Ithaca, New York: Cornell University Press, (1979), [21b-e, 29b].

18. [Ed.] Plato, *Hippías Major*, trans. with commentary by P. Woodruff, Oxford, Blackwell, (1982), [282c-d].

19. [Trans.] The word recalls the crossroads [*Kreuzung*] of the trivium and anticipates Heidegger's move in a later essay, "On the Question of Being," to place *Sein* beneath the "mark of crossing out" [*Zeichen der Durchkreuzung*].

2

Truth, Science, Thinking, and Distress

David E. Cooper

The contributions of great philosophers to educational thinking are not confined to remarks that they explicitly address to educational matters. Heidegger is no exception. Perhaps it is from his account of, say, authentic human existence, or of language and art, that theorists and practitioners of education have most to learn. Certainly, writers on professional education—nursing education, for example—have exploited his discussions of "care" and "solicitude" in *Being and Time*, just as teachers of art and its history have drawn on his lectures *The Origin of the Work of Art*.[1] Nevertheless, during his long career, Heidegger did offer many explicit remarks on education, although he never devoted a substantial work to the subject. Most of these remarks belong to writings during the decade or so after *Being and Time* (1927), although he continues to address the subject in the relatively late lectures, *What Is Called Thinking?* (1954).[2] Whether or not it is in these remarks that Heidegger's main contribution to educational thought resides, they certainly invite consideration, for it is possible that they aid reflection on the condition of education in modernity and may even indicate certain directions for education.

To focus on Heidegger's remarks explicitly relevant to education is not, however, to ignore his wider philosophy. Indeed, a central theme in this chapter will be that the force or depth of those remarks only emerges when they are set in the context of discussions of topics, such as the nature of truth and the status of science, that preoccupied Heidegger over forty or more years. This makes any full understanding of the remarks a difficult task, not least because their context is, for the most part, the famously elusive philosophy or thinking of later, "post-turn" Heidegger. One aspect of the difficulty involved is that the most important later text, composed during 1936–38, *Beiträge zur Philosophie (Vom Ereignis)*, was only published in 1989 and did not appear in English translation (as *Contributions to Philosophy (From Enowning)*) for another decade. This huge and opaque work has yet to be digested, especially by those whose German was not up to the demanding standard required for reading the original. Because of the difficulty of placing Heidegger's remarks on education within the wider constellation of his thought, I make no apology for devoting the bulk of this chapter to elucidation and interpretation. Only towards the end do I raise critical issues concerning the viability and possible application of those remarks. To raise those issues without having first placed the remarks would be pointless.

SCIENCE AND "THE ESSENCE OF THE UNIVERSITY"

In the 1930s, both during and after his Rectorship of the University of Freiburg in 1933–34, the bulk of Heidegger's remarks on education addressed the state of university education. Reflecting, twelve years later, on the Rectorship, Heidegger wrote that his primary concern around that time had been with the grounding of "the essence of the university," an essence he perceived as increasingly compromised in modern times. Three related threats were discerned. To begin with, the traditional scholar was disappearing, to be "succeeded by the research man," a man of a "different stamp," committed to a rigid methodology and increasingly at the beck and call of publishers and outside bodies eager for useful "results."[3] Second, universities were increasingly perceived as answerable to the needs of the professions—law, medicine, politics, and so on. This was a perversion of the proper relationship, for "knowledge is not in the service of the professions, but vice-versa."[4] The university should be "providing [society] with a measure," and not, therefore, be measured by its contribution to transient and extraneous goals. Finally, and most importantly, it is of the essence of the university to be a "living unity," its members sharing a perception of a common, "essential ground" of inquiry. The modern trend, however, is one of the dispersal and encapsulation of the sciences into special faculties. Already in his 1929 inaugural lecture, Heidegger had lamented that the only unity remaining was that provided by "the technical organization of universities and faculties," for "the rootedness of the sciences in their essential ground has atrophied."[6]

These concerns of Heidegger will strike today's university teachers, no less worried than he by a utilitarian perception of the university's vocation, by the mechanisms of "quality assurance," by the influence of external funding bodies, and by increasing fragmentation of the disciplines, as remarkably prescient. Things have indeed gone as Heidegger saw them going. It is not, however, in these prescient remarks that Heidegger's special contribution to educational thinking resides. After all, he was hardly alone in his perception of the threats faced by universities: it was one shared by many other conservative *Schwarzseher* of the time. We go some way toward bringing out the deeper dimensions of Heidegger's observations on the compromised "essence of the university" by noting that these nearly always occur in the context, or proximity, of discussing "the essence of science." In Heidegger's view, the atrophy of the university has intimately to do both with the growing dominance of "the new science of modern times"[7] and the atrophy, noted above, of the rootedness of the sciences themselves in their "essential ground."

Care needs to be be taken with Heidegger's use of "science" (*Wissenschaft*). Like German speakers generally, he applies *Wissenschaft* to any disciplined search for knowledge—to history, say, as much as to physics. In another respect, however, he normally applies it more narrowly than our "science"—to "the new science of modern times." Hence, in calling history, as pursued by modern historians, a science, he means to bring out the way these historians model their inquiries—their search for "laws," for example—on the approach of the natural sciences.[8] Like Heidegger, I take modern physics as paradigmatic of the "new science": what makes it new and modern is something that will emerge later.

Heidegger predicts that universities will become "merely operational institutions," "sites for scientific research and teaching," which for a while, at least, will retain the traditional humanities as "cultural decorations."[9] It is the dominance of science, then, that is immediately responsible for the threats to the essence of the university remarked on earlier. It is in the sciences that the scholar gives way to "the research man," for it belongs to the very character of modern science that it is 'research,' in the sense of trying to secure a preset plan of inquiry through the application of a rigorous methodology, of techniques of measurement and calculation.[10] It is the sciences, on account of their manifest "usefulness" and their complicity with technology, that render the university subject to "adjustable shifting to various purposes, depending on [the] need[s]" of society and the professions.[11] It is the sciences, finally, that threaten the fragmentation destructive of the university's unity. Because each science, or branch of a science, has its own special "object-area" and method of research, it becomes necessary to delimit and compartmentalize them. Specialization is "a necessary consequence . . . of the coming to presence of modern science."[12]

Specialization does not entail fragmentation, but that will be the result in the absence of "reflection on the totality of the sciences," on their "essential grounding." Unfortunately, it is precisely that kind of reflection that gets treated as "cultural decoration."

Relating Heidegger's observations on the condition of the university to his understanding of the new science and its dominance does something to confer depth and distinctiveness on those observations. Again, though, Heidegger was not alone in discerning the decisive impact of modern science on his culture, including its educational climate. His teacher, Edmund Husserl, for one, had been sounding this theme for several years.[13] To identify what is truly distinctive in Heidegger's reflections on education, we need to widen the context in which to place them.

PHILOSOPHY, TRUTH, AND "DISTRESS"

Usually, I noted, Heidegger's remarks on education occur in the neighborhood of discussion of the nature and dominance of science. Both those remarks and that discussion, moreover, typically occur in the neighborhood of reflections on further topics—notably, the nature of philosophy, the nature of truth, and the 'distress' of the modern human condition.

Just as care was needed over his use of "science," so Heidegger's use of the term "philosophy" requires circumspect handling. In *Contributions*, he distinguishes between philosophy as "thinking-mindfulness of the truth" and philosophy as "historical erudition that constructs 'systems.'[14] This second characterization is an early sign of Heidegger's increasingly pejorative use of the term, and in later works "philosophy" has joined— indeed, been equated with—"metaphysics," as the name for something which is anything but "thinking-mindfulness of the truth." By 1954, he writes that "preoccupation with philosophy . . . give[s] us the stubborn illusion that we are thinking."[15] Now he prefers to refer to his own kind of inquiry as "thinking" or "reflection," with "philosophy" and "metaphysics" surrendered to those who, in Heidegger's judgment, have turned the forms of inquiry originally named by those terms into branches of science.

As that remark suggests, it is always with the sciences that Heidegger wants to contrast philosophy (in the "good" sense) or "thinking." Let's call this "philosophy/thinking." And it helps one to understand his conception of science and the university "in modern times" to attend to this contrast. It is precisely because philosophy/thinking 'has no place in the "university"' that the essence of the university is lost. The quotes around "university" indicate that an institution in which philosophy/thinking has lost its place is a university only in name. Two related reasons were given for this in the Rectoral Address. First, a university must be a "unity," and this requires that its members reflect upon "beings-as-a-whole"—upon the interrelations between beings and, therefore, between the various disciplines in which different domains of beings or entities are examined. Second, it is in the university that there should be reflection on the grounds or foundations of the various disciplines. This is the task of philosophy/thinking, for it can be no part of, say, physics proper—which presupposes the existence of a particular object-area—to reflect on the grounds and possibility of its access to this area. "All science is philosophy, whether it knows and wants this or not"[16] not because scientists must be philosophers, but because, in the absence of reflection on the grounds of science, its claims float, "unthinkingly," in the air, its pretensions to truth unfounded.

As the characterization of philosophy/thinking as "thoughtful-mindfulness of the truth" indicates, Heidegger's contrast between philosophy/thinking and science is often made in the context of reflections on the nature of truth. If philosophy/thinking has a privileged concern with truth, the implication is that science does not. And Heidegger indeed refers to "the lack of truth in all science."[17] More typically, however, and less radically, he speaks of the sciences as engaged with, and furnishing, truths in a "derivative" sense of truth, of their concern for truth as "correctness" rather than for truth of a more fundamental, "primordial" kind.

If the notion of truth figures prominently in Heidegger's discussion of the essence of science, so it does in his observations on education. The message, which he endorses, of the allegory of the cave in Plato's *Republic* is, according to Heidegger, that "the essence of 'education' is grounded in the essence of 'truth.'"[18] The point here is not the banal one that teachers do and should aim to impart truths rather than falsehoods to their pupils. It is, rather, that in order for any process to count as a genuinely educative one, it must be self-consciously concerned with reflection on the nature of truth in Heidegger's favored, primordial sense. What that sense is will emerge in later sections of this chapter. For the moment, one should observe an obvious implication of Heidegger's point: to the extent that schooling or university teaching fails to be engaged in reflection on truth, it relinquishes its title to being education.

It is already apparent, perhaps, that Heidegger's remarks on the university and the dominance of science are connected with his perception of the modern human condition. "Distress" is one of a battery of terms he employs to register that perception. Ours is an age of distress, a "destitute age" in which "meaninglessness" reigns and human beings are "abandoned" and "homeless."[19] The connection is quite explicit in the Rectoral Address. Unless the essence of the university can be reestablished, and the sciences rooted once more in philosophy/thinking, the "spiritual strength of the West" will collapse, as will what remains of culture, "dragging everything that is strong into confusion and letting it suffocate in madness."[20] It is not simply that the natural sciences, as "part of machine technology,"[21] are deeply implicated in the "gigantism" of the technological enterprise, the "total mobilization," that threatens to bring about the "devastation of the earth." In addition, though relatedly, the natural sciences, with their monochrome view of the world as merely so many "spatiotemporal magnitudes of motion,"[22] contribute to a levelling down, a flattening out, of everything. They render the world "boring," and the boredom they inspire is only warded off by the frenzied pursuit of "life-experiences," pointless titillation and "kicks."[23] No wonder that, to the degree the humanities survive in the modern university, they do so as so much cultural decoration. In the terminology Heidegger was increasingly to employ from the mid-1930s on, these various aspects of a contemporary "distress" belong to a late stage in that long process that he refers to as "the abandonment of be-ing."[24]

Two things may be emerging from my discussion. The first, already previewed, is that the interest and importance of Heidegger's reflections on the university and education more generally reside, if anywhere, in their integration into a whole constellation of related themes—those of science *versus* philosophy/thinking, of truth, and of the "distress" of modern humanity. So far, the connections among those themes have only been suggested, and several crucial terms, including 'the essence of science' and 'thinking' have been left unexplicated. A strategy for making the connections and explicating these terms is suggested by something else that may have emerged from the discussion. This is that that the central theme in the constellation, the one around which the others revolve, as it were, is that of *truth*. It was, recall, in terms of a special concern with truth in a special sense that Heidegger characterized the very idea of education. The contrast between science and philosophy/thinking was also drawn in terms of their respective relations to truth. And Heidegger's diagnosis of "distress" as the outcome of an "abandonment of be-ing" is one that he elaborates in terms of his notion of truth. There is abandonment of be-ing when be-ing no longer "holds sway" as the "en-joining," "sheltering," and "occurrence" of truth.[25]

Heidegger would approve of the metaphor of the notion of truth standing at the center of a whole constellation of further concepts. He is sympathetic to what he takes to be the point of the description, in Plato's allegory, of the prisoners' emergence from the cave and eventual ability to look at the sun. It is the description of an educative process that culminates in an understanding of truth, without which nothing is genuinely understood. In the following sections, I attempt to explain, in some detail, the centrality or priority of the notion of truth in Heidegger's thinking about the various notions, including education, that are under discussion.

THE ESSENCE OF TRUTH

Let me start with a brief overview of Heidegger's discussion of truth and of the momentous effects, in his view, which a change in our understanding of truth has carried in its wake. The primordial notion of truth was the early Greek one and was clearly indicated in their word for truth, aletheia—"unhiddenness" or "uncoveredness." The true is the unhidden, what is brought into the open or clearing, and for us to be in the truth is for us to be party to the uncovering of things, to their emergence into the open. That notion, however, was gradually to be displaced until, in the modern era, a quite different conception of truth dominates: that of the certainty and correctness of "representations," such as statements, which correspond to how the objects represented actually are. With that displacement, at least three other concomitant changes in our conceptions have come about. Philosophy/thinking, a meditative attention to the source and occurrence of the unhiddenness of things, gives way to science as the primary form of inquiry, for science is precisely the disciplined endeavor to arrive at correct, certain, and objective representations of the world. Second, the early Greeks' combination of wonder at the opening up of a world for them and a sense of being at home in a world where they are, so to speak, the shepherds of this "event" and the shelterers of what comes into the open, atrophies.[26] It is eventually replaced by the "distress" of modern men and women who, when they are not "tranquilising" themselves with "life-experiences," experience the world as an alien array of objects set over against themselves *qua* the "rational subjects" who represent and calculate these objects. Finally, one observes, even as early as Plato, a shift, now complete, from a conception of education as a process whereby people are brought to an experience and understanding of things in their unhiddenness to a conception of education as the amassing of information, of knowledge in the form of correct representations of objects.

It needs to be stressed that, for Heidegger, these concomitant changes are closely related functions or aspects of the shift from truth as aletheia to truth as the property of certain and correct representations of objects. Modern "distress"' fuels a mania for utility and expensive diversions that only technology and its bedmate, natural science, can quell. The consequent dominance of science, made central to modern systems of education, serves to drive out other forms of inquiry from educational institutions. Conversely, the conception of education as serving the accumulation of information reinforces the idea that it is only the sciences, not the "decorative" humanities of previous centuries, that are genuinely educative. This, in turn, serves to cement, among educated people, that "boring," "levelling," natural scientific conception of reality which is part of our modern distress.

To appreciate the position just sketched, we need to understand in more detail the shift in the conception of truth that Heidegger identifies and how, in his view, this episode in a seemingly abstract region of philosophical speculation could have such momentous consequences.

The currently dominant conception of truth as correct, certain representation is, for Heidegger, one among several possible versions of a wider, traditional conception of truth, the ontological foundations of which he examines in section 44 of *Being and Time* (from which the citations over the next few paragraphs all come). According to that traditional conception, the vehicles of truth are assertions or judgments, and their truth resides in their agreement with objects or facts. While this conception is not simply mistaken, Heidegger levels two criticisms against those who subscribe to it. First, they treat "agreement" as a matter of similarity between two entities, a representation and the object or fact represented. Like many Anglo-American critics of correspondence theories of truth, Heidegger rejects, as unintelligible, the idea of some likeness—some isomorphism—between such entities. Instead, he argues, we should think of a true assertion as disclosing or uncovering an object. "To say that an assertion 'is true' signifies that it uncovers the entity as it is . . . 'lets' the entity 'be seen' in its uncoveredness." Assertion, that is, is a kind of vicarious performance whereby, in lieu of bringing someone before an object, we uncover it for him.

But this means, second, that proponents of the traditional conception fail to recognize, typically, that it is not, after all, assertions or judgments which are the *primary* vehicles of truth. For it is *we—Dasein*—who disclose and uncover. "What is primarily 'true'—that is, uncovering—is *Dasein*." There are many ways in which "entities get snatched out of their hiddenness" by us: making true assertions is only one of these, and hence the truth of assertions derives from truth *qua* disclosing as a way of *Dasein*'s "being towards," "comportment towards," the world. The primordial conception of truth, therefore, from which traditional and current conceptions derive, is the Greek one of aletheia—"taking entities out of their unhiddenness and letting them be seen in their unhiddenness."

There are two implications of this account drawn by Heidegger that are especially relevant for understanding how the emergence and dominance of the derived conception are, in his view, of such moment. The first is that if *Dasein*, through disclosing and opening up things, is "in the truth," it is equally "in untruth": for *Dasein* can and, in "average," everyday "chatter" (*Gerede*), generally does at the same time disguise and cover up how things are. Indeed, this is inevitable, for if we reveal things in certain ways, then there are other ways in which they are not being revealed. Not all the veils can be snatched away simultaneously. Second, the derivation of the traditional and current conception from a primordial one is not just some interesting fact of history or etymology that we can note and then ignore. This is because the truth of assertions *remains* parasitic on truth as *Dasein*'s disclosive comportment towards the world. "Primordial 'truth' . . . is the ontological condition for the possibility that assertions can be either true or false." Only when domains of objects have been disclosed for *Dasein* through its "projects" and activities in the world, can we then go on to say anything true or false about these objects. This presupposition of factual discourse is something we forget, for quite generally, *Dasein* tends to get "absorbed" in the objects which concern it, hence to forget its own contribution to the very possibility of experiencing and encountering objects, and so to "understand itself in terms of what it encounters within-the-world." It is due to this forgetfulness and absorption that we treat truth as simply a relation between worldly entities, representations and their objects.

Before examining the relevance of these implications for Heidegger's discussion of science, philosophy, education, and distress, one needs to note certain changes in his account of truth that accompany—perhaps inspire—the "turn" in his wider thinking. In crude terms, the effect of the 'turn' is to attribute to being a good deal of what, in *Being and Time*, had been attributed to *Dasein*. In particular, truth now gets spoken of as "the fundamental trait of being itself," as the "clearing sheltering" of the "event of Be-ing."[27] It is now being that at once discloses and hides, uncovers and covers up. What gets "forgotten" is now the role of being itself, not *Dasein*'s, in opening up domains of objects to encounter and make assertions about. Even if, however, the change here is more than the largely terminological one that Heidegger liked to portray it as, one should not exaggerate the distance between the earlier and later accounts of truth. Aletheia remains the primordial notion of truth on which later conceptions remain parasitic. While *Dasein* is no longer the locus of truth, it is still essential to truth, since it is *to* human beings that anything is open or revealed: without them and their language, there would be no "clearing" for things to appear in, hence no truth *qua* unhiddenness. While being, not *Dasein*, hides as well as reveals, it remains that the penalty for any way of revealing things is that, in other ways, they are concealed. And while it is now a trait of being, not *Dasein*'s way of engaging with the world, that is "forgotten," it remains that the form of this amnesia is "absorption" in worldly objects at the expense of attention to the preconditions for there being a world to experience, encounter, and describe in the first place.

THE CENTRALITY OF TRUTH

We are now in a position to confirm and elaborate the sketch, at the start of the previous section, of how, for Heidegger, various related and momentous changes hinge on a shift in the understanding of truth.

Both within and without the university, the dominant mode of inquiry has become research: hence the dominance of those paradigmatic vehicles of disciplined research, the sciences. This "arriv[al] at science as research" occurred, says Heidegger, precisely because "truth has been transformed into the certainty of representation."[28] According to its own self-image, science is on the way to providing a uniquely correct and certain account of the world, one that corresponds to the way that reality independently is. As such, it is guilty of a failure to appreciate that, however correct its representations, it is also "in untruth": for, like any other way of revealing or disclosing the world, science is just "one way . . . in which all that is presents itself to us." Nature, as depicted by the sciences, is "only *one* way in which what presences . . . reveals itself." Relatedly, the sciences as such are "utterly incapable of gaining access to . . . their [own] essence"—to the preconditions that make scientific inquiry, and the true or correct assertions and theories which result, possible.[29] In particular, science fails to recognize that it operates upon an "*a priori* ground-plan" that only admits as "real" those entities which lend themselves to exact measurement, subsumption under law-like regularities, and experimental investigation.[30] It neither is nor could be a matter of scientific *discovery* that the world is simply a network of such entities, for scientific discoveries presuppose a determination so to regard the world.

If the reasons "science does not think" are that it fails to appreciate its own preconditions and that it is blind to its status as only one way of disclosing,[31] the implication is that philosophy/thinking, in not "forgetting" the more primordial notion of truth, is not similarly thoughtless. In *Being and Time*—the completed parts, at least—the primary task of philosophy is fundamental ontology, the existential analytic of *Dasein*'s way of being. Since truth, primordially understood, has a "primordial connection" with *Dasein*'s being, then truth crucially "comes within the range of . . . fundamental ontology."[32] A central role—*the* central role, perhaps—of philosophy is therefore reflection on the various ways *Dasein* discloses and covers up, is "in the truth" and "in untruth," and on the preconditions for any given way of disclosure, including science's, to be possible. With the emphasis switched to the disclosing role of being, similar remarks, suitably modulated, inform Heidegger's later conception of philosophy as thinking. If philosophy has decayed into "metaphysics," "historical erudition" and "system-building," this is because it has fallen prey to the understanding which prevails in the sciences. Revival of the great "first beginning" of philosophy/thinking among the Greeks requires, therefore, a "reverent paying heed to the unconcealment of what presences," "mindfulness" as "inquiring into . . . the truth of be-ing," including the manner in which *Dasein* serves as the medium, so to speak, through which the unconcealing of things by being is "shepherded" and made possible.[33]

That modern humanity no longer pays heed to, is no longer mindful of, this is at the root of its contemporary distress. For the general form of this distress is an unthinking absorption in, a being beseiged by, objects that, since they are no longer experienced against the background of a process of being's unconcealment, lose all depth, resonance, and mystery. "Hollowed-out" and thought of as simply *there* for objective measurement, they no longer invite wonder. With truth conceived of as a fixed relation between entities, assertions, and their objects, human beings lose all sense of themselves as being essentially engaged in the emergence of truth, in a process, that calls for "deep awe," whereby things emerge out of hiddenness into the light.[34] It is no objection, Heidegger explains, to the description of the present condition as one of distress that few people are aware of their distress. On the contrary, beseiged as they are by objects, absorbed in the world around them, people are without recollection of what has been lost. The symptoms of distress are everywhere, however: in frantic pursuit of life-experiences, in hysterical participation in mass-meetings, in adulation of sporting heroes, in blind devotion to technological progress, and so on.[35] Lives so lived are palpably bereft of the deep awe and wonder that obtain when there is mindfulness of truth—of a world arising from concealment.

It is, finally, the shift in the understanding of truth that underlies the mutation of paideia as a "passage" from one condition to another into "schooling" as the "calculated, swift, massive distribution of unununderstood information to as many as possible in the shortest possible time."[36] For the Greeks, education is an overcoming, of a condition of *apaideusia*, "lack of education," a condition of being "in the dark" where the young person is, as yet, unable to distinguish genuine ways of disclosing things from opinions, and mental habits that cover them up, leave them hidden and confused.[37] (Ironically, for Heidegger, it is Plato, whose allegory of the cave is the best testament to the Greek understanding of paideia, who is distantly responsible for its atrophy: for Plato replaced the notion of truth as unhiddenness by that of truth as "the correctness of the gaze," directed at the Forms. It is that latter conception which, after several modulations, results in the contemporary conception of truth as correct, measurable, certain representation of objects.)[38] The 'schooled' person piles up information, but it is "unununderstood" since he is without appreciation either of the status of the information—as belonging to just this or that particular way in which things are revealed—or of the possibility of, and the conditions for, access to the types of information he gathers.

APPRAISAL AND APPLICATION

I have tried to establish that Heidegger's remarks on education, schooling, and the university integrally belong to a much wider discussion of a
constellation of notions—science, distress, and so on—that revolve
around the notion of truth. It is, as Heidegger sees it, a momentous shift
in our understanding of truth that has brought in its wake the dominance
of science, the atrophy of philosophy/thinking, our contemporary distress, and a stunted conception of education. And it is here, in this vision,
if anywhere, that the depth and originality of his remarks reside.

Philosophers of education will want to ask what credence is to be given
to this vision and, if it can be, whether the vision is capable of informing,
at a tolerably concrete level, both criticism of modern education and pro-
posals for its redirection.

By making his discussion of education, science, and so on revolve
around his account of truth, Heidegger would seem to play hostage to fortune. That account is, at the very least, contentious and has been subjected
to sharp criticism by several commentators. It has been argued, for instance, that, despite the etymology of the word, the Greeks never meant
"unhiddenness" by "aletheia" and generally regarded assertions and beliefs as the primary bearers of truth. It has been contended, too, that it is
illegitimate to describe what may well be presupposed by the truth (and
falsity) of assertions—access to things through some manner of revealing
them—as truth itself. And it has been argued that Heidegger's characterization of truth as disclosure is either insufficient or marks no advance on
the traditional correspondence view. Disclosure or revelation *tout court*
cannot be true, since something may be falsely disclosed: but if one adds,
as Heidegger sometimes does, that the disclosure must be of something
"as it is in itself," it is difficult to see how this differs from the idea of truth
as correspondence with a fact.[39]

I shall assume that these criticisms are well taken. What, then, remains
of Heidegger's account of truth? If, by "his account," one means the definition of truth as disclosure or unhiddenness, then very little remains.
But if, more generously, one means a set of reflections germane to truth,
nearly everything does. That, in the Greeks' lexicon, "aletheia" did not
mean unhiddenness, does not show that they did not experience the
world in a manner that is lost to us—as an emergence or blossoming into
the open of dark, occluded processes. That it may be odd to describe as
truth what is presupposed by there being truths does not mean that there
are no such presuppositions and that accounts of truth which ignore those
presuppositions are stunted. That any disclosure may itself be mistaken
does not erase a crucial distinction between what is disclosed, accurately
or not, and what remains hidden. Nor, therefore, does it impugn Heideg-

ger's point that any given way of disclosure, by elbowing others out, entails that we are also "in untruth."

Granted that Heidegger's claims about truth, suitably rephrased, survive the criticisms I rehearsed, in what ways, if any, can they inform contemporary educational practice? It would be disappointing if they could not, given that, as I have tried to establish, his remarks on education revolve around those claims. At least two related reasons might be given for doubting any concrete engagement of these claims with practice. First, by the mid- to late-1930s—with the "turn" to the talk of Being, rather than of *Dasein*, as that which discloses, sends, and "holds sway"—Heidegger's position, for some commentators, has become a mystical, postmonotheistically religious one.[40] That position, whether intelligible or not, and whether attractive or not, is simply too remote from the preoccupations of our secular culture to have any impact on how young people are to be brought up in that culture. Second, doesn't Heidegger himself disavow the practical bearings of his reflections? The optimism of the Rectoral Address, in which Heidegger hoped for a "renewal of the people" through a new movement, National Socialism, under the guidance of universities that had rediscovered their philosophical roots, soon faded.[41] In writings shortly to follow, Heidegger accepts the inevitability, for the foreseeable future, of the dominance of science and technology, the reduction of the humanities to "cultural decoration," the transformation of education into information-grubbing "schooling," and so on. Only "the few and the rare" can hope to resist these processes, and they will do so, not through the efforts of schools and universities, but by attending to the poetry of Hölderlin—words in which Being itself "speaks." If Heidegger himself thinks that "the saving power" can only come from a direction so totally removed from the present and foreseeable realities of educational practice, why should we demur?

It is true, in my judgment, that the tone of Heidegger's later thinking is mystical and certainly its prevailing mood is quietistic. "Only a god can save us," as he put it in the famous interview of that name by *Der Spiegel* in 1966.[42] Two things should be noted, however, before concluding that Heidegger's reflections are without practical educational bearing. First, as argued above, the main threads of Heidegger's conception of truth remain relatively constant, despite "the turn." Second, even during the quietistic decades, Heidegger sometimes indicates respects in which, even in educational institutions, the message of his reflections on truth, science, and distress may be at least partly and modestly heeded. We do not have *just* to wait for the advent of "the last god." He writes, for example, that while science per se can never understand its own essence, "still every . . . teacher of the sciences . . . can keep reflection vigilant."[43] Again, some years later, he remarks that while, indeed, "the danger is still very great" that, in the universities, philosophy/thinking will be regarded as "hostile" and irrelevant to the sciences, there nevertheless exists scope for addressing scientists and for promoting "clarity concerning [science's] essential nature." There exists scope, too, for a kind of teaching that does not stuff with knowledge, but "lets learn," not least through enabling students to unlearn the fixities of thought in whose grip they are.[44]

Modest as the ambitions indicated in these remarks are, they are genuine and feasible ones with which many people critical of the current culture of education must sympathize. The outstanding feature of that culture, which Heidegger was already remarking on in the early 1930s, is the dominance of the natural sciences and of other forms of inquiry closely allied to, or modelling themselves upon, these. This dominance is attested to less by the volume of resources—money, slots on the curriculum, and so on—devoted to the sciences, but by a deeply rooted perception that it is the sciences alone that are the proper and finally authoritative repositories of knowledge and understanding. This is a perception evidenced as much by what is denied of the humanities as by what is proclaimed on behalf of science. The humanities are not vehicles of knowledge or truth, for there, all is "interpretation" and "opinion." The point of moral and religious reflection, for example, is not to arrive at truth, but to set out what choices of values, lifestyles, or beliefs are available to the individual. With such a conception of the humanities prevailing, they indeed become "cultural decoration," for who is to take with due seriousness convictions and tastes that, as contemporary rhetoric continually proclaims, are nothing but "individual preferences"? ("No one dies for mere values," Heidegger once remarked.)[45]

If Heidegger is right, this culture of education—indeed, of society at large—is deeply flawed. The sciences cannot be the repositories of objective, presuppositionless truth that is imagined, for they are the products of a determination to restrict what is to count as knowledge of the world to a particular domain. The sciences are no more *the* way of truly revealing or disclosing how reality is than the modes of thinking and activity which they have driven out—or driven into the realm of subjective impression and "choice." Here is not the place to elaborate on the shape of an educational enterprise in which these considerations are given due weight.[46] And perhaps such elaborations would be a waste of time. Perhaps Heidegger was right, in his most pessimistic mood, to predict "a gigantic progress of sciences in the future . . . advancements [that] will bring . . . rearing and training of humans into conditions . . . whose onset can neither be hindered nor even held up in any way."[47] But some of us would hope that he is right when, in a less fatalistic mood, he discerns the "signs" of a "world-age in which that which is worthy of questioning will someday again open the door" to reflection on "what is essential."[48] Lacking a crystal ball, we may as well play our small part in trying to pry open that door.

NOTES

1. See, for example, Stephen Horrocks, *"Heidegger and Nurse Education"* (Ph.D. thesis, University of Durham, England, 1998). On the implications for teaching generally of Heidegger's wider philosophy, see Michael Bonnett, *Children's Thinking* (London: Cassell, 1994).

2. The texts on which I mainly draw, with abbreviated titles in brackets for further references, are: *Die Selbstbehauptung der deutschen Universität* [*Universität*] (Frankfurt: Klostermann, 1983); "The Rectorate 1933/34: Facts and Thoughts" ["Rectorate"], trans. K. Harries, *Review of Metaphysics*, 1985; "The Age of the World Picture" ["World Picture"] and "Science and Reflection" ["Reflection"], in *The Question Concerning Technology (and other essays)*, trans. W. Lovitt (New York: Harper & Row, 1977); "Plato's Doctrine of Truth' ["Plato"], trans. T. Sheehan, in *Pathmarks, ed. W. McNeill* (Cambridge: Cambridge University Press, 1998)); "What Calls For Thinking? (from *What Is Called Thinking?*)" ["Thinking"], trans. F. Wieck & L. Glenn Gray, in *Basic Writings: Martin Heidegger* [*Basic Writings*], ed., D. F. Krell, (London: Routledge, 1993); *Contributions to Philosophy (From Enowning)* [*Contributions*], trans. P. Emad and K. Maly, (Bloomington: Indiana University Press, 1999); and *Being and Time*, trans. J. Macquarrie and E. Robinson (Oxford: Blackwell, 1980).

3. "Rectorate," 483.

4. *Universität*, 12. It is regrettable that this lecture, delivered in 1933 on Heidegger's assumption of the Rectorship at Freiburg, is usually read only as a testament to his National Socialism. Not only is this to ignore the lecture's main theme, the "essence" of the university, but it primes one to misunderstand the points Heidegger is making. Thus, as Julian Young rightly observes, Heidegger was calling for, "not the subordination of the university to the state, but precisely the reverse." *Heidegger, Philosophy, Nazism* (Cambridge: Cambridge University Press, 1997), 20.

5. "Rectorate," 483.

6. "Rectorate," 482; *Universität*, 13; 'What is Metaphysics?" in *Basic Writings*, 94.

7. "Reflection," 157.

8. See, for example, *Contributions*, 104–7.

9. *Contributions*, 108.

10. "World Picture," 120.

11. *Contributions*, 103.

12. "Reflection," 170.

13. See especially Husserl's *The Crisis of European Sciences and Transcendental Phenomenology*, trans. D. Carr, (Evanston: Northwestern University Press, 1970). The book proper is a late work of the 1930s, but the appendices in the English edition contain earlier material.

14. *Contributions*, 108.

15. *Thinking*, 371.

16. *Universität*, 11.

17. *Contributions*, 99.

18. "Plato," 170.

19. On "distress," "homelessness," etc., see, for example, *Contributions*, Parts I & II, and *Discourse on Thinking*, trans. J. Anderson and E. Freund (New York: Harper & Row, 1966).

20. *Universität*, 19.

21. *Contributions*, 107.

22. "World Picture," 119.

23. See *Contributions*, Part II. The theme of boredom had been explored at length in *The Fundamental Concepts of Metaphysics* (1929–30), trans. W. McNeill and N. Walker (Bloomington: Indiana University Press, 1995). The theme of "levelling" or "averaging," though not in connection with the sciences, had also been an important one in *Being and Time*, section 27.

24. In *Contributions*, Heidegger uses 'be-ing' (his translators' rendering of the archaic German "*Seyn*") for being as it should be thought of, as distinct from how, in Western metaphysics, it has generally come to be thought of (as a kind of fundamental entity, like God, say, or as a "formal" property of everything that exists). One should note, too, that the expression "abandonment of be-ing" is intentionally ambiguous, referring both to our abandoning (forgetting) of be-ing and to be-ing's abandonment of us.

25. *Contributions*, 22.

26. Such metaphors abound in "Letter on Humanism," in *Basic Writings*, 213–65.

27. "Plato," 179; *Contributions*, 22.

28. "World Picture," 127.

29. "Reflection," 156, 174, 177.

30. "World Picture," 118ff. It is, incidentally, because of this preemptive "ground-plan" to admit only what is measurable and experimentally manipulable that, for Heidegger, science partakes in "the essence of technology" ("Thinking," 379). That science also and importantly contributes to the technological enterprise is a further and, for him, less essential point.

31. "Thinking', 373.

32. *Being and Time*, 34, 256.

33. "Reflection," 164; *Contributions*, 31.

34. *Contributions*, 91.

35. See, for example, *Introduction to Metaphysics*, trans. R. Mannheim (New Haven: Yale University Press, 1959), 36–7.

36. *Contributions*, 85.

37. "Plato," 167.

38. "Plato," 177.

39. For these criticisms see, especially, Ernst Tugendhat, "Heidegger's Idea of Truth," in *Critical Heidegger*, ed. C. Macann (London: Routledge, 1996), 226–40.

40. See, especially, Herman Philipse, *Heidegger's Philosophy of Being: A Critical Interpretation* (Princeton: Princeton University Press, 1998), Sections 11 & 16.

41. "Rectorate," 483ff.

42. Trans. M. Alter & J. Caputo, *Philosophy Today*, 20, 1976, 267–84.

43. "Reflection," 181–82.

44. "Thinking," 378 and 380.

45. "World Picture," 142.

46. A couple of fairly recent attempts at this sort of elaboration are John White, *Education and Personal Well-Being in a Secular Universe* (London: University of London Institute of Education, 1995), and David E. Cooper, "Educational Philosophies and Cultures of Philosophy," in *50 Years of Philosophy of Education: Progress and Prospects,* ed. G. Hayden (London: University of London Institute of Education, 1998), 23–40.

47. *Contributions,* 108.

48. "Reflection," 181.

3

Martin Heidegger, Transcendence, and the Possibility of Counter-Education

Ilan Gur-Ze'ev

Normalizing education has many faces. At its best it is power realizing its responsibility for the efficient subjectification of the subject and its pleasures. Within the process of subjectification it produces the "I." In the course of its production, the "I" is constituted as a focus of selfhood in a manner that ensures the identification of the subject with the present order of things, reinforces its justifications, and makes possible the invisibility of the violence which construct and represent it as "reality." Normalizing education guarantees efficient orientation in the given order of things, perfects competence in its classification and representation, and allows communication and functional behavior, success, security, pleasure, and social progress.[1] It distributes these competences, knowledge, and powers in a socially uneven manner, creating or reproducing social and cultural asymmetries and violences within the system. It not only permits human social life and its normalities, it even constitutes its telos. This success, however, has its price: it opens the gate to reflection, resistance, alternative orders, and unexpected new versions of normalization and standardization. Even in such situations, not solely in situations of stability, it must ensure the constitution of the normalized subject as a false not-yet-"I"; as an unproblematic product of the subjectification processes. As long as normalizing education is unchallenged, the human comes upon her relation to the Other, to the world, and to herself while imprisoned in the framework of never-fully-deciphered representation apparatuses. Even if unconsciously, she faces the full toll of the efficiency of the representation apparatuses in the form of "the given" limitations and possibilities. As existential, political, and theoretical "realities," these horizons actually manifest her very existence as a constant downfall. This is so since "reality" and her own self are constructed by the manipulations, traditions, structures, and powers that she can reflect on or challenge only through the ways, tools, and manner imposed on her by the very system whose logic and "vocabulary" are to be questioned, resisted, and overcome. Normalizing education does not "influence" or "limit" the self: it actually produces the "I" and the self-evidence of the self. In this respect, normalizing education produces the human subject as some-thing and prevents her from becoming some-one, a true subject. Normalizing education achieves this by internalizing in the subject from "outside" the conceptual apparatus, the moral yardsticks and ideals, the consciousness, and the main actual possibilities for reflectivity and social behavior. It governs even the human possibilities for encountering the otherness of the Other and knowledge about knowledge. Even knowledge and evidence about the otherness of the "I" are fabricated by normalizing education. The annihilation of the subject's otherness is a bona fide manifestation that the human subject is more than the product of the powers that fabricate and control her, that reduce her to an object of care, education, salvation, and oppression. She is much more than what she was directed to become.

But what if not only knowledge and knowledge about knowledge, but even yardsticks to categorize, evaluate, and receive/reject knowledge, values, fears, and quests are nothing but manifestations of the productivity of normalizing education, which is effective enough to hide its violence from its victims, who are created by, and to make them, its most devoted agents? What if, in the end, our sense of evidence, certainty, and desirability manifest the efficiency of the creative violence of normalizing education? In this light we should ask: Is there room for "genuine," "authentic" reflection, dialogue, and transcendence from omnipotent meaninglessness? Is there room at least for a tragic sense of life, real nihilism, or even real overcoming of the quest for life, for meaning, or for happiness in such a closed system? There are several answers to this challenge, but here I offer only one, which is a conditional "yes." Yes—but only if this closure is not quite entire or unchallenged. That is, the world and the human are infinite in a way that also includes antagonistic elements of a kind that might fertilize an essential alternative to normalizing education, one that is not just another version of normalizing education. "But," one should ask, "is there any serious justification for talking about the possibility of counter-education as a different stance in life, which transcends the conflicting versions of normalizing education, many of which pride themselves on being emancipatory, different, ever more radical, or anti/counter-educations?"

Below I suggest that the philosophy of Martin Heidegger is of much relevance for the elaboration of an attempt to open the gate to counter-education as an open possibility. An attempt of this kind already challenges the triumph of normalizing education. From its part, counter-education is far from an unproblematic alternative. It is a very dangerous path, and the reconstruction of Heidegger's philosophy of education suggested here will manifest this danger.

The centrality of the concept of transcendence results from the severity of the struggle over meaning, from the despair invested in the search for a meaningful manner to relate to the human as a subject. Such a search is conditioned by the possibility of a very special moment. It is a moment of transcendence from thingness. This "moment" in itself is the beginning of elevation. It is immanent to life as an effort for overcoming the closure of contextualism, of the situateness of each perusal, quest, and act. Every such moment, indeed, every "moment," incubates a promise for transcendence. It is embedded within this special kind of relation to human existence as transcendence, as elevation in, but also from, the context which constructs the human as an object of manipulation, as one among countless beings, materials, or merchandise. Is it justified to speak about the human if she or he does not ask the question of Being and cannot but become but a mere manifestation of the violence of the context—be this as an effect of the manipulations, traditions, or present horizons that are arbitrarily imposed by social-cultural-technological structures? If the context, the situation, or the human enframing merely reflect the omnipotent contingent arbitrariness of the context, then what it actually ensures is this: a perfect dehumanization of the human subject. If the situatedness is totalistic, closed, and contingent, and has no invitation or room for the presence of the totally other, talk of dehumanization processes is unjustified. This is because from the very beginning, in her essence, the human subject has no room to exist as a subject or to engage in a meaningful relation to her stolen subjectivity as a manifestation of her humanity.

Nor is there any air for the human to breathe within conditions of total "freedom"; where nothing within the "I," the context, or the transcendental can reveal/enforce alienation and becomes sparse in terms of an aim, meaning, yardstick, or impetus—as in the Utopia of the cyberoptimists. The category of transcendence as an open possibility manifests or preconditions the humanity of the subject. It manifests itself as a social and individual process of overcoming the given horizons, the present conditions, or the fabricated/revealed truths, internalized strivings, fears, and hopes, as well as the power of the hegemonic representation apparatuses. The minimalist claim is that the subject can be human as a subject of discourse, as a manifestation of a position he or she holds within a system, whereby she can offer resistance and repositioning—although not transcendence.

Yet even this claim is still grounded on a concept of transcendence.[2] But, one can ask, what if this quest or this reasoning, too, is nothing but one of the manifestations of the hegemonic representation apparatuses? What, then, would be the first step in challenging normalizing education, which often manifests itself in the form of extreme skepticism, relativism, escapism, and antiphilosophical orgies? For centuries Western and Eastern philosophies committed themselves to respond to this challenge, and Heidegger's contribution here is of special importance. It is particularly so in face of postmodern conditions in which traditional dichotomies such as subject-object, real-imaginative, center-margin, same-different, and even human-machine or culture-nature, have been transformed.

Heidegger too is occupied with the question that concerns us here in various articulations, relating to the possibility of overcoming meaninglessness or the possibility of transcending from unauthentic to authentic life.

At first glance Heidegger "solves" the traditional problem of the gap between the known/unknown object and the knowing/failed attempts/vain attempts of the knowing subject. This is apparent in his refusal to develop the subject-object problematic within the framework of traditional Western realism, relativism, skepticism, and solipsism. Accordingly, in his philosophy the possibilities and limitations of transcendence from ignorance to knowledge or from evil to worthy life, or the question of redemption come to a turning point in Western thought.

According to Heidegger the human being as *Dasein* is not like a stone, one of the beings who is positioned as an object among other objects. The presence in the world of *Dasein* differs from that of a stone or a table in the sense that these are parts of *Dasein's* world who is the center of this world within which the *Dasein* works, concerns, uncovers, forgets, or transcends himself from or in face of nothingness. The world of appearances, or reality, is not to be understood as "objective," in the sense that its existence is unconditioned by the will or recognition of the human being. For Heidegger, the being-there of the *Dasein* is not to be understood as if it merely exists within a physical space or within another essential content. The human "being-there" is exclusively human. While rejecting the traditional attempts to overcome skepticism or produce proofs to the existence of reality,[3] Heidegger's being-in-the-world of the *Dasein* projects human creativity on all other beings. It is not "within" but part of being-in-the-world in which the human becomes a meaningful reality and reveals the world within a mode of existence as a human existential. "If *Dasein* is understood correctly, it defies such proofs, because, in its Being, it already *is* what subsequent proofs deem necessary to demonstrate for it," says Heidegger.[4]

Transcendence is the fundamental structure of the subjectivity of the subject. This is why in the traditional sense for Heidegger there is no transcendence: for him it is immanent in human existence. If the subject were not constantly on the move, did not transcend beyond the given, she would not be a subject. "To be a subject means to transcend. This means that *Dasein* does not exist as something that transcends from itself from time to time—the fundamental meaning of his existence is the transcendence beyond the given."[5] While being-in-the-world as a creator of the world and as concern (*Besorgen*), *Dasein* manifests itself simultaneously in authentic and in unauthentic life. Freedom manifests itself in both. This is how existence manifests itself not as a fact, or reality, but as a possibility.

A dialectical tension exists between the concept of the constant partiality of the *Dasein*, as being-there which is committed to self-overcoming, and Heidegger's concept of the human subject who conceives herself as a constant possibility to become wholeness. This tension manifests the uniqueness of the human as a special being among beings, who, as in the traditional concept of God, creates/subordinates all beings, all nonhuman beings as a manifestation of her freedom.

Heidegger's concept of freedom avoids moral or other hierarchical models of concern. In his philosophy, authentic life possibilities do not stand in hierarchical relation with unauthentic life. Both are but manifestations of the exile of Being. In this respect, at first glance "genuine" transcendence seems impossible in Heidegger's philosophy, given the human condition. Later on we will see two versions of transcendence in his philosophy. These are two levels of problematizing the possibility of transcendence in the sense of confronting the possibility of overcoming meaninglessness. The two versions of transcendence are of special importance for the evaluation of Heidegger's contribution to philosophy of education, offering a theoretical framework for the elaboration of the possibility of counter-education.

The existential possibilities of normalizing education as well as those of counter-education are always manifested in concrete relations and in specific historical arenas, even if they are never reducible to power relations and to efficiency of political struggles. This stance makes a special contribution to the attempt to avoid self-contained, easy going, "emancipatory" educational projects. Often these projects introduce pedagogies for the oppressed, for overcoming contextualism in the form of hegemonic consciousness and unjust structural power relations. They avoid being swallowed by instrumentalist-oriented educational projects. These are normally functionalistic in their nature and are committed to improving the adaptation of the human being to the governing facts, improving humans' productivity, "success," and pleasures while serving as an agent of the governing violences. Both "conservative" and "emancipatory" trends represent normalizing education, which counter-education should resist. A possible resistance should refer to Heidegger's concept of transcendence.

As we have seen, for Heidegger, transcendence is immanent to the *Dasein*, yet at the same time it has an ontological framework which positions as a normal human situation unauthentic concern and oblivion of the call of Being. Heidegger's conception of the ontological conditions for transcendence makes transcendence to authentic life or a worthy struggle such a rare situation on the one hand and ultimately imaginary and futile on the other. Before examining this any further, we should revisit his dividing lines between the categories of authenticity and unauthenticity.

For Heidegger, the human subject can exist only by self-overcoming, which as an authentic existence reveals itself in the moment of conceiving herself—and her surroundings—as some-thing, and will open herself to the call, to her or his mission of revealing the openness of Being in beings and in herself. She manifests herself as a creator in realizing the call of Being and manifests her uniqueness in disclosing the thingness of the world. *Dasein* is "the location of the truth of Being."[6] For Heidegger, "the essence of man consists in his being more than merely human, if this is represented as being a rational creature."[7] This is revealed when he responds to the call of Being: "Man is the shepherd of Being. Man loses nothing in this 'less'; rather, he gains in that he attains the truth of Being. He gains the essential poverty of the shepherd, whose dignity consists in being called by Being itself into the preservation of Being's truth."[8] Man in his authentic existence, as the shepherd of Being, is in an ecstatic "homelessness."[9] This is the Heideggerian understanding of realizing human responsibility as "ecstatic dwelling in the nearness of Being"[10] which enables the *Dasein* to face meaninglessness, to confront the question of Being, and to exit authentically in face of the *Daseinfrage* (question of Being).

The possibility of authentic life is inseparable from the question of truth. But here the question of truth is not revealed as an epistemological question within a correspondence theory but as an erotic posing of the question of the truth of Being. As the shepherd of Being, the human subject is not a mere thing, one of the beings which does not concern for the question of Being and the truth of his mission. He has a responsibility, an aim to fulfill—to face the absence of the call by which he is to be awakened. The response to the absent call fertilizes a creative self-positioning which is anti-instrumental or anti-goal oriented.

The Heideggerian concept of truth as *a-letheia* as *Ent-bergung* (dis-covery, un-covering, un-veiling) confronts *Verbergung* (concealment), closure, and thingness. Transcendence in the authentic ex-istence realizes concern as un-covering, as opposed to the possibility of oblivion of human responsibility and being swallowed in an opposite, unauthentic concern in the given appearances as an alternative mode of existence.

Angst (anxiety) normally drives the human subject away from himself. It prevents him from facing his situateness as being—thrown (*geworfen*) into meaninglessness (as manifested in accepted truths, values, and ways of life), of the Man and of a way of being-in-the-world which is contrasted to itself, and as such realizes itself in an unauthentic existence (*Uneigentliches Dasein*).[11] Authenticity is here revealed as a human existential in which the presence of the absence of wholeness manifests itself as a human question. It is exactly the absence of the presence of wholeness which enables the authentic human subject to face the partiality and creative meaninglessness which surrounds him—as a precondition to turning himself to the wholeness, to the infinity of nothingness beyond the given reality. This is manifested in being-towards-death.[12] Anxiety is not only the way for a human to experience her or his authentic experience of death as being-towards-not-being. This is where, for Heidegger, freedom manifests itself: when deciding for authenticity and against unauthenticity not as a realization of a positive Utopia but as a manifestation of realizing responsibility for overcoming all false promises of optimistic, purpose-oriented projects. Freedom reveals itself in letting-things-be.[13]

To be authentic the human subject must overcome the governing world of facts, the realm of self-evidence or "proved" truths and resist the threats and temptations of security, pleasure, and success offered by the Other, by society. Then, and only then, in face of the anxiety,[14] of confronting the infinity of nothingness and of homelessness, will the overcoming of the given be possible and truth as uncovering realize itself in human transcendence.

Da-sein means: being held out into the nothing. Holding itself out into the nothing, Dasein is in each case already beyond beings as a whole. This being beyond beings we call "transcendence." If in the ground of its essence Dasein were not transcending, which now means, if it were not in advance holding itself out into the nothing, then it could never be related to beings nor even to itself.[15]

This kind of unveiling as letting-things-be is essentially different from normal violence directed at imposing realities and meanings. It represents a concept of transcendence as enlightening—and not as a violent penetration. It is this alternative concept of transcendence, which allows this *Lichtung* (enlightening) in which Being, which is normally veiled and exiled, reveals itself.

Threatened and utterly disquieted as man is by the infinity of nothingness, the authentic subject approaches the things in the world in a unique, never-determined or instrumentalized manner. In this sense she transcends from unauthentic existence, faces things in their veiled situateness, and sees in light of Being the original, not-yet-revealed meaning of the things as they actually are. In this anti-utopian concept of transcendent freedom, in authentic existence, there must at the same time be a binding-to what-is. Precisely the authentic human in an act of free creation manifests her infinite openness, letting-a-being-be what it actually is.

> But when the gods are named originally and the essence of things receives a name, so that things for the first time shine out, human existence is brought into a firm relation and is given a basis.[16]

This authentic self-positioning, while transforming the human condition and realizing transcendence from unauthentic into authentic existence, ultimately manifests human freedom as openness. This openness makes possible infinite possibilities and realizations of the letting-be of things in the sense of unveiling the Being within beings. Only as such does it reclaim the truth of Being, which is what poets and philosophers—when true to their mission—represent:

> To "dwell poetically" means: to stand in the presence of the gods and to be involved in the proximity of the essence of the things. Existence is "poetical" in its fundamental aspect—which means at the same time: in so far as it is established (founded), it is not a recommence but a gift.[17]

It is not only that morally there is no difference between authentic and unauthentic life. An authentic decision to realize human freedom which uncovers what normally is veiled and abandoned is ultimately revealed as one of the manifestations of the veiling/unveiling games of Being which in itself manifests the infinity of nothingness, its aimlessness, and meaninglessness. This is so, even when the human is transcended into authentic life and "dwells poetically" as an ecstatic creator. In this sense, in Heidegger's philosophy, there is no redemption.

Freedom manifests itself here as a transcending power: as a binding call to the human mission as the shepherd of Being and as a Dionysian response to the call of Being—which ultimately is revealed as the call of his own lonely, finite, consciousness. As such it cannot but reveal the illusions and the abyss of untruth—as part of the a priori structure of the essence of truth. But mostly the human subject is far from authenticity and from the kind of openness that makes possible transcendence, self-creation, and unveiling the truth of Being. She is deprived of sensibility and power for responding to her mission and to the call of her own conscious mind.[18]

The normalized subject is swallowed by the meaninglessness of the "Them"; she forgets herself as a finite openness towards infinity, exiled from the possibility of living in the nearness of Being. This is the starting point of transcendence from unauthenticity towards authenticity, when the human subject faces nothingness as the only gate to the endless struggle for worthy life, for true, frightening, religious existence. The traditional category of God is here replaced by nothingness, and the traditional concept of love of God as the ultimate manifestation of religiosity is here replaced by true transcendence into authentic life. It is of vital importance, however, to acknowledge that ontologically, for Heidegger, transcendence alone does not offer a positive Utopia into truth as something positively attainable and as a gate for rest or nirvana. The various versions of unauthentic life and their concerns offer transcendence too, but only as an escape from the anxiety of facing nothingness and the infinity of empty freedom; an escape from an endless, never-guaranteed, struggle for fulfilling the responsibility which does not offer a new Garden of Heaven in the form of dogma or a formed "way of life."

The historical fascinating success of normalizing education is offered a grounded explanation by Heidegger's philosophy: the possibility of unauthentic concern and unauthentic transcendence opens the gate for the human subject to flee from herself, from her responsibility, and from freedom as a danger. This is in the form of retreats into the "Them," into the Other after he was deprived of his otherness. The "Them" replaces the Being-there as part of the possibilities of being-there. In contrast to authentic dialogue with the Other, normalizing education offers escape from loneliness and from the anxiety of ecstatic presence of the exile of the truth of Being. The "poetic dwelling" is represented by poets such as Hölderlin, whose poetry targets the essence of language, the exile of the gods, and the possibility of being *"between"* "the gods" and "the people"[19] as manifestation of "this conversation, which we are."[20] The surrendering of the subject to the manifestations of normalizing education is not to be reduced to mere power relations and manipulations, as suggested by critical pedagogy or the postcolonial, multicultural, and feminist pedagogies of the day. In their rush for optimistic critique, "solutions," and languages of "possibilities," these alternatives ignore what Heiddeger's thought teaches us: that the abandonment of the subject contains much more than a mere self-neglecting enhanced by "exterior" manipulations. It is one of the ways by which Being reveals itself. Only as such does it represent an existential tiredness. And as such it constitutes the human's eternal companion. Like other modes of being-towards-death, this one, too, makes possible concern for the given realities as an escape. An escape from the human's mission to face the exile of the gods and the omnipotence of meaninglessness (from which accepted truths, meanings, values, yardsticks, perspectives, and identities spring).

This escape is responsible for creating objective validity, justifications for the "realities" and the calculative logic of control, production, and representation in science, technology, and society. The rationality and

efficient, functionalist, objective justifications of the "They," or of normalizing education, to which the subject flees in his Fall (*Verfall*), are
not "false." In the present order of thing,s it "really" offers more efficient understanding of human life and constitutes an unproblematic
promise of redemption, security, truth, justice, pleasure, or success,
compared with the "unrealistic" reflective, transcendental impulse as it
is galvanized in counter-education. The "Fall" expresses not a historical "mistake" or an outcome of unfortunate conditions to be optimisti-
cally replaced or corrected by efficient political struggle and emancipatory education; "Falling" here expresses the essential ontological
structure of *Dasein* itself: "Dasein evades its very self."[21] This "Fall" is
manifested in modern science and technology and indeed in the very
possibility of genuine thinking, learning, and teaching.

According to Heidegger, modern science and technology are instrumental-
oriented. We may even use the word "oppressive," even if he does not, since
he tries to avoid dichotomies such as oppressive-emancipatory. Modern science and technology challenge truly human possibilities and demolish the
uniqueness of the things in the world which might have some call upon
human beings in their unconcealment to a life in which they may come to realize freedom in truth. In its essence technology is a central element of openness towards life and a flourishing of nonstandardized life possibilities:
"Technology is a mode of revealing. Technology comes to presence in the
realm where revealing and unconcealment take place, where aletheia, truth,
happens."[22] Technology is no mere means. Quite the opposite. In its origin, in
its essence, technology is *techne*, which for the Greeks did not refer only to the
activities and skills of the craftsman but also to the arts of the mind and the
fine arts. "*Techne* belongs to bringing-forth, to *poiesis*; it is something poetic."[23]

Modern technology and modern science also display—but in an essentially different way, namely in an instrumental, calculating, and subordi-
nate manner—a diminishing of the otherness, the uniqueness of the object.
"Everywhere everything is ordered to stand by, to be immediately on
hand, indeed to stand there just so that it may be on call for a further ordering. . . . We call it the standing-reserve (*Bestand*)."[24] Within this process,
modern science and technology transform man himself into a standing-
reserve. Enframing and unconcealment as roads to realizing human
freedom are blocked in a manner that does not enable the human to acknowledge and challenge it. Modern education is part of this process of dis-
mantling the possibilities for self-constitution, of life as unconcealment. Instead life becomes a concern and a response to the call of instrumental,
calculated thinking and its fabrications. This is where education can celebrate its victory over the possibilities for counter-education. "When thinking comes to an end by slipping out of its element it replaces this loss by

procuring a validity for itself as *techne,* as an instrument of education and therefore as a classroom matter and later a cultural concern."[25]

As we can see, Heidegger makes no effort to contribute to normalizing education or to scientific thinking and its successful reduction to the progress of technology, elevation of "the standard of living," propagating "joy," or enhancing "success." Nor can he contribute, as some scholars would suggest, to the improvement of schooling and the elevation of teacher-pupil relations. He is interested in something very different: in life. This is where his conception of transcendence is anchored.

Within the framework of his attraction to thinking as a mode of transcendence but never as means, medium, or instrument, he offers an important alternative to normalized human relations and to the kind of schooling and teacher-pupil relations which are only too common and so well known to us. This is exemplified especially clearly in his "What calls for thinking?"

The situateness of the human determines his possibilities for reflection[26] and the kind of resistance she will put up to the closure of "her" horizons. In modern *Ge-stell,* in the human's being framed in modernity as advanced by modern science and technology, human situateness ensures the oblivion of the mission of the human, of life as something more than mere life. But for Heidegger, framing has deeper roots and is not to be reduced to a specific historical situation. It springs from the very fact of situateness of human life, of always living enframed. In this sense there is not much truth in the rhetoric of emancipation and the promises of all positive utopias. Thinking itself is actually exiled while alternatives such as science celebrate their triumph. "Science does not think."[27] But if there is no air left for thinking for the modern human subject, how might true learning and teaching be experienced? In what sense is authentic transcendence possible?

According to Heidegger, who does not make the differentiation between a teacher and an educator, "to learn means to make everything we do answer to whatever addresses itself to us as essential."[28] We can, however, struggle for possibilities for learning, even in the face of the exile of thinking. In a certain respect it is exactly the absence of thinking that makes learning, thinking, and transcendence possible. But this is possible insofar as we start by radically unlearning what thinking has been traditionally. Heidegger's antifunctionalist, antipositivist, and anti-instrumentalist attitudes are manifested here, too. Genuine teaching is not a successful transmission of knowledge. "What teaching calls for is this: to let learn."[29] This is also the reason why teaching is more difficult than learning. The teacher is ahead of his apprentices in this alone, that he has still far more to learn than they—he has to learn to let them learn.

This is also why he has to be far less sure of his material than those who learn are of theirs. This conception of teaching is very close to Heidegger's concept of unconcealing, which opens free relations between the human and beings in their openness, or of relating to the open-being. Since this kind of teacher is not instrumental and does not transmit information, "his conduct, therefore, often produces the impression that we really learn nothing from him."[30]

So even in face of the success of modern science and technology, even in face of the present situateness, even in face of the absence of thinking, transcendence into learning to think is still an open human possibility. The presence of the absence of thinking does not halt genuine learning—and unlearning: it is its starting point.

> Once we are so related and drawn to what withdraws, we are drawing into what withdraws, into the enigmatic and therefore mutable nearness of its appeal. Whenever man is properly drawing that way, he is thinking—even though he may still be far away from what withdraws, even though the withdrawal may remain as veiled as ever.[31]

But in what sense is that which calls us to think preferable to concealment, framing, and unauthentic life? For Heidegger there is no way to justify the one rather than the other. In this sense, on Heideggerian grounds there is no way to favor this kind of learning over the conventional kind. The two ways represent opposing versions of concern.

The reception of Heidegger's ideas in the field of philosophy of education and within different pedagogies varies. Some scholars claim that it has no relevance whatsoever, or at least that he never really had a great deal to say about education.[32] Some see Heidegger's educational implications as nothing but "nonsense."[33] Others are basically critical of his "abstractness" and still others propose various means to "implement," instrumentalize, or domesticate Heidegger's philosophy and make it "relevant" to actual teaching in schools.[34] For all their differences, these responses to Heidegger's thought consider it in respect of schooling and normalizing education. Even at their best, when following Heidegger they refer to teaching as an artistic, noninstrumental process.[35]

Normalizing education, as was shown, guarantees not only security, prosperity, cooperation, and reproduction; it offers even concern and transcendence. This kind of concern, however, represents an abandonment of another kind of concern, an authentic one, which does not satisfy itself by successful imposition on the things in the world; it does not fulfill itself as technological success or social cooperation and solidarity.

This other kind of concern makes another kind of transcendence possible. Here truth as letting-be the otherness of beings realizes human freedom. It is transcendence not as "progress" or self-oblivion but as an outcome of the worthy suffering of facing meaninglessness and living-towards-death. As such, transcendence faces the infinity of nothingness and makes the absent freedom and truth present. It becomes what Heidegger never speaks of: worthy suffering. It sheds light on the futility of the mere thingness in the beings which have been stripped of their uniqueness by human instrumentalism. Worthy suffering makes possible a kind of transcendence, which allows reflection on the production of meanings, identities, and quests. It even reflects on the representation apparatuses and their manipulations.[36] But can it also offer transcendence from pain/pleasure into the worthy suffering/happiness of facing the truth of Being/nothingness as a transcendence into a worthier way of life? Into the terrain of truths which are not fabricated by successful violent manipulations? Is there a way of transcending metaphysical violence itself in the form of the closure/arbitrariness of enframing (*Ge-stell*), of human beings as standing-reserve (*Bestand*), of the limits of language and the effects of the essence of Being as ontological exile?

The kind of counter-education to which Heidegger's concepts of "unlearning," unconcealment," and "transcendence" are not foreign is still voiceless. It cannot become institutionalized or avoid becoming a dogmatic positive Utopia. It should avoid the quest for "authentic authority" and the acceptance of mundane violence as a tool for overcoming metaphysical violence as it is invested in normalizing education. When counter-education is not true to itself, in the name of authenticity and transcendence it will speak, with Heidegger, the vulgar language of National Socialism and other positive Utopias and create a rhetoric of this kind:

> The knowledge of true scholarship does not differ in its tradition from the knowledge of farmers, lumberjacks, miners and craftsmen. For knowledge means being at home in the world in which we live as individuals and as part of a community. Knowledge means growth of resolve and action in the performance of a task that has been given us. . . . Knowledge means being in the place where we are put.[37]

From here the way easily leads to the conception of "we are but following the glorious will of our *Führer*."[38] Every historical collectivistic-oriented situateness or normalization process has its *Führer*: even the process of McDonaldization of reality or the infantilization processes in cyberspace as a totalistic pleasure machine.

But counter-education can find in Heidegger's philosophy a different kind of concept of transcendence. In it transcendence is conditioned by overcoming authority, any authority, especially that of the one who "knows"[39] or sets the standards, quests, or telos. Here it is impossible to differentiate between self-overcoming as "let-learn" and unconcealment as let-things-be what they already are in their essence. In both, thinking manifests itself, and the presence of the exile of Being allows authentic transcendence or a kind of religiosity in which redemption as a relevant pole of existence is saved. Transcendence into thinking, which is normally absent, is transformed into a special existential "moment." Facing the presence of its absence is already thinking:

> And what withdraws in such a manner keeps and develops its own incomparable nearness. Once we are so related and drawn to what withdraws, we are drawing into what withdraws, into the enigmatic and therefore mutable nearness of its appeal. Whenever man is properly drawing that way, he is thinking—even though he may still be far away from what withdraws, even though the withdrawal may remain as veiled as ever.[40]

But even here, when it is not the *Führer* who calls for transcendence into thinking—but that to which the *Führer's* voice responds or that call which he betrays—it is always "the call" which chooses us. It is always "the call" which selects us, challenges us in a way which, while it gives itself to the human, swallows the not-yet-really-human as an act of its creation. The transcendence from contingent human power relations and the contextualized, imposed production of truths, values, identities, consciousness, and representation apparatuses in its turn offers another kind of arbitrariness. It manifests the other face of metaphysical violence:

> And what it gives us to think about, the gift it gives to us, is nothing less than itself—itself, which calls on us to enter into thinking. The question "What calls for thinking?" asks for what wants to be thought about in the preeminent sense: it does not just give us something to think about, nor only itself, but it first gives thought and thinking to us, it entrusts thought to us as our essential destiny, and thus first joins and appropriates us to thought.[41]

Here, as a danger, counter-education unveils its essence and makes human transcendence possible—with no security, no promised "success," consensus, or pleasure. And this is only the first step in the long way of counter-education, which should at the same time address the most concrete and banal manifestations of reality and the politics of the distribution of evils.

NOTES

1. Ilan Gur-Ze'ev, "Introduction," in *Conflicting Philosophies of Education*, ed Ilan Gur-Ze'ev (Dordrecht: Kluwer Academic Publishers, 2000), p. 1.

2. Michel Foucault, *Power/Knowledge: Selected Interviews and Other Writings 1972–1977*, translated by Colin Gordon, Leo Marshal, John Mepham, and Kate Soper (New York: Pantheon Books, 1980), p. 117.

3. Martin Heidegger, *Being and Time*, translated by John Stambaugh (New York: Harper & Row, 1996), p. 248.

4. Heidegger, *Being and Time*, p. 249.

5. Martin Heidegger, *Gesamtausgabe, 26: Metaphisische Anfangsgruende der Logik im Ausgang von Leibniz* (Frankfurt: Klostermann, 1978), p. 33.

6. Martin Heidegger, "The Way Back into the Ground of Metaphysics," in *Existentialism from Dostoevsky to Sartre*, ed. Walter Kaufmann (Cleveland: Meridian Books, 1969), p. 213.

7. Martin Heidegger, "Letter on Humanism," in *Basic Writings* (London: Routledge 1996), p. 245.

8. Heidegger, "Letter on Humanism," in *Basic Writings*, p. 254.

9. Heidegger, "Letter on Humanism," in *Basic Writings*, p. 242.

10. Heidegger, "Letter on Humanism," in *Basic Writings*, p. 246.

11. Martin Heidegger, *Being and Time*, p. 233.

12. Heidegger, *Being and Time*, p. 234.

13. Martin Heidegger, "On the Essence of Truth," *Basic Writings*, p. 125.

14. Martin Heidegger, "What is Metaphysics?" *Basic Writings*, p. 106.

15. Heidegger, "What is Metaphysics?" *Basic Writings*, p. 103.

16. Martin Heidegger, "Hölderlin and the Essence of Poetry," in *Existence and Being* (London: Vision Press, n.d.), p. 305.

17. Heidegger, "Hölderlin and the Essence of Poetry," *Existence and Being*, p. 306.

18. Martin Heidegger, *Being and Time*, p. 269.

19. Martin Heidegger, "Hölderlin and the Essence of Poetry," in *Existence and Being*, p. 312.

20. Martin Heidegger, "Hölderlin and the Essence of Poetry," in *Existence and Being*, p. 303.

21. Martin Heidegger, *Being and Time*, p. 179.

22. Martin Heidegger, "The Question Concerning Technology," in *Basic Writings*, p. 319.

23. Heidegger, "The Question Concerning Technology," in *Basic Writings*, p. 318.

24. Heidegger, "The Question Concerning Technology," in *Basic Writings*, p. 322.

25. Martin Heidegger, "Letter on Humanism," p. 221.

26. Ilan Gur-Ze'ev, Jan Masschelein, and Nigel Blake, "Reflectivity, Reflection, and Counter-education," *Studies in Philosophy and Education* (forthcoming).

27. Martin Heidegger, "What Calls for Thinking?" in *Basic Writings*, p. 373.

28. Heidegger, "What Calls for Thinking?" in *Basic Writings*, p. 373.

29. Heidegger, "What Calls for Thinking?" in *Basic Writings*, p. 380.

30. Heidegger, "What Calls for Thinking?" in *Basic Writings*, p. 373.

31. Heidegger, "What Calls for Thinking?" in *Basic Writings*, p. 381–382.

32. George H. Douglas, "Heidegger on the Education of Poets and Philosophers," *Educational Theory* 22 (Fall 1972): 449. Frank Margolis, "Heidegger and Curriculum," *Philosophy of Education* 42 (1986): 101.

33. William Bruening, "Heidegger on Teaching," *Philosophy of Education* 37 (1981), p. 238.

34. Angelo A. Giugliano, "Heidegger, Authenticity and Education: The Move from Existentialism to Phenomenology," *Philosophy of Education* 44 (1988): 150–156.

Helen Khoobyar, "Educational Import of Heidegger's Notion of Truth as 'Letting-be,'" *Philosophy of Education* 30 (1974): 47–58. Michael Dwyer, "The Educational Implications of Heidegger's Authenticity," *Philosophy of Education* 44 (1988): 146. Ignacio L. Goetz, "Heidegger and the Art of Teaching," *Educational Theory* 33, no. 1 (1983): 8. Donald Vandenberg, *Being and Education: An Essay in Existential Phenomenology* (New Jersey: Publisher, 1971).

35. Ignacio L. Goetz, "Heidegger and the Art of Teaching," *Educational Theory*, 33, no. 1 (Winter 1983): 7.

36. Ilan Gur-Ze'ev, Jan Masschelein, and Nigel Blake, "Reflectivity, Reflection, and Counter-education," *Studies in Philosophy and Education* (forthcoming).

37. Martin Heidegger, "Follow the Fürher," in *German Existentialism*, translated by Dagobert D. Runes (New York: Publisher, 1965), p. 40.

38. Heidegger, "What Calls for Thinking?" p. 42.

39. Heidegger, "What Calls for Thinking?" p. 380.

40. Heidegger, "What Calls for Thinking?" p. 382.

41. Heidegger, "What Calls for Thinking?" p. 391.

4

The Origin: Education, Philosophy, and a Work of Art

Paul Smeyers

In his essay *The Origin of the Work of Art*, Heidegger departed from earlier theories concerning the essence of art, rejecting the notion of art as reflection or imitation of nature, and presented instead an appraisal of art closely tied to his own metaphysical views, an appraisal explaining the essence of art in terms of being and truth. Art is a way in which truth comes to "happen" and "be" in the "real" world, a way in which "that which is," is revealed and clearly preserved. The creator discloses the truth-of-all-being within a design and illumines a new, unfamiliar world beyond the existing realm. It is crucial to appreciate that this essay reflects the position of the "later" Heidegger. Where in *Being and Time* the place of ontological clarification, for example where Being is revealed, is situated in (the) *Dasein*, now the initiative is located in Being itself—to stress this he will express this orthographically with the neologism *Seyn*. Though the human being, more precisely in what humans do and say, remains the place where Being reveals itself, a dimension of passivity is introduced in order to overcome the anthropocentrism of traditional philosophy but still be able to account for authentic existence. The technical term *Seinsgeschick* expresses that the human being is at the mercy of the manner in which Being reveals itself in an epoch in a particular mode, a happening of bringing into the openness of what was concealed, yet at the same time concealing of what was in plain view. Thus Heidegger tries to think Being itself and not from the already existing shapes (beings) it has taken on.

Heidegger's reflections on the sphere of art may be of some relevance these days where in all kinds of areas performativity rules. Thus the question is addressed whether this realm is not too different from what is supposed to go on between adults and children, teachers and pupils, professors and students. Though there is already in some circles within the context of education a criticism of focusing almost exclusively on particular outputs to judge and evaluate educational processes, this approach might add to the mentioned "review" and shed some light on those neglected aspects that are deplored. In this chapter I will investigate whether Heidegger's insights can be used to understand educational activities: what does education seen as a work of art look like? I will do the same for the study of education and seek inspiration in the essence of art in terms of being and truth. It will be argued that the present-day preoccupation with performativity has to be understood as a *Seinsgeschick*; and moreover, that the materiality of education can be understood from a Heideggerian position in this way—that, at the same time, it rules out the obsession with measurement and ranking without implying that education could do without a materiality whatsoever. By doing this it will be made clear that though the educator cannot but do particular things, engage in certain activities, pass on certain values and deal with particular (curriculum) content, she has to be aware of the fact that she only represents a particular mode of the openness of Being. Thus she has to realize that though this is the only thing she can do, the response of the child and the educator's response to this answering is also required in order for education to take place and truth to set forward, recommendation Being to take shape over and over again. Before turning to educational activities and its philosophical counterpart I will summarize and highlight some of the crucial insights of Heidegger's beautiful and inspiring essay.

HEIDEGGER'S *THE ORIGIN OF THE WORK OF ART*

Heidegger accords the work of art a special status which sets it apart from the entities in *Being and Time*, defined as present-at-hand (*Vorhandene*) and ready-to-hand (*Zuhandene*). The work of art is neither of these, but rather an entity through which the truth of beings is disclosed—it has a privileged relation to Being, similar only to that accorded to *Dasein*. He starts with the question concerning the origin, or "source of the essence" of the work of art. This appears, at first, elementary, says Heidegger; of course it is the artist, but one could also say that the artist derives from the artwork. Just as the artwork could not exist without the activity of the artist, so the artist could not exist without the work of art. Neither is without the other; nevertheless, neither is the sole support of the other, they both derive from art. The question is now, how can we seek out the essence of art? Possibly, we could examine some artworks and judge for ourselves what they all have in common. Such a maneuver, however, would only take us in circles—we encounter an impasse and seemingly cannot proceed from here. Defying the ground rules of logical thought, Heidegger decides arbitrarily upon a new way to continue with his study: either seek out the essence of art or the essence of artworks, and since works are the more concrete of the two, we should seek out their essences first. Clearly, we are all acquainted with them: artworks hang in museums, in churches, in homes. There is however no simple, neat answer to the question of what they consist of: they have numerous traits, but at least they seem to be "things." The question is now what is the nature or essence of things?

Again, to answer this question is not simple. In general a thing is "that which exists," which is "not nothing." Looking in a narrower sense, "mere things" are mundane, lifeless objects such as the clod in the field, the stone on the road. In what do these consist? Heidegger now examines three classical theories of Western thought describing the nature of mundane things. The first view contends that mere things are no more than "the bearers of their traits." The second maintains that such things are "a unity of sensations." And the third asserts that such crude, lifeless objects are mere "combinations of matter and form"—a description quite often applied to the work of art. Though each of these theories presents an entirely valid view (describes correctly some property of mere things), they also serve to describe *every* thing which exists in the "real world" and therefore cannot help determine the nature or essence of any one thing. Moreover, these thing-concepts obstruct the way toward the "real" being of things, therefore, we ought to try to approach somehow the mere thing in a simpler, more direct manner. In order to do this we have to choose one and then try to judge what the nature of it is—as previously, this is also a move which defies logic.

Heidegger selects a pair of peasant shoes painted by Van Gogh—again this selection will lead us around in a circle as the so-called mere thing is really a work of art. Describing them as "constructed of leather" etc. would not help to reveal the nature of the shoes but would only serve to define their apparent form and matter. Moving beyond this, Heidegger will look for an answer by referring to their purpose:

> From the dark opening of the worn insides of the shoes the toilsome tread of the worker stares forth. In the stiffly rugged heaviness of the shoes there is the accumulated tenacity of her slow trudge through the far-spreading and ever-uniform furrows of the field swept by a raw wind. On the leather lie the dampness and richness of the soil. Under the soles stretches the loneliness of the field-path as evening falls. In the shoes vibrates the silent call of the earth,

its quiet gift of the ripening gain and its unexplained self-refusal in the fallow desolation of the wintry field. This equipment is pervaded by uncomplaining worry as to the certainty of bread, the wordless joy of having once more withstood want, the trembling before the impending childbed and shivering at the surrounding menace of death. This equipment belongs to the *earth,* and it is protected in the *world* of the peasant woman. From out of this protected belonging the equipment itself rises to its resting-within-itself. (Heidegger 1993, p. 160)

The mere peasant shoes seem to embody much more than their own mundane form, they appear to project and secure the existence of the peasant as well. By virtue of this reliability she is admitted into the silent call of the earth, she is certain of her world. So much for equipmental things then, but we still do not know whether these are the only mere things which possess this trait and/or what the nature of other mere things might be—he will return to this later in his essay. Heidegger now remarks that we have learned, perhaps by chance, something about the nature of the work of art: Van Gogh's painting disclosed what the peasant shoes really are, unveils their truth by means of the work of art. Thus it seems, Heidegger says, artworks reveal the "actual nature" or "being" of things and serve to unveil " . . . the truth of what is" in the "fixity" of the work of art: "the truth of that which is has set itself into work" (Heidegger 1993, p. 162). This is not to say that works represent or imitate things that exist, or that works reproduce or depict the so-called universal essence of things, but that they serve to bring out the actual being of that which exists in the work of art. We have come full circle: artworks disclose in their own way the truth of that which is.

To answer the question "What is truth that it happens in art?" Heidegger turns to another particular work of art—a massive Greek temple which stands in the midst of a ragged rock-cleft valley—chosen because it copies or represents nothing at all thus allowing us to study it "resting-in-itself":

The building encloses the figure of the god, and in this concealment lets it stand out into the holy precinct through the open portico. By means of the temple, the god is present in the temple. This presence of the god is in itself the extension and delimitation of the precinct as a holy precinct. The temple and its precinct, however, do not fade away into the indefinite. It is the temple-work that first fits together and at the same time gathers around itself the unity of those paths and relations in which birth and death, disaster and blessing, victory and disgrace, endurance and decline acquire the shape of destiny for human beings. The all-governing expanse of this open relational context is the world of this historical people. Only from and in this expanse does the nation first return to itself for the fulfillment of its vocation.

Standing there, the building rests on the rocky ground. This resting of the work draws up out of the rock the obscurity of that rock's bulky yet spontaneous support. Standing there, the building holds its ground against the storm raging above it and so first makes the storm itself manifest in its violence. The luster and gleam of the stone, though itself apparently glowing only by the grace of the sun, first brings to radiance the light of the day, the breadth of the sky, the darkness of the night. The temple's firm towering makes visible the invisible space of air. The steadfastness of the work contrasts with the surge of the surf, and its own repose brings out the raging of the sea. Tree and grass, eagle and bull, snake and cricket first enter into their distinctive shapes and thus come to appear as what they are. The Greeks early called this emerging and rising in itself and in all things *physis* (φύσις). It illuminates also that on which and in which man bases his dwelling. We call this ground the *earth*. What this word says is not to be associated with the idea of a mass of matter deposited somewhere, or with the merely astronomical idea of a planet. Earth is that whence the arising brings back and shelters everything that arises as such. In the things that arise, earth occurs essentially as the sheltering agent. (Heidegger 1993, pp. 167–168)

The Greek temple embodies two fundamental characteristics: it sets up "a world" and also sets forth "the earth." Heidegger distinguishes between "existing reality" (*das Seiende*) and "the being of existing reality" (*das Sein des Seienden*). With the former he points to man and those things which we often refer to as "entities" in the real world; the latter is the context in which we view these things, the unified fabric of relationships which gives meaning to the day-to-day world. Existing reality is ever-concealing and self-withdrawn and never reveals an absolute nature or essence on its own. To know existing reality, man must transcend reality and relate to reality within a context, a realm of being. He must also transcend himself to the realization of his possibilities—the essence of his existence is that there is no essence (no given nature) but "to exist," for example he must and cannot but realize himself than through what he does. Likewise the work of art exists on two different levels which are called here "the earth" and "the world." The earth is the existing reality of the work of art (the paint, the stone, the words), and the world is the being of existing reality of the work of art, the setting of higher relationships which gives meaning to the artwork. Thus what is (*seienden*) may be transcended and new ways of Being can take shape. In unfolding a world, the temple rests on the earth, that which shelters the emergence the Greeks called φύσις: in the things that arise, earth abides as the sheltering. The earth of the work is ever-concealed, ever-enclosed, always withdrawn in itself; it is unrevealed, by its nature to be undisclosed and resists all attempts to uncover its innermost characteristics. It is essentially irrational and incomprehensible; it retreats when we want to give it form, it withdraws when we attempt to appropriate it. To make "earth"

apparent we must set forth the earth in a context of being, an open relational context which will enable the earth to be, for example the world.
While the world consists of the familiar, earth represents otherness, the
limitations of human existence, the difficulty and indeed the impossibility of making intelligible all the aspects of entities, complete truth.

Every artwork erects or sets up such an open and spacious world; at
the same time the earth of the work serves to anchor, secure, and protect
the world, defending and guarding the world within an enduring firm
foundation. The world serves to uplift and to open the hiddenness of the
earth; the earth serves to ground and protect the transcendent, intangible
realm of the world. Both elements make up the unity of the work of art.
The world and earth do not join in a tranquil or motionless manner; they
are engaged in a struggle in which each opponent—more precisely, each
element in this dialectical relationship—attempts to assert its own self in
the art work. In strife each element carries the other beyond itself. This
struggle is never entirely resolved. It is here that truth emerges, that truth
happens. The unity of the setting-up and setting-forth of world and earth
accomplished by the work is the self-subsistence of the work which consists in an ever-increasing struggle that cannot be resolved in the sense of
delivering the truth instigated by the work to another more complete
truth.

The source of the essence of works (of art) is elusive. Starting from the
artist who makes or produces works of art, Heidegger initially concludes
that he does not hold the key to the artwork, as many things are created
or crafted. Though we cannot find the source of the work thus in the act
of the artist, we might still discover it in the fact of the artist's action (for
example the fact of creation). The artwork such as the painting by Van
Gogh, has no defined function or use, except to happen or be—evidently,
the temple is in some respects a different case. The canvas is admired
because it exists. Not because it is made or produced by an artist, neither
because it is fashioned or crafted in some artistic sort of a way, but rather
because the fact of the act of creation stands out. Works become works of
art when the fact of creation stands out in their essence. The fact of creation is not the sole source of the art work, it also must be preserved. This
is done when the work is observed and absorbed as a work, when those
outside the artwork respond to the work as a new and unusual thing, respond to the truth in its being, which stands forth in the struggle of world
and earth. As guardians, in their preserving, they enable the work to be
an art work, and are thus just as essential, Heidegger says, as those who
create it. A work thus becomes a work of art when it is created to set forth
the truth of that which is and when the uniqueness of the work is known
to those who respond to the work. Works of art are free of residual inauthenticity. Beings lose their meaning and slide into triviality until they are

integrated into the new world constituted by the work of art. The artwork needs the response of those who admire it, and thus it makes authentic existence possible, it discloses the nature of all entities and thus grants and guarantees to us humans a passage to those beings that we ourselves are not, an access to the being that we ourselves are. The earth within the work of art challenges each successive generation anew to realize, preserve, and interpret its inexhaustible meaning.

In his additional observations, Heidegger makes the point that art is poetic, in both the broadest and the narrowest sense of the word. Respectively, it occurs in a linguistic realm, and the truth of what is emerges in an evocative manner because it is guided and governed throughout by the openness of language. Art institutes truth in three senses: first, by bestowing the truth as a new unique thing, by presenting it as a gift which transcends "that which is" in the real world; second, because it serves to institute truth by projecting or grounding the truth of what is by revealing the truth in the overt unhiddenness of the unconcealed; and third, by beginning the strife which accomplishes truth, for example, by renewing the struggle of world and earth, of *das Sein* and *das Seiende*, which brings about truth, and thus art initiates new worlds. Every time that art brings into being the truth of what is, it is established within the historical realm of the unconcealed. Art thus also originates human existence, beginning man's history as a whole, by revealing to man the "appointed historical tasks" which are his to fulfill. By placing man at the periphery and the work of art at the center of his endeavors, Heidegger overcomes the anthropocentrism of traditional philosophy and gives an account for authentic existence. In this way man's destiny (*Seinsgeschick*) bears on his authenticity: only within a particular givenness can he give shape to his existence, responding to Being by the meaning he realizes in what he does and the words he utters. Works of art open up new horizons by drawing in advance the paths for authentic existence.

THE CONTEXT OF EDUCATION NOWADAYS

In more than one aspect, education is an Enlightenment notion. It is the result of the modern idea that man and society to some extent can be "made"—in Heideggerian terms this is a *Seinsgeschick*, a mode of the openness of Being. For Kant education was seen as the "means" to become human, for example, rational; the person is nothing but what education makes of him. This was itself a reaction to an earlier period, characterized by the inculcation of values, the uncritical learning of facts or bodies of information, and a concern with discipline understood as obedience to (persons in) authority. With the Enlightenment, rationality becomes the proper end of what a human being is. This does not result in a means-end reasoning: in becoming free from one's inclinations and passions, one realises one's true nature, for example, to put oneself under the guidance of reason. Because of his freedom, man is a task to himself: he has to realize himself at a rational level which implies the need for a morality. Man has to realize himself as a subject of practical reason, and he can do that in as far as he binds his acting to the law of his powers of judgment, for example, his rationality. As the ultimate aim is to become moral, education is shaped according to moral understanding. Thus, liberal education is concerned with the initiation of the learner into forms of thought and understanding which are part of the cultural heritage. In the German tradition, where at least initially this academic endeavor particularly flourished, the concept of education also encompasses child-rearing as well as more formal schooling.

The primary aim of the educational relationship between the adult and the child undergoing education is for the child to become an adult. The influence adults exert on children will bring them to the point where they can take up for themselves what is called a dignified life-project. Adults, supposedly being a representation, though certainly not the ultimate embodiment, of what is objectively good, are in a position to educate, since they themselves have already achieved adulthood. Responsibility for realizing one's life-project is dictated by reason. Adulthood shows itself by being in command of oneself, able to bind oneself to a law of one's choosing, to maintain steady relationships both morally and practically and not being reliant upon the judgments of others; to put this more positively, having personal access to objective standards of value and being able to place oneself under a higher moral authority. This will show itself in the adult's taking part in societal life in a constructive manner. The child, on the other hand, is helpless in a moral sense. He does not know what is good and therefore cannot yet take responsibility for his own actions. He cries out for guidance, and only if such guidance is offered, if adults (first the parents, and subsequently the teachers) make the necessary decisions in relation to the child, will he be able to reach adulthood. Central to this traditional concept of education is this intention on the part of the educator, and it is that which makes an activity educational. What the educator undertakes can only be justified as education in so far as it aims and contributes to adulthood and to the autonomy of the young person. The educator is, thus, responsible by proxy, and his relationship with the child is based on trust. This is no simplistic reasoning of a manipulative kind. The adult decides on behalf of the not-yet-rational child and in his best interests. By confronting the child with rationality in this way, the adult seeks to awaken the child's potentialities to become a rational human being. Such a view of the justification of parental authority belonged to the conception of a just, well-ordered society.

As indicated, the Enlightenment tradition is being concerned with the initiation of the learner into forms of thought and understanding which are part of a critical cultural heritage. Here, discipline is primarily an attuning of the mind to the inherent norms of these forms of understanding. The learner is initiated into forms of thought which are public but as yet beyond the child's understanding. In their strongest formulation these norms of rationality were thought to be stable and valid for all cultures. Such a view necessarily implies a transmission model of education and upbringing. The child may be conceived of as a passive recipient of rationality and culture or as recalcitrant material to be molded or inscribed. Alternatively, he must, like the barbarian outside the citadel, be lured in and skillfully initiated into the stock of worthwhile knowledge, sentiment, and inherently valuable activities and practices of civilized life.

Because of the "carrying" idea of freedom, education for Kant is an *art* which can be exercised mechanically or thoughtfully. The mechanical aspect needs to be changed in a science in order to form a system, so that not each generation has to start over again. A well-thought-out science of education lifts education from the mere facts and from the tradition, thus children might be better educated, better than their parents and free from their example. "Science" is, according to Kant, *always* a system: knowledge built on the basis of principles. What is expressed has to emerge as necessary for the mind. A science whose foundations and principles are only empirical can only produce false knowledge. Therefore, a proper educational science has to be based on *a priori* ideas. Our reason was not to found theoretical knowledge, he argues, but is practical: it should give the norms which bind our acting unconditionally. Only after this will Kant speak of developing our natural capacities and of a society, thus bringing education and politics together. The educational theory that emerges is a science of principles, a philosophy. And though he was not indifferent to how society develops, as a *scientist of education* he was neither interested in empirical falsification, nor in outcomes, nor in prediction. Within this ideal (theory), educational practice finds its own place (situated within a particular societal and historical context). But Kant's interest is not focused on the individual, but on humanity and on how it actualizes, and gradually realizes the perfection of a human being. One's realization as a being of pure practical reason is actualized in as far as one commits one's acts to the law of one's own reason. In order to be able to do that, an education that is orientated by ethics is required as the main task of a human to become moral. A historical-teleological orientation will express the way in which the human being is shaped. For Kant then, the science of education was a philosophy of education, and practical educational activities clearly were not his primary concern. In as far as he says something about these, they have to do with restraining the animal tendencies (drives) in order to be able to place oneself under the demands of reason. Nevertheless, his approach has set the stage for education for centuries to follow.

In some sense, the debate initiated by Kant has continued ever since. Johann Friedrich Herbart's reformulation of the issue, outlining that philosophy should give us the aims, and psychology the means, to achieve them, reconceived the place of empirical facts, but left the over-all design almost untouched. It will become radicalized in the positivistic blend where a science of education is seen as only able to deal with the means in relation to achieving certain ends, not with the ends themselves. Such an empirical approach, which finds itself within the idea that we can control reality, is strikingly argued for by Wolfgang Brezinka in his *Von der Pädagogik zur Erziehungswissenschaft* [From Educational Theory to the Science of Education] published in 1972. In this kind of positivism, educational science is defined as that approach in which one looks for general laws and thus tries to explain, predict, and use technology. Hypotheses are seen as only temporarily valid and are carried by intersubjective repeated observations. He accepts that it is not possible to discover "real" laws, that one has to content oneself with statistical regularities; but value judgments can never be scientific, as they involve, in his opinion, subjective decisions. His idea of education is well known: the educator exerts influence on the child with the aim for him to achieve certain mental dispositions. The main problem for an educational science is therefore to work out which conditions have to be fulfilled in order to reach particular aims. It is therefore a teleological, statistical (or causal), analytically-oriented science. Brezinka's idea about education is *the* paradigmatic way in which activities in the context of education and child-rearing are conceived. Indeed, teacher as well as parent often infer their successfulness from the effect of their interventions, and so does society in its preoccupation with output, performativity, and effectiveness, and thus do educational sciences in general as well.

Though the Kantian rationalist presuppositions would soon have to be given up, the development of the natural sciences, and of social sciences mimicking the methods of the natural sciences, will radicalize the distinction between the *a priori* and the *a posteriori* on the one hand and between facts and values on the other. Among other reasons, this too contributed to the emergence of a wider crisis of rationality. The question of whether reason, and reason alone, can decide what should be done, and if, moreover, rational thinking is even possible at all, are at the heart of the matter. This can be made clear particularly with the use of two key ideas: performativity and nihilism. The quest for efficient solutions to problems is characteristic of modernity, and of course we owe to modernity much that makes our lives safer and more comfortable. Solutions have been sought, and found, for all kinds of conditions afflicting the human race. But there comes a point where modernity begins to parody itself, pursuing answers without any sense of the original questions, proliferating devices for achieving ever greater "efficiency," in education as in other spheres. This is the point that some call "high modernism," and others the condition of postmodernity. A profound objection to modernity has always been that the modern technical genius for finding effective means to ends has too much diverted attention from serious consideration of our chosen or implicit ends themselves, whether ethical, economic, or educational. Modernity is instrumentalist. Under performativity, deliberation over ends is eclipsed and all kinds of business and activity are measured and ranked against each other, with ever less concern for the rationale for doing so. Thus performativity obscures differences, requiring everything to be commensurable with everything else, so that things can be ranked on the same scale and everyone can be "accountable" against the same standards. This in turn entails the disvaluing, and perhaps the eradication, of what cannot be ranked (Cf. Blake et al. 1998, for a further development of these ideas). Already, Nietzsche complained that values have devalued themselves: that there is no goal anymore, that values have become merely conventional, that they are experienced as external to us, as things we do not recognize ourselves in or identify ourselves with. Education nowadays is characterized by a similar nihilism, by a lack of commitment which we conceal with the reduction of complex educational aims and purposes and with this a positive refusal to devote real thought to questions of the aims and purposes of education. The only sure value of education lies in the maintenance and extension of the system itself, in "efficiency" and "effectiveness," at the service of government in the quest for "what works" (Cf. Blake et al. 2000, for a further development of these ideas). It is to withstand this kind of reasoning that I propose to investigate how Heidegger might offer us another approach.

EDUCATION AS A WORK OF ART

It goes without saying that educators are interested in what they achieve through their interventions. But there are different aspects to the results they envisage which have to be taken into account to appreciate this more fully—what they are interested in is indeed not necessarily limited to empirical generalizations. First, though they are interested in "results," these are not to be aimed at at whatever cost. A simple means-end reasoning is therefore out of the question. Not only are certain procedures or means within a particular concept of a human being unacceptable (for instance on the basis of moral considerations or because they lack wittingness or

voluntariness on behalf of the learner), the particularities of the child
and/or the situation the *educator* and *educandus* find themselves in also
have to be taken into account—which implies that in some cases it may
gradually become clear that certain ends are out of reach, for instance, because of the limitation of talents, interests, etc. Second, it is not so much
that education is directed exclusively to certain outcomes (skills or knowledge of), there are more important, deep insights and attitudes the educator cares for and hopes they might appeal to the child. The teacher and
parent are particularly interested to get their message across, for instance,
about values or the fascination for certain worthwhile activities. This is at
the heart of their educational endeavors. Looking at educational activities
with this in mind, from the perspective offered by Heidegger's ponderings on a work of art, what does follow then? And what are the crucial
concepts in which this has to be envisioned?

In some theories, education is seen along the lines of the metaphor of
the potter. The educator shapes, or "molds," the child in the manner the
potter processes clay. For some educational activities, this indeed seems to
be the right way to think of them. We want our children to be polite, to
have particular manners, to behave (in such and such a way), to know the
capitals of the European Union countries, the formulas of this or that
chemical element, mathematical algorithms, what happened in 1789, and
so on and so forth. And though we will, to some extent at least, give them
some reasons (explain why we think this ought to be done), it is nevertheless basically "just" what *we* think is right (in our shared culture). This is
the materiality of education that is offered, the (Heideggerian) "earth,"
the material for the world to come forward. Evidently, this behaving of
the educator in a particular way "opens up a world," makes the child a
member of the larger community, prevents her from being isolated. This
seems to be the case for instrumental skills such as reading and writing,
but also for all those things we need to know to cope with everyday life.
The activities we want the child to master are the material *substratum* of
the educational intentions. Without these, education cannot take place.
Clearly, however, they are not the essence of education, which for now
can be indicated as helping the child to give shape to *her* life, but without
thus being equipped, there is no education at all.

A widespread model for education is "initiation." The educational activities that are thus described differ from the previous ones, not only concerning the subject matter (for example, the content), but more importantly, about what the educator hopes to achieve. Where, above, particular
skills and simple facts were focused on, which can be assessed in terms of
outcomes evinced in particular tasks, here it is not that clear how one can
evaluate the "progress" children have made. We want pupils to get acquainted with history in terms of knowing some facts and, above all, un-

derstanding some insights, but surely we also want them to develop some kind of historical attitude. This can be as little as being able to see the point of a historical question or as much as being fascinated by historical research. Not only is there the context of education where one may conceive a place for the disciplines in this sense, but the model of initiation also applies for child-rearing generally.

From a Wittgensteinian stance for instance, to consider a more subtle and balanced position in as far as this model is concerned, "education" can be conceived as a dynamic initiation into a "form of life." As he argued in *On Certainty*, doubt comes after belief: "If you tried to doubt everything you would not get as far as doubting anything. The game of doubting itself presupposes certainty" (Wittgenstein 1968, p. 115). And, moreover, he holds that, in what I do, it will become clear what I stand for, the things I value, and the way I go on and "follow a rule." From this position, parents are seen as the "first educators," and from this responsibility, the responsibility of the state concerning schooling can be "derived." Children are important to parents—what they are, and what they achieve, doesn't leave them indifferent. These educators offer the child the truths by which they live: what moves them, what appeals to them, what supports the idea of "human being" they offer to the child hoping that she will participate. This is an initiation into what is self-evident, or the initiation into the "form of life," as Wittgenstein puts it. Their offering of, and making present the horizon of, meaning is at the same time a taken, or accepted, responsibility, or the intentional aspect of the process of child-rearing. "Aims of it" can be conceived as summarized formulations, as elucidations of the idea of human kind, as anticipations from the point of view of the parent, which are embedded in the "form of life." This is not to say that having certain basic propositions is merely the result of an external process that happens to us. In the end, through a number of experiences, what matters is the acceptance of an offered meaning. The subject is embedded in the culture in a certain way. She is immediately grasped in the human order, structured by certain relationships, and identified by language. In the personification of the parents is shown what it means to live a human life. It is into this that the educandus is beckoned.

Precisely because of the particularity of the context, as an educator I am answerable for what I do. The lack of an ultimate foundation makes me long for a universality which would free me from this burden and give me certainty. But the kind of absolute certainty that is longed for will reveal itself as a fraud. It haunts my existence and asks for an answer that cannot be given because we cannot live but in the particular. This position is threatening to the individual, as it confronts her with the fact that not *the* but only *a* solution is possible; that things are very complicated, that no simple answer will do and that all solutions are conditional; it leaves her very literally alone and ascribes responsibility for one's choice. The only way to deal with this un-groundability consists, according to Wittgenstein, in the acceptance of this unavoidability and, with that, its correlative: one's engagement. That we cannot but act out of what appeals to us and that we cannot answer questions of ultimate justification is the essence of our tragic human existence. To act morally in an educational context concerning child-rearing presupposes being prepared to question one's own position in relation to the input of the educandus; to think it over and over again, given his or her "contribution." This could mean that we will look to discussion with others as well to reveal what we do share and what we do agree upon. It can also mean that we will try to convince the other person, to "convert" her, as Wittgenstein puts it, so that she sees what I see and is prepared to look at the problem in a "new" way. It is clear that, given that several options are possible, there is not necessarily only one that is so certain, so vital for the happiness of the educandus that it urges the educator to choose it necessarily. Things are rarely that clear-cut.

A similar position can be argued concerning the justification of the education that goes on in schools. Here, as elsewhere, it is claimed that if education ought to provoke new ideas, ideas which are different from the existing ideas of "human society" and "human dealings," it nevertheless has to start from somewhere. Michael Oakeshott (1959) indicates the aim of education as being to enter a relationship of "conversation" informed by familiarity with the traditional literary, philosophical, artistic, and scientific expressions of European civilization. Therefore, "contemporary" efforts to simplify teaching into a set of technical functions so that it might become "fail safe" are a disastrous misunderstanding threatening to destroy the possibility of genuine learning, thus to confuse it with "behavior modification." He reminds us that what has been lost is the idea of a school, a college, a university. Learning is seen by him as a specific transmission which may go on between the generations of human beings, in which newcomers to the scene are initiated into the world they are to inhabit; in using these languages one invents them each time again and adds to their resources. Oakeshott also stresses that a teacher is someone in whom some part or aspect or passage of this inheritance is alive. She has something of which she is a master to impart, she has deliberated upon its worth, and she furthermore knows the learner. The transaction between generations has no extrinsic end or purpose: education being acquiring in some measure an understanding of a human condition in which the "fact of life" continuously is illuminated by a "quality of life." Instead of thinking of education as a form of liberation, of emancipation, and in this way a progression in human activities, it can be thought of as an initiation into what is considered "worthwhile for us." It is not the case that one becomes human by being educated, but it is the case that education tries to convey what is regarded, at least by a certain number of human beings, as worthwhile to them. To accept this historicization and, at the same time, decentralization of what one is engaged in, makes the justification of the content of education a risky business. What is important to them, what proves to be important to those who share a culture, is guarded and bestowed upon the persons being educated, whom they care for. There should not only be a place where new ideas can grow, there should also be a place where what is worthwhile can be kept. What should be aimed at, however, is a personal way of dealing with "what matters": how people have struggled in the past with what troubled them most and how they dealt with it. In this process one gets acquainted foremost with questions rather than with answers, and to be initiated, to be touched by the questions, seems to be what it is all about.

The initiation model has been criticized from various angles. The Heideggerian position offers us some insights to appreciate it more fully. What else than initiating can we do, one may wonder? Surely deciding not to initiate in a particular content, in a particular way of life, is also an initiation in something. Moreover, what else could we do for those we love or the students who are entrusted to us. Again, a world is created first for the *educandus*, in opening particular perspectives on life, on others, on society, which, of course, she might or might not get enthused by. Similar to what Heidegger says about the work of art, this work of education stands within a world, yet the work itself opens up the world in which it stands. In this opening up (*Aufstellen*), the world worlds (*die Welt weltet*), granting time and space to all things—which gain their lingering and hastening, their remoteness and nearness, their scope and limits. In the content the teacher offers, through textbooks, poems, particular activities she wants the children to engage in, the process of education is materialized. In this sense, a "canon" has to be offered, the work of education cannot but be made out of particular material: activities which the educator prescribes for the child, particular experiences she wants her to have, to go through. Through this work, different aspects of this material are set forth. This setting forth (*Herstellen*) happens as the work sets itself back into the material of the work, for example, when the child engages in these. The educational activity is materialized in what is done by the educator, yet the act of education seems to withdraw itself from the scene. Importance is given to history, science as such; to particular "behaviors" in themselves. In this sense, the work of education lets earth appear in world, but precisely as earth, that is, as self-secluding (*Sich-verschliessend*). There are many more things which could be done with this material, with the interaction between human beings and so forth, and this in itself retreats in the background—as the work of art which is neither of the mode of the present-at-hand nor of the ready-to-hand, its basic nature is that it "refers to." "Earth" shatters all attempts to penetrate it by calculative thought. This may be clear if one realizes that the possibilities of the content that is offered are never fully realized, can never *be* fully realized. There is always so much more, which means that, in assessing how far children have proceeded, no simple testing of degraded, complex aims will do. The inspiration the child finds in what is offered to her will keep alive the spirit of what is passed on.

In some respects, the teacher is analogous to the artist, to the actor, who performs, behaves as . . . hoping the child will "critically" respond. He practices the evocative. In this he is representing, much more than just presenting, what is "beyond doubt." Even when he deals with so-called real things, he represents rather than presents (he shows a flower out of context, speaks of France by the use of diagrams, of animals using documentary programs, etc.). In this, at the same time, he reveals some parts of the world, puts particular facts of life in the picture, but other things, facts, meanings, and values are necessarily "concealed." Though a particular content is offered, "what" is in it is a matter for constant evaluation (and debate). The Heideggerian position makes clear that to be truthful to the Truth, to Being, requires an amendment to the initiation model. It is not "only" initiation in what is already there that matters, it is moreover the response of the child that has to be taken into account. And as an answer to this, the way in which the educator deals with the child's responsiveness, for example, with her particular answer is also imortant. Only in such a way can real education come forward. Clearly, this particular human endeavor, as a part of our way of living, of our civilization, can only be there as long as it is practiced. It may be in danger because of the way society evolves. It too needs to be preserved, and the content of education itself needs to be gone through, not as a mere repetition of what previous generations hold important, but as a way of going through, for oneself, what is seen by the educator as valuable. To be protected against dullness and decay no mere rehearsal or repetition of the valuable suffices: the content has to be deepened through one's own wrestling with it, one's own completion, in order for truth to come forward.

Above it was indicated that Heidegger considers resistance to be an essential element of the strife of the artwork that instigates the *Ur-streit* of revealing/concealing and refers to the inaccessibility of the ground of the appearing process. There is so much more about the subjects, about human life, that indicates the many possibilities for being fascinated by human creations and endeavors. They appeal, evoke, give witness of what they are carried by. In the strife, the self-assertion of each striving member is protected—the opponents raise each other into the self-assertion of their natures. There is, however, no sense of surpassing and retaining of the striving members as moments of a deeper or further movement. All subjects and ways of life exhaust the attention of the learner, exhaust her potential, compete with each other for the best place, pretend to bear the ultimate answer, and want to be seen as capturing the essence of education. And yet, education can only exist in this struggle of offering something on the one hand, but keeping the possibilities open on the other. "Strife" also makes clear the everlasting need to be opposed, not to acquiesce with what one "is," but to find oneself in responding to challenges. In answering these, the very best will be brought out, thus giving opportunity for the child to develop her gifts.

In the activities, the teacher involves the learner, and the learner becomes the *educandus*. Correlatively the educator, too, exists as a consequence of her activities, for example, as *educator*. She will be recognized by the child and by others on the basis of what she does. For her, too, a world is created, through which she may realize her existence in which educating will find a place. In some sense she is at the mercy of the response of the child. The educator's potentialities, what she "is," is drawn out of her, among other things on the occasion of how the child answers her appeal. Again there is no precisely circumscribed realm of activities she has to perform. She may "only" give herself as she "is." This is therefore (again) not an area of skills or outcomes, but of being human in the broad sense. In her life outside the education she is "giving," she will be seen by others as educator, which may lead to new experiences (in the context of new expectancies), to a rearrangement of what she generally does, a new order of priorities in her life; for instance, she might get involved in school activities, in representative bodies and, thus, acquire new insights, have different experiences, even develop new relationships. By what she does, and she organizes to some extent the life of the child: here particular values she holds will come into the open, she also brings about and preserves a way of living together, which implicitly or explicitly opens a political dimension. She is a model for the child, giving here a particular example of what being human means. The initiation that is offered makes clear that decisions have to be taken on the background of what is not completely lucid, or comprehensible, that instead some darkness always remains. At the same time she exemplifies that "identity" is not something to be realized once and for all, that "one finds oneself" in the particular things one does, but that, later, other aspects of life, other experiences, other things to do may appeal. And this too she passes on to the child.

Thus another aspect of the educational relationship becomes visible: the singularity which characterizes the work of art. It was argued that striving for a further or deeper truth would destroy the self-subsistence of it, being disrespectful of the singularity of its occurrence. The movement, here, is a movement to more strife, deeper into the truth of art, but not beyond this truth into a deeper context whose truth would surpass that of

the artwork. Similarly, educational activities occur within human relationships. For these, no final "solution" for the essence of what makes us
human, for the quest of the meaning of life, can be offered. It was argued
that to be human means, first of all, to go a way for oneself, to be on this
road again and again and thus to realize one's humanhood. In a double
sense, thus, there cannot be a final answer: each answer is only *an* answer,
and it has to be given over and over again. As the artwork does not presuppose a world whose enveloping truth would be revealed, but opens its
own world on the spot in a singular event, and where, in its strife, the
"earth" appears, as self-secluding, this holds too for the human being.
One cannot realize one's existence but through doing this or that, yet
what one does conceals the essence of what exactly is going on. As in
other areas, in an educational activity *a*, not *the*, way of being human is
shown—a way which realizes education and, through this, one's existence. Concealment conceals and dissembles itself. Concealment can be
either refusal or dissembling, in which one being presents itself as other
than it is. Dissembling takes place within the clearing, while refusal is the
refusal of the beginning of the clearing to become accessible. One can
never be sure if in any one case concealment is contingent (dissembling)
or essential (refusal). And it is possible to forget the essential concealment
resulting in an "oblivion of Being." Such an oblivion forgets that clearing
is not a fixed stage but a happening in which clearing happens as double
concealment, that is, beings come to appearance in a distribution whose
origin withdraws, or refuses, itself.

Gradually, the identity of the child takes shape as the realization of
some of her potentialities. It is important for the educator to create many
opportunities in which she can realize herself, bearing in mind as well the
fact that there is no end point to this, because subjects, in essence, are a
plurality of identities—ascribed to them by others or experienced by the
person herself in the activities and dealings with others she engages in.
Heidegger's reflections may help us to keep the non-fixity of identity in
mind. His insistence on the necessity for a work of art for those who preserve—not understood as conservation but as cocreation—may apply to
the following in the context of education. On the one hand there is only
education for as long as the child is responding to it; on the other there is
only education as an expression of a particular kind of human existence,
for as long as society sustains it. The former refers to the natural ending
of a particular process and thus of the educator and educandus as such in
this relationship; the latter a particular mode of existence which presupposes a particular kind of human existence in which some educate others
and all that goes with it. If society dissembles, if there are "just" individuals or if the distrust toward each other is carried by a discourse of rights
and duties instead of framed in "caring for," then education is in danger

to disappear. Thus it also becomes clear that education is, in essence, not directed toward extrinsic ends, but finds within itself its true nature.

Through education the world—in the ordinary sense—will become "my world." But again, while we are familiar with the things that have become accessible to us in our world, this appearing process itself is uncanny, its ground withdrawn. Refusal is the origin of clearing: truth occurs precisely as itself in that the concealing denial, as refusal, provides its constant source to all clearing, and yet, as dissembling, it metes out to all clearing the indefeasible severity of error. The opposition between clearing and concealing in the essence of truth is named by Heidegger the originary strife (*Ur-streit*). The world does not equal the open of clearing, nor does earth equal the closed of concealing, rather, world as the opening of paths of decision always contains what outstrips the decider, what can never be fully accessible. The strife of earth and world in the artwork occurs only insofar as the *Ur-streit* of clearing and concealing occurs; the *Ur-streit* is the essence of truth/untruth, the appearing process whose origin withdraws itself. In the way in which truth is pulled into a work so that the open may take its stand, we find a way of allowing ourselves to linger over this particular happening of truth (the singularity of the art occurrence). This is not seen as an instance of truth: the difference between the elemet must be thought as a "difference as such" (an originary split as it grants a particular flow of time. Any attempt at finding a *Grund* bring us to face an unknowable *Ab-grund* The world goes on to nourish the philosophical wonder of the human existence. Life is never in its fullness revealed. One can never be completely at home. Education opens up the possibilities for the child, it promises yet "frustrates"—to think that compete openness was possible would imply the destruction of the subject. Are there no technical aspects then to education? Of course there are, as there are particular results as well. But one should be careful with this concept.

A special experience of being occurs in φύσις: beings open themselves to man in a unique way—bringing to presence, the Greek experience of the world as different from the Egyptian, et cetera. The Greek artist does more than create "beautiful objects" that are then paradigmatic and thus effective for the future. A co-responding to the fundamental experience of φύσις takes place in their production—yet they are not an imitation or copy of what is already present. It is this belonging together of art and φύσις that determines the Greek world. The knowledge (or understanding) guiding the production of a structure and a work is called by the Greeks τ'εχνη—a knowledge which also concerns the production of works of science and philosophy, poetry, and public speech. Art is τ'εχνη, but not technology, and the artist is τεχνίτης—distinctive is the fact that somehow a kind of knowledge is concerned. This knowledge looks toward something not yet present in such a way that it makes it possible to give form to the work. In this sense education is marked by the technical, yet surpasses the technological. And thus research concerning this area will totally fail to bring out what is at stake if it occupies itself only with the means-end, with instrumentality.

STUDYING AND SEEING: BEYOND THE PERFORMATIVE

The scientific world, like the cybernetic world, is based on the supposition that the fundamental trait of all calculable world processes is steering. But a world where these accomplishments of technology are focused on does not question its own limitations. For education, a philosophical approach is demanded in which the evocative, the artist like doing, plays an important role. Clearly, in some sense, the educator does not know what he is doing, therefore a language of means and ends will never do. Here the work of education shows itself as a happening of truth, which in some sense is, for the educator, also marked by passivity, by something that happens to her. She is only partly the originator in her authentic acting—with the *Seinsgeschick* at the background, she will, as the artist, inspire, respond, answer the dealings of the child, enabling to bring forward an answer to a mode of Being. Clearly only a language which evokes what is going on will do to bring this to mind. Thus to speak truthfully of what has to be studied in a theory of education necessarily demands that the hostility to a poetic language is given up; and though there may be a place for empirical generalizations, educational theory thrives on the evocative. An education which dwells with the child, with her possibilities, in a world which is more than what can be manipulated and measured, thus goes beyond the instrumental attitude. It shows a way to a future which cannot be spelled out but the possibility of which can only be cherished and longed for. Heidegger's insights make it abundantly clear that we cannot do without the materiality of education but helps us at the same time to avoid falling into the trap of the terror of performativity. As the Wittgensteinian stance he urges us to transgress, to go beyond output and ranking, when the human is concerned. The way of the work of art, its bringing forward the unseen, should thus guide education and its study.[1]

NOTES

1. For comments and suggestions on an earlier version of this paper, I am indebted to Bert Lambeir, Stefan Ramaekers, and particularly to Paul Standish.

REFERENCES

Blake, N., P. Smeyers, R. Smith, and P. Standish. 1998. *Thinking Again: Education After Postmodernism*. New York: Bergin & Garvey.

Blake, N., P. Smeyers, R. Smith, and P. Standish. 2000. *Education in an Age of Nihilism*. London: Falmer Press.

Heidegger, M. 1993. The origin of the work of art. Trans. D. F. Krell. In *Martin Heidegger. Basic Writings*. Ed. D. F. Krell. London: Routledge. The German text for this translation is originally published in a collection edited by H. G. Gadamer. Stuttgart: P. Reclam, 1960.

Okeshoot, M. 1959. *The Voice of Poetry in the Conversation of Mankind: An Essay*. London: Bowes & Bowes.

Wittgenstein, L. 1953. *Philosophical Investigations/Philosophische Untersuchungen*. Trans. G. E. M. Anscombe. Oxford: Basil Blackwell.

Wittgenstein, L. 1969. *On certainty/Über Gewissheit*. Ed. G. E. M. Anscombe and G. H. von Wright. Trans. D. Paul and G. E. M. Anscombe. Oxford: Basil Blackwell.

5

Comfortably Numb in the Digital Era: Man's Being as Standing-Reserve or Dwelling Silently

Bert Lambeir

"Dichterisch wohnet der Mensch auf dieser Erde." (Poetically man dwells on this earth.)
—Hölderlin

By referring to the poet Hölderlin at the end of his essay "The Question concerning Technology," Heidegger shows that technology is not, or should not be, at the heart of man's life, that *Being* cannot be understood in a purely technological manner. This strongly contrasts with the contemporary hype concerning technological advancement in general, and information and communication technology in particular. Although Heidegger never encountered the computer as such, his analysis captures the contemporary situation sharply, as I will indicate. First, questioning the information and communication technology in a Heideggerian way leads to the undermining of the illusion that man stands deliberately above the machine, as an autonomous creator. Second, it will become clear that our perception of reality is largely digitally mediated, and that more than ever before, man himself has become standing-reserve. At the same time, Heidegger's philosophy sets a stage for an alternative understanding of the computer phenomenon, which provides a space for altering educational practice in present-day schools.

FROM VIRTUALITY TO REALITY:
THE OMNIPRESENCE OF NEW TECHNOLOGY

Two decades ago, people went to the grocery around the corner and saved their money under the pillow, children played games in the street and went to school two kilometres away. What then seemed to be a mission impossible, is nowadays accomplished thanks to the computer and the internet. Since computer operations include a lot of daily practices, one can go online shopping, banking, applying for jobs, learning, and playing. Furthermore, the Internet has become the world's largest library as it provides an immeasurable amount of information of all kinds, open to anybody at anytime, anywhere. Even the weekly visit to the pub, just to meet some neighbors, is being replaced by having a drink in the cyber cafe. We log in to communicate with persons on the screen as if it were face-to-face conversations, regardless of the fact that your chat partner is playing the keyboard at the other side of the Pacific. In no time at all you can contact fellow cyborgs logged in anywhere in the world—rather than a planet, the earth became a global village to us, as Marshall McLuhan put it[1] (Levinson 1999). The world (truth) is no longer "out there," we carry it in one hand (not even on our shoulders as Atlas was supposed to)—as it is all there at the interface.

Apart from the *"what"* of information and communication technology (ICT), that is, all the aspects, the opportunities, and facilities it embodies, another and even more striking feature of computerization is that it became so quickly widespread. The idea of the PC, "personal" computer, is no longer fictional. Almost all over the western world, every adult and child has a computer at their disposal in their daily environment, certainly since various digital operations, such as word processing, have made the computer part of their ordinary activities. Finally, the pace of this evolution is as considerable as its influence. It took hardly a decade for men to *co*-operate with new technology in the way in which we do nowadays. In almost no time at all the computer has become a sine qua non. Either we learned to perceive the computer in that manner or it just happened, unquestioned (like our assimilation of the motor car and, more recently, the mobile telephone).

At first sight, digitalization is a beneficial change for human beings, as is shown by the major part of commercials. But they do not only refer to web addresses for more information about a product, they also make us believe that it is very important to *be online* and to be able to surf the net as fast as we can. Occasionally, authors warn us about a new kind of deprivation, a new structural and social phenomenon: *e-poverty* (De Ceulaer 2000). However, since the computer has been integrated into education at all levels, human beings will become even more familiar with electronic

technology. But, the important connection between education and computers is not only the issue of social deprivation, because new technology
seems to have benefits for learning as such. First there is the way in which
the total availability of all kinds of information, together with the mode in
which it is at hand (as a conglomerate of texts, sounds, and images), enables
the student to obtain a more complex idea of reality. She can cut and paste
information from various sources to "complete" the puzzle with which she
is dealing. Second, and related to the feature of the internet just named, the
hypertextual presentation of electronic information frees the student from
the barriers of authorial thinking and linear reading. Contrary to the book
where everything is explained in a particular order, with hypertext the student can link the text chunks at her own discretion—she can, as it were, create her own story. For Nicholas Burbules and Paul Callister, this fits very
well with a way in which we often learn, namely nonsequential, dynamic,
interactive, associative, and by means of exploration (Burbules and Callister 1996). Another benefit concerns the implementation of communication
technology in educational contexts. This means for both the learner and the
teacher a possibility to bridge geographical distances, and the freeing of
physical or speech disabilities which might hinder a good educational relationship (or an educational relationship at all). Furthermore, ". . . much of
what is screened out or clouded in online education is precisely the kind of
personal characteristics that can interfere irrationally in human interaction,
and in education can distort, disrupt and at the extreme pervert the interaction of tutor and student" (Blake 2000, p. 190).

Besides these positive voices about the opportunities of information
and communication technology for education, a broader, even more optimistic vision in this concern is the romantic euphoria of Douglas
Rushkoff. He states:

> "Human beings have evolved significantly within a single creature's life-
> span, and this intensity of evolutionary change shows no signs of slowing
> down. What we need to adapt to, more than any particular change, is the fact
> that we are changing so rapidly. We must learn to accept change as a con-
> stant. Novelty is the new status quo. (Rushkoff 1997, p. 3)

For adults, Rushkoff continues, it is hard to assimilate to this recent habitat of rapid alternations, because they will always try to assimilate these
into their familiar habits. On the contrary, the capacity of children to
adapt to evolving situations is almost inexhaustible. Therefore, with an
eye on a brighter future, it might be better for grown-ups to perceive the
child as a standard for their own actions.

The other side of the cyberstory, which takes on different shades of gray,
is a hesitating, or even skeptical, attitude toward the ongoing *e*-volution.
These examples illustrate some of the "unwanted" consequences to be

expected or to be feared: the end of the reading of books; the unsuitability of hypertext to form the core of teaching materials; the destabilization of political and juridical borders; the disappearance of physical social contact; the end of privacy; and so on.

Whether this technological evolution is good or bad, *Rock'n Roll is here to stay* and so is the computer. *"Education unplugged"* is expelled from the contemporary pedagogical debate. It is indeed a sweeping change, affecting us in every aspect of our life, touching us where we live, with promising but uncertain features. It cannot be brought to a halt—perhaps it does not need to. Therefore it might be worth the effort to investigate the digitalization in a way that goes beyond the polarity euphoria—skepticism—beyond the opposition technocrats—neo-luddites.[2]

In this respect, Heidegger's profound analysis concerning the relationship between technology and Being illuminates the way in which the ongoing technological evolution strikes us at our innermost life.

HEIDEGGER QUESTIONING TECHNOLOGY

Reality can never mean *the* reality, but it is for Heidegger always *our* reality, within which people live and stand in relationships. He speaks in *"Der Ursprung des Kunstwerkes"* of the earth and the world, to mark sharply the distinction between the material world and the world in which we live. The now famous shoes of the peasant in an artwork of Van Gogh belong to the *earth* in the sense that they exist ". . . whether or not we disclose them; they present themselves as independent of our awareness of them" (Weinberger 1984, p. 104). We as human beings however, do not live on that earth but inhabit a world—this is the place that allows us to disclose the earth, that enables announcements, the place within which reality finds its meaning and becomes intelligible. The worldliness of things, originated in a relational context, is a specific manner in which the earthly things become unconcealed. The shoes named above belong to the world, that is, the world of the peasant, since they are part of her life, her habitat. By putting them on or placing them by the fire, by cleaning them or seeking them when they are lost, the peasant reveals these things as her shoes. This unconcealment of reality only makes sense against the background of concealment—where there is no option for nondisclosure, there is no chance for revealing either. This paves the way for Heidegger's idea of our Being as *Da-sein*, a Being characterized by the threefold past-present-future, and therefore a Being, meaningful within the limited interpretation of reality. Because there is no direct knowledge of the world, the relationship between human being and reality is necessarily mediated. As the correspondence theory of truth is generally no longer accepted, every statement about the world is necessarily historically and socio-culturally embedded, and therefore limited.

In this unfolding of reality, this showing and withdrawing of nature, technology plays an important role. According to Heidegger, the question concerning technology, which asks for the essential relationship between technology and nature, cannot be answered by referring to something technological. "Technology is no mere means. Technology is a way of revealing" (Heidegger, QCT, 1993, p. 318).[3] For Heidegger, technology is not so much something with wood or iron or fuel, but is in the first place a way of doing things, a way of being in the world, or a form of life. By stating this, Heidegger understands technology as a mode of human existence, an essential feature of Being. To arrive at this point, he returns to the Greek meaning of *techne*.

> One is that *techne* is the name not only for the activities and skills of the craftsman but also for the arts of the mind and the fine arts. *Techne* belongs to bringing-forth, to *poësis*; it is something poetic. The other thing that we should observe with regard to *techne* is even more important. From earliest times until Plato the word *techne* is linked with the word *epistēmē*. Both words are terms for knowing in the widest sense. They mean to be entirely at home in something, to understand and be an expert in it. Such knowing provides an opening up. As an opening up is it a revealing. (Heidegger, QCT, 1993, p. 318–19)

Concerning the first meaning of *techne*, the more instrumental and thus more familiar one, Heidegger denotes a three-phased evolution in western history. For the ancient Greek, *techne* was an activity in the first place, a practical know-how. They understood it as craftsmanship, a skilled working with materials and tools. In this sense, *techne* was very much comparable to the work of an artist who is related to the material he is working with, and thus related to nature in a particular, respectful manner. The work of art is the way to disclose reality, to reveal reality, it is *Dichtung*. The second meaning of *techne* "is characterised by factory production geared towards the satisfaction of needs, and the reduction of the human being to the labouring animal" (Standish 1997, p. 444). In the third phase, this production is part of an overall systems theory, and the satisfaction of needs is supplemented by an ongoing creation of other needs, a persistent feeding of desire.

As the quotation above shows, *techne* is more than just a way of using tools, or a mode of working and producing. Referring again to the Greek, Heidegger's additional understanding of the concept reveals the relation with *epistēmē*, which points to a tight connection between technology and knowledge, or even stronger, technology and truth. "Technology is a mode of revealing. Technology comes to presence in the realm where revealing and unconcealment take place, where *alētheia*, truth, happens"

(Heidegger, QCT, 1993, p. 319). In other words, technology incorporates a particular relationship between human beings and reality, in which a specific interpretation of what counts as real, holds sway. Consequently, technology is the framework, the standard for our interpretation of the world. It is the way in which the earth becomes our world. By means of technology, man transforms the world into its comfortable home—technology then is a mode of *In-der-Welt-Sein*.

Analogous to the three kinds of *techne*, the mode of Being, the revealing of truth evolved from *poiēsis* to ". . . a challenging, which puts to nature the unreasonable demand that it supply energy which can be extracted and stored as such" (Heidegger, QCT, 1993, p. 320). According to Heidegger, the way in which we approach nature, is no longer comparable to the contemplative, artistic, and skilled dwelling of the ancient craftsman. Rather it is an exploitation of nature by our own discretion, supported by the drive for quantity, availability, mastery, and power. We are all miners of the earth, searching for energy to unlock, transform, store, distribute, and switch about.

> Everywhere, everything is ordered to stand by, to be immediately on hand, indeed to stand there just so that it may be on call for a further ordering. Whatever is ordered about in this way has its own standing. We call it the standing-reserve [*Bestand*]. . . . It designates nothing less than the way in which everything presences that is wrought upon by the revealing that challenges. Whatever stands by in the sense of standing-reserve no longer stands over against us as object. (Heidegger, QCT, 1993, p. 322)

Modern technology as a way of revealing, Heidegger continues, is not our deliberative choice at all—it is not our disclosure of the truth because we want it to be, but because it is the omnipresent, dominant way in which the world becomes meaningful to us. Technology ought to be understood as our "way of life." The contemporary sense of *techne*, "the challenging claim that gathers man with a view of ordering the self-revealing as standing-reserve [is called]: *Gestell* [enframing]" (Heidegger, QCT, 1993, p. 324). We frame the world as raw material at our disposal, as a stock from which we can order. The "enframing" is the way in which we encounter the world. The Rhine, Heidegger illustrates, is no longer that river floating through the valley, but supplies pressure for the hydroelectric plant, to set the turbines turning. Man masters the machine and by doing so, masters nature. For the subject, truth is no longer a "happening" but a collection of objects (on order).

However, the seemingly comfortable world picture described above brings with it an unpleasant consequence. In the age of modern technology, Heidegger warns us for a particular form of *"das Gestell,"* what he calls *"das Geschick"* (destiny), because herein, the danger slumbers to become comfortably numb within the "enframing." If destining unfolds it-self only within the context of the enframing, the concealed nevermore comes into unconcealment as "*Gegenstand*." That is to say that ". . . the challenging-enframing not only conceals a former way of revealing (bringing-forth) but also conceals revealing itself and with it that wherein unconcealment, that is, truth, propriates" (Heidegger, QCT, 1993, p. 333). When man is nothing but the orderer of standing-reserve, the unavoid-able consequence is that he is endangered to become standing-reserve himself. While thinking himself to be the king, man is no more than the pawn on the game board of the enframing. Being a waiter of the chal-lenging-forth of *das Gestell*, he misinterprets the far reaching power of his master, he fails to see the enframing as an overall mode of unconcealment, "he fails to see himself as the one spoken to" (Heidegger, QCT, 1993, p. 332). and thus as being ordered himself. That this kind of *techne* trans-forms Being while carrying an air of harmlessness and ease probably is Heidegger's greatest concern. Perhaps one of the most striking expres-sions of this phenomenon in modern times is the discourse of "human re-sources" (and "human resources management"). In industrial contexts, namely, man is approached as a particle of a huge manpower stock, ready to be ordered and fired depending on the continuing profit calculations. Man is stored to be unemployed, to *be* a reserve worker and to keep the economical discourse alive. In this chess game between the company managers and the world economy, man isn't addressed personally but as one of all the numbered pawns. He became nothing but standing-reserve, managed by the laws of *das Gestell*. The subject has been transformed into an object himself, hardly distinguishable from the other ones.

Heidegger's compelling questioning of technology still "works," that is, it reveals truth in the era of new information and communication technology.

THE QUESTION CONCERNING INFORMATION AND COMMUNICATION TECHNOLOGY

The human condition, Hannah Arendt states, implies that man is a condi-tioned being in the sense that everything, made by man or not, immedi-ately conditions the being of man. Man has adapted himself to the world and its machines, from the moment of their invention (Arendt 1994). In the era of digital technology, however, this adaptation seems to be more intriguing than ever before, since man seems to submit himself passion-ately to the computer. Remember the "millennium bug" that "threatened" our world at January 2000—a global "dysfunction" lurking around the corner. This shows how the computer became the engine that keeps our "world" turning, and the frame through which we perceive reality.

As described above, the computer, and its technical possibilities, became a crucial part of a wide range of ordinary practices. We perceive it, in other words, as a very helpful tool in the arrangement of our life, in the encounter with nature, as Heidegger would have put it. This goes for writing, shopping, and banking, as well as for chatting and playing—and additionally, this happens in an air of total convenience. Simultaneously, our language (the house of being) is thoroughly "brushed up" with concepts such as "surfing" and "downloading." The way we digitally organize our daily life in all its aspects. no doubt resembles Heidegger's notion of *techne* as a way of revealing reality. Through the monitor, the world comes into presence for us. But as we saw above, the coming into unconcealment of the concealed, the happening of our world through *techne*, can take different shapes in conforming to the three interpretations of the Greek concept. At first sight, there does not seem to be a reasonable comparison between artistic craftsmanship and worldwide digital technology, since the latter creates a reality rather than letting it come into presence. Where the artist is dependent on the material she is laboring with, the one sitting at the interface seems to be more in control of the ongoing process. Both of them deliberately manipulate input and outcome, but the latter does not encounter the material as such, rather she creates it. This is not to say that there do not arise new art forms, original ways to express delight and concern, recent modes of fusion between sounds and moving images, reflecting the characteristics of the new media at hand. Furthermore, there is no reason to turn a blind eye to the ongoing creation and revision or updating of websites, the production of software and accompanying gadgets, the flourishing economy and information technology companies, and so on. Obviously, the equation of ICT and *techne* as factory production can have its relevance but is a limited one because it does not take into account the interactivity and the rapid change of the medium. A lot of (industrial) production comes to the fore, but reducing men to laboring animals when it comes to information and communication technology is rather hasty and simplistic. Indeed, for some activities digital technology is merely used as a simple tool, as is the case for ordering books or tickets, or for making financial transfers. But there is more at stake than a mere satisfaction of needs, as I have already suggested when I described the new technology phenomenon above. In short, the opportunities ICT offers us influence our daily life so thoroughly that we cannot speak of a simple production process—the relationship between man and computer is fundamentally different from the connection between man and factory machine, as I will elucidate below. Furthermore, the numerous possibilities make us look for something different, something more challenging or attractive; they encourage us to look for more applications of digital technology in our daily life. Finally, there is at least one feature of new technology that characterizes our relation with it in a particular way. The modes of interactivity of ICT can touch us on a social, or more personal, level, for example, when we communicate with cyberfriends or when we seek digital liaisons. The different modes of communication the machine has to offer transform it into something we will not shut down for a long time—we hope for an answer, a reaction, recognition. *Techne*, in the mode of information and communication technology, thus seems to be first and foremost an enframing of nature, or more precisely, of reality in the sense that information and communication technology become the lens through which we mainly perceive our environment (which was the third meaning of *techne*, Heidegger described).

In the way that Heidegger describes this kind of revealing, this enframing, man perceives nature as a reserve, and that counts for the last two digital decennia, too. The computer, with the included virtual reality and the accompanying cyberspace, brings the world into our home, into our offices, and into classrooms. Any search engine traces *all* the information about the subject of interest. One can choose the most suitable web page and sometimes even add additional comments on it, or one can design a website oneself, that is, creating a piece of virtual *reality* to be ordered. Every interface is a window, a passageway to cyberspace, an artificial world, a laboratory in which we can experiment with reality in a manner that suggests virtual reality to be a transparent representation of the "outer" reality. Consequently our relationship with reality is altered, enframed in a way so that we seem to be in control. By entering the medium that can provide a complete knowledge and an overview, and given the fact that we can alter the input (thus the output), we know *the* world, and moreover, we are able to recreate it endlessly. We not only reach the level of a Platonic mind—the ability to acquire pure knowledge—but we can also, by entering "reality" through cyberspace, take a look at the world with God's eyes. We have access to all information (the earth), enabling ourselves to determine the mode of entering with the velocity we want, leaving it up to us whether we will manipulate it or not. We have a complete overview of reality, and simultaneously, we are not bound by it. We live the solipsist's illusion.

Though, immediately, the risk to lose control even before it has been attained is reiterated again, it reveals itself as an illusion. The world, dwelled on with cybershoes, is interpreted as essentially transparent and representable, and this has become, in its turn, the paradigm for our thinking, our way of speaking of the world, and due to the fact that the computer has become an ingredient of human knowing, an integral part of our thinking—we are interfacing, interacting, collaborating with computers. Arendt's perception of the relationship between human being and technology, the immediate adaptation to equipment, thus becomes more sharply defined as an *affair*. Our link with the computer is not merely one of appliance—taking the computer for no more than a useful object. It is indeed the case that applied technology fills our lives with familiar routines, but as in a marriage, the partners influence each other. We go from appliance to the interface level. This means that ". . . two or more information sources come face-to-face. A human user connects with the system, and the computer becomes interactive. Tools, by contrast, establish no such connection. . . . The software interface is a two-way street where computers enhance and modify my thinking power" (Heim 1993, p. 77–78). This cannot but remind us of Heidegger's concern that man, contrary to his own beliefs, loses control over the things he himself made. The reciprocity of the bond between man and machine leads to the point where the computer influences human behavior (as proved the hype concerning the millennium bug)—man makes the machine makes man. Michael Heim speaks of the computer as a mental prosthesis. Another way to denote the connection can be found in McLuhan's work, wherein he describes man as "the sex organs of the machine world, as the bee of the plant world, enabling it to fecundate and to evolve to ever new forms" (McLuhan, in Levinson 1999, p. 63).

Heidegger's analysis of nature *and* man as *Bestand* (standing-reserve) remains highly accurate these days. Not only is the reality on order, but also it is simultaneously as if modern technology uses men as fuel in an ongoing production process. Additionally, besides man awaiting the computer, man awaits man, that is, man is to be ordered by others who have logged on in cyberspace. Tak,e for example, MUDs (multi user dungeons) and MOOs (MUD object oriented) or other kinds of chatrooms bringing people together around virtual tables. Men log in to become cyborgs, seeking some virtual social contact, wanting to talk, to play, to have cybersex, etc. The ways in which these possibilities of modern communication technology reshape man as *standing-reserve* have two aspects: on the one hand, by logging in, often at times known to be crowded, the man at the interface orders some contact, some response, of those logged in as well—in other words he perceives them as a stock of non-bodily incarnate codes on the cable, as *Bestand*. A reinforcement for this attitude is the opportunity offered by technology to break every contact "when the time is right"—when the needs are fulfilled and the relationship tends to lose its meaning or when the interaction might become too unpleasant or confronting. On the other hand, man must realize that by looking for *e*-contact, looking for instant camaraderie with total strangers, he is on order also. He thus volunteers as *Bestand* and therefore reduces himself to a bare means for satisfaction.

This digital *Gestell*, and its additional picture of the standing-reserve, doesn't shun the educational discourse either. On the contrary, it transforms it into a performativity contest on the playground. According to Paul Standish, modern technology "has created a world in which we are caught up in a never-ending business where no one seems to be fully in control and where, while some may ponder the significance of this, we are generally lulled into a tranquillised acceptance of technology's values— witness the common difficulty of even seeing a problem with current pre-occupations with efficiency and effectiveness" (Standish 1997, p. 448; see also Standish 2000). This interpretation transfers adequately Heidegger's fear, that man becomes subordinated to the technology he developed himself, to the contemporary computerization.

Following Standish, this evolution expresses itself in the emphasis put on (transferable) skills, a modularized and even self-sufficient curriculum (the need for subject expertize of the teacher is reduced), and above all, there are league tables. Imagine an educational system dominantly based on new technologies—thus a web-based pedagogy. No doubt, the desirable goal in such a pedagogy is ensuring that everyone becomes technologically literate. To L. Blasi and W. F. Heinecke, this means that students are no longer encouraged to participate, persuade, and to produce. Rather, a technologically innovated education aims at the creation of effective consumers of information. "The passive acceptance of technology into the classroom," they state, "may actually damage the social fabric within which corporations are enmeshed. Integrated learning systems and 'drill and skill' software move students away from active citizenship toward the intellectual prowess more suited to passive consumerism" (Blasi and Heinecke 2000, p. 83). The ceaseless invention, development and innovation of technological applications and the ongoing and growing interference of large-scale business in the nonprofit sectors make the computer an indispensable partner of education. Furthermore, we are stuck with the impression that information and communication technologies feed off the limitations teachers often have to face. The emphasis put on time management, class management and efficiency, individualization and autonomy, information processing and problemsolving strategies "promote pedagogy based on drills and quantitative data that circumvents the expertise of the teachers and the learning styles of the students" (Blasi & Heinecke 2000, p. 86). Teachers are "deprofessionalised." And when the "teaching-to-the-test" is being stressed and the overall educational process has become leaner, there is little incentive and merit left for those teachers who cultivate the interaction, communication, and productive practices—as is characteristic of the ancient concept of education and technology.

The efficiency of the educational system as overall standard reduces the subject content, as well as both teacher and student, to *Bestand*. Herein, the computer keeps playing the same double role mentioned above: on the one hand, the extraordinary relationship we have with digital technology makes the enframing an even more demanding reality. The peculiar meaning we attribute to the digital machine—or the particular place it takes in our life—makes the computer and its systems and functions into a form of life. On the other hand, the bare fact that we have the computer at our disposal as a tool facilitates the challenging-forth of reality; the world becomes get-at-able by means of databases and simple search engines. The process of data input and information output is significantly simplified, thus the results can easily be shown. The computer is equipped with programs to deliver the data we want and such at the blink of an eye. It fulfills our lust for efficiency and effectiveness. The idea of on-line education, for example, realizable by placing courses on the Internet and contacting teachers via email, reorganizes curriculum material and the teacher's comments to a stock which can be ordered from at all times. In this context, P. Levinson speaks about the "intellectual safety net" of on-line education: remarks made by members of an electronic discussion group are stored for an indefinite period, just to be retrieved (or not) someday and to be discussed one more time. Thus the computer capacities make information of all kinds (means, scores, grades, statements, etc.) totally available, in order to compare, calculate, sort out, replace, or delete.

ON SPEAKING, SAYING, AND THE CRUMBLING OF WORDS

What is the state of the English language? No state at all. It is in process. Our language is being word processed. If languages have states of health, sick or well, then ours is manic. (Heim 1993, p. 3)

Why would we have to be concerned with the state of the English language—with the condition of any language at all? Why is it important to consider language while interpreting Heidegger's question concerning technology within the scope of ICT and education?

If we consider what is happening to our language in a time governed by new technologies, we observe at least the following alterations: firstly, we are using quite new words as if we have been using them for centuries—this is certainly the case when English terms such as "downloading," "chatting," and "surfing" are integrated into other tongues. Without even being fully aware of these changes in speech, we fluently use these terms that "enrich" our language. Besides the emerging of new words, there is an increased use of acronyms such as ASAP, CU, and LOL,[4] due to the fact that a lot of interaction is mediated by written language—a major part of our communication gets shape via SMS (short message service) on mobile phones, e-mail, and other chat opportunities. This leads us to a third linguistic aspect that is changing, namely, the manner in which sentences and even whole messages are constructed. Whereas letters used to have a proper salutation and a grammatically correct body, messages nowadays incorporate many abbreviations, unfinished sentences, and very informal opening lines. It is as if our language has adapted itself to a new writing style, constantly exercised with the new information and communication technologies. Finally, when investigating the influence of modern technology on language, we must acknowledge that the familiar mode of reading and writing is under construction too. As Heim states, our language is being word processed: writing is as much cutting and copying, pasting, inserting, and deleting numerous text chunks as it is typing a linear story. He says: "Digital writing is nearly frictionless. You formulate thoughts directly on the screen. You don't have to consider whether you are writing the beginning, middle, or end of your text. You can snap any passage into any place with the push of a key" (Heim 1993, p. 5). The same goes for reading, since a lot of texts are available on the Internet in a hypertextual mode. Consequently, reading is no longer studying a complete text, but becomes an active scrolling and clicking, looking for the most interesting and useful parts on the screen. In this way, reading seems to be a participation in the construction of the text and its meaning.

What Heim is drawing attention to is that literacy and literature, language as such, are under pressure since electronic text is becoming an almost dominant language form. We experience language as if it is raw material to us, ready to be molded in a desired shape. It is small wonder that we get the impression that language is awaiting us; that words are at our disposal; that meaning is on order; that speech is under deliberate construction. Modern information and communication technology tends to transform language into a mere instrument, a *Bestand*. This is obviously the case for computer or programming languages such as JAVA, which serve as a bare means to an end, and which are constructed in that respect. Heidegger, however, warns us: "Speech is challenged to correspond to the ubiquitous orderability of what is present" (Heidegger, WTL, 1993, p. 420) .He observed already that the *enframing*, the challenging of nature by means of modern technological equipment, also applies for language that is endangered to become a formalized one. Heidegger states that the language machine is one way in which modern technology takes control over the mode and world of language. Following him, this means that the machine is infecting our thinking, since both aspects are unconditionally tightened to each other—speaking, and thus writing, is materializing thoughts. But when our speech is altering, our thoughts are changing at their turn. For Heidegger this is to say that our thinking is in danger of losing its sense, because language becomes *Bestand* and thus "speech, when posed in this fashion, becomes information" (Heidegger, WTL, p. 420).

Language changes and we, in using it, with it. The conviction that language is under deliberate construction and words (meaning) are on order as standing-reserve is, according to Heidegger, deceitful.

> Speech, taken on its own, is hearing. It is listening to the language we speak. Hence speaking is not *simultaneously* a hearing, but is such in *advance*. Such listening to language precedes all other instances of hearing, albeit in an altogether inconspicuous way. We not only *speak* language, we speak *from out of* it. We are capable of doing so only because in each case we have already listened to language. What do we hear there? We hear language speaking. (Heidegger, WTL, p. 411)

Language is the house of Being, the place we find ourselves in, and is, as such, a sine qua non for men to dwell on this earth. Speaking is showing, verbally pointing at something, and by doing so letting the things come into unconcealment, without revealing them completely. Saying is paving the way to our world. This *happening* is restricted in at least three ways: Firstly, there always remains something concealed or hidden. Saying is as much remaining silent as it is uttering words; secondly, there is only the spoken way—silence too is a corresponding; and finally, we find the paving stones on our way instead of choosing them explicitly.

> We human beings, in order to be who we are, remain within the essence of language to which we have been granted entry. We can therefore never step outside it in order to look it over circumspectly from some alternative position. Because of this, we catch a glimpse of the essence of language only to the extent that we ourselves are envisaged by it, remanded to it. (Heidegger, WTL, p. 423)

We thus can replace, insert, and delete; we can construct computer languages and use new terms; we see our use of language altering in the age of information and communication technology; we get the impression that language is *Bestand*. Does there still remain some poetry in man's life, some articulation unspoken, some pointing without touching, some words unsaid?

Clearly, the impoverishment of language brings with it the impoverishment of life. This could mean that, following Heidegger, a web-based education, as is encouraged by the government, becomes information processing in the first place and such an evolution can no longer be perceived as a diminishment for education. Such a concept of education fits in very well in the contemporary performativity discourse and puts the rest—that which is more than information (standing-reserve) or different from skills—and the lack possibly expressed by students into oblivion. This comes as no surprise, that is, when there is no ultimate truth or no firm foundation, there is only the usefulness of things valuable to us. Is this gloomy picture all there is left for us?

THE INTERFACE AS *BESTAND* OR *GEGENSTAND*

In the last section, I wish to consider if there is some space left for *Dichtung* in this techno-centric universe. What can it mean to dwell in a world overrun by the compute,r and what is in it for education? Is it indeed the case that *Being* does not have to be understood in a purely technological manner, as stated above, even in this digital era?

If man dwells poetically on this earth, as Heidegger following Hölderlin argues, there can be some stage for *Dichtung* on the interface too. It only seems to be about keeping some distance from what appears on the screen, that is, letting the web materials speak for themselves as they pop up, instead of feverishly clicking further. It is not hard to see that the computer enables us to express our delight or appreciation for a peculiar verse when we install it as our personal screensaver, our enjoyment of a particular painting when we set it as our wallpaper. Though the verse is not complete and takes another style, though the painting is not the masterpiece on canvas, though the sound of the song downloaded from a website has lost quality, we show our appreciation and we confront ourselves every single day with the beauty—and its related meaning to us—of the specific piece of art. By saving some bits and bytes for these special "objects," we continually express what could not be described otherwise. We create ourselves by reading and rereading, looking and then looking again. Before shutting down the computer, there was at least a little moment of attention, this short stop (of the machine in our head), or a second to be touched.

Perhaps this sheds light on a different manner in which the Internet can be *used*. There are websites escaping the paradigm of speed, ignoring the criterion of efficacy and accuracy, inviting the visitor to sink back for a while and to look slowly at what is presented, stimulating the surfer to use her imagination. Take, for example, the website of a college, which features a project on poetry. The movements of images and words are out of control for the visitor, and surfing is nothing more than letting appear the next poem and paying attention to all the details included.[5]

As mentioned earlier, *education unplugged* is no option—there are different kinds of revealing, but no chance to escape from *das Geschick*. It became clear that the integration of the computer in educational contexts can hardly avoid the pitfalls which Heidegger described in his question concerning technology. The enframing he spoke of counts for education in the age of digital technology, too. So we might want to look for an alternative use of the computer rather than for its replacement. We might want to search for a use beyond the contemporary, monotonous "drill and skill," beyond the decent attention paid to problem solving strategies, beyond the thin perception of the machine as database or as a typing and computing machine. In the beginning of the chapter, I outlined some discussion topics in the debate of web-based education. Let us also consider the following quote: "In the press to integrate technology into classroom instruction, teachers may adopt an uncritical stance toward curriculum materials found on the Web. What works may be defined as what is readily available for quick, mass consumption" (Blasi & Heinecke 2000, p. 89).

Contrary to this tendency, ICT is able to uncover another concept of education if we *point at* some broader understandings and permit some unexplored perspectives into unconcealment, if we dare to question the overall idea of education as practicing information processing skills and problem-solving strategies. The computer, in all its diversity and complexity, can open a window to the world, and bring the latter back into the classroom. Teachers do not have to slide down into pure consumption when the Internet, as an information storage and as a communication medium, is perceived as the source for an open-minded discovery. At least three domains ought to be explored: First, there is the World Wide Web which contains huge amounts of information. It seems worthwhile to surf the web together, that is learner and teachers, to see what shows up and to react to it. Why not dwell in cyberspace with an open mind and see all that is there, without searching for something in particular? Since the internet has become an integral part of our life, this in-depth exploration certainly is an educational challenge: "helping students learn to operate in an environment that is inherently 'dangerous,' to deal with what may be unexpected or unpleasant, to make critical judgments about what they find. . . . Educationally, we need some of the 'bad' in order to create some of the 'good'" (Burbules & Callister 1997). Obviously, such practices contain some risks, but at least not the risk that one would not be educating. Reacting to what comes into the classroom through the interface is learning to deal deliberately with all kinds of information. If one tries to avoid this confrontation in education, one does not avoid the child being confronted with web pages in extracurricular contexts.

But there is more than discovering the information overload and perceiving virtual reality as more than a stock, as something that shows and withdraws, as *Gegenstand*. In letting the uncertainty of content slip into the classroom, the teacher cannot but show her colors in at least two ways. On the one hand, in dealing with the information overload, she cannot pretend as if she herself does not hold particular things valuable, prior to the "choice" of the learner. Whatever the teacher offers as education content, she will have to legitimate and thus speak as the person she is, more than as the teacher. On the other hand, every hyperlink might contain new information of all kinds, that shows up unexpectedly and at any time. The teacher, then, cannot but take these texts, sounds, and pictures into account, again, in the first place, as the person whom she is, being confronted herself by this material for the first time. Here, the information itself and the reactions of both teacher and peer can draw the student's attention to something which is worth the effort to learn.

Finally, in actively using the diversity of the web, the teacher can pay attention to various modes of the creative potential of her students. These might emerge in unexpected associations they make and in the use of information in an original way. The opportunities the web offers enable the students to express their concerns and delights. They can, for example, build their own website, thus choose the colors, the images and sounds, the moving elements, the words, and the characteristics of the hyperlinks. Can reality not show and withdraw itself in such a work? Can we not perceive such activity as a kind of poetry? It seems that new technology lends itself to an artistic kind of expression that comes closer to Heidegger's notion of dwelling poetically.

Rather than ordering the information and the persons one needs, rather than perceiving all the educational components as standing-reserve in this digital era, this concept of education emphasizes a broader and more risky use of the computer. It stresses some unusual ideas concerning ICT and education, based on the idea that education cannot be merely a factory production of skilled persons who are able to survive in a computerized world. Not everything, according to Heidegger, is reduced to bare information, and it is in educational contexts, in the first place, that this should be highlighted. At the time that our fantasy, contemplation, and attention are mainly put aside by the ordinary Internet use, the teacher can give room to a broadened use of ICT and, by doing so, stimulate the attention of the learner. The main condition to this is that some time is saved to be enraptured, to be troubled and touched by a particular subject, and that one can give expression to this. Learning can be a process of confrontation for both the teacher and the student, when room is given to the unexpected, when one surfs the Internet *together* and takes time for the concerns that pop up. This, too, is what learning can be in an age of new media and by means of this technology.

IT IS NOW SAFE TO TURN OFF YOUR COMPUTER

In this chapter, we saw how the computer and the Internet, as one of the most fascinating and powerful technological developments, have been integrated in our daily life. To understand the consequences of such a fundamental evolution, Heidegger offers us a very adequate framework. His important analysis of technology enlightens the way in which computerization alters our understanding of reality and affects the concept of human being, as such. Nature and man are endangered to become merely standing-reserve, and man is not even aware of what is going on. We have become comfortably numb in the world of digital technology. The reduction of man and nature to *Bestand* and the compelling enframing have entered our education as well, since the implementation and integration of the computer in school practices is on the political agenda. Here, too, every content tends to become bare information.

It is possible, however, to think of an alternative relationship with technology. If we follow Heidegger in what he tells us about language, and if we try to combine this with an altered use of information and communication technology, something of the contemplative, artistic, and skilled dwelling of the ancient craftsman is revealed again, as well as another concept of education—as a personal and challenging undertaking. As did Heidegger's questioning, this investigation articulates our bond with technology and enables us to keep some distance now and then. In becoming aware of the role the digital machine began to play in our life, a different kind of *techne?* opens up. Virtual reality might be a place where truth happens, where nature reveals itself, speaks to us, and remains silent. And since the computer does not need to be our iron lung, it is safe to turn it off from time to time.

Though when the computer is satisfying most of our needs, who will be inclined to turn it off actually? The more the machine plays a crucial role in the aspects of our life that we find important, the less we can and want to function *offline*. But are electronic conversations as captivating as face-to-face contacts? And is online education as intriguing as listening to the teacher who is explaining something enthusiastically? That human beings are present as human bodies in social contexts tells us that teachers and students might still want to walk through the classroom door to encounter each other as *Gegenstand*.

NOTES

1. Interesting to see is how McLuhan spoke of a global village even before the rise of the new, digital technology, denoting a village of voyeurs instead of an interactive one.

2. The Luddites, historically, were not opposed to technology as such, but to technology that deprived men of work and a livelihood. In a modern use of the term, neo-luddites are described as being opposed to nearly all technology.

3. QCT refers to Heidegger's "The question concerning technology."
WTL refers to Heidegger's "The way to language."

4. These frequently used words mean respectively "as soon as possible," "see you," and "laughing out loud."

5. Available at: www.xaveriuscollege.be/poezieproject/index.html

REFERENCES

Arendt, H. 1994. *Vita activa*. Amsterdam: Boom.

Blake, N. 2000. Tutors and Students without Faces or Places. *Journal of Philosophy of Education* 34: 183–196.

Blasi, L., and Heinecke, W. F. 2000. From Rhetoric to Technology: A Transformation from Citizens into Consumers. *Issues in Web-based Pedagogy: A Critical Primer*. Ed. R. A. Cole. London: Greenwood Press.

Burbules, N. C., and Callister, T.A. 1996. Knowledge at the Crossroads: Some Alternative Futures of Hypertext Learning Environments. *Educational Theory* 46: 23–50.

Burbules, N. C., and Callister, T.A. 1997. *The risky promises and promising risks of new information technologies for education*. Available online at: http://faculty.ed .uiuc.edu/burbules/ncb/papers/risky.html

De Ceulaer, J. 2000. Digibeten aller landen! *Knack* 30 (18): 32–36.

Heidegger, M. 1993. The origin of the work of art. Trans. D. F. Krell. In *Martin Heidegger. Basic writings*. Ed. D. F. Krell. London: Routledge.

Heidegger, M. 1993. The question concerning technology. Trans. D. F. Krell. In *Martin Heidegger. Basic writings*. Ed. D. F. Krell. London: Routledge.

Heidegge., M. 1993. The way to language. Trans. D. F. Krell. In *Martin Heidegger. Basic writings* Ed. D. F. Krell. London: Routledge.

Heim, M. 1993. *The Metaphysics of Virtual Reality*. Oxford: Oxford University Press.

Levinson, P. 1999. *Digital McLuhan: A Guide to the Information Millennium*. London: Routledge.

Rushkoff, D.1997. *Children of Chaos*. London: Flamingo.

Standish, P. 1997. Heidegger and the Technology of Further Education. *Journal of Philosophy of Education*, 31: 430–459.

Standish, P. 2000. Fetish for effect. *Journal of Philosophy of Education* 3:, 151–168.

Weinberger, D. 1984. Earth, World and Fourfold. *Tulane Studies in Philosophy* 32: 103–110.

ich the sedimented layers of distorting interpretations are cleared

6

Heidegger on Ontological Education, or How We Become What We Are

Iain Thomson

HEIDEGGER'S DECONSTRUCTION OF EDUCATION

Heidegger sought to deconstruct education. Rather than deny this, we should simply reject the polemical reduction of "deconstruction" (*Destruktion*) to "destruction" (*Zerstörung*) and instead be clear that the goal of Heidegger's deconstruction of education is not to *destroy* our traditional Western educational institutions but to "loosen up" this "hardened tradition and dissolve the concealments it has engendered" in order to "recover" from the beginning of the educational tradition those "primordial experiences" which have fundamentally shaped its subsequent historical development.[1] In fact, Heidegger's deconstructions are so far from being simple destructions that not only do they always include a positive as well as a negative moment, but this negative moment, in which the sedimented layers of distorting interpretations are cleared away, is invariably in the service of the positive moment, in which something long concealed is recovered. To understand how this double deconstructive strategy operates in the case of education, then, we need simply clarify and develop these two moments: What distortions does Heidegger's deconstruction of education seek to cut through? And, more

Reprinted from "Heidegger on Ontological Education" by Iain Thomson from *Inquiry* (www.tandf.no-inquiry), vol. 44, no. 3, pp. 243–68, by permission of Taylor & Francis AS.

importantly, what does it seek to recover? Let us answer this second, more important, question first.

Through a hermeneutic excavation of the famous "allegory of the cave" in Plato's *Republic*—the textual site where pedagogical theory emerged from the noonday shadows of Orphic mystery and Protagorean obscurity in order to institute, for the first time, the "Academy" as such—Heidegger seeks to place before our eyes the most influential understanding of "education" in Western history: Plato's conception of paideia. Heidegger maintains that aspects of Plato's founding pedagogical vision have exerted an unparalleled influence on our subsequent historical understandings of "education" (its nature, procedures, and goals), while other, even more profound, aspects have been forgotten. These forgotten aspects of paideia are what his deconstruction of education seeks to recover. Back, then, to our first question: What hermeneutic misconceptions or distortions stand in the way of this recovery and so must first be cleared away? Heidegger's focus here is on a misconception about education which also forms part of the legacy of Plato's cave, a distortion embodied in and perpetuated by those institutions which reflect and transmit our historical understanding of education.

Now, one might expect Heidegger's assessment of the future prospects for our educational institutions to be unremittingly pessimistic, given that his later "ontohistorical" (*seinsgeschichtliche*) perspective allowed him to discern so presciently those interlocking trends whereby we increasingly instrumentalize, professionalize, vocationalize, corporatize, and ultimately *technologize* education. Heidegger's powerful critique of the way in which our educational institutions have come to express a nihilistic, "technological understanding of being" will be developed later. But before assuming that this diagnosis of education amounts to a death sentence, we need to recall the point with which we began: Heidegger's deconstructive strategies always have *two* moments. Thus, when he seeks to recover the ontological core of Platonic paideia, his intent is not only to trace the technologization of education back to an ontological ambiguity already inherent in Plato's founding pedagogical vision (thereby demonstrating the historical *contingency* of these disturbing educational trends and so loosening their grip on us); more importantly, he also means to show how forgotten aspects of the original Platonic notion of paideia remain capable of inspiring heretofore unthought possibilities for the *future* of education. Indeed, only Heidegger's hope for the future of our educational institutions can explain his otherwise entirely mysterious claim that his paideia "interpretation" is "made necessary from out of a future need [*aus einer künftigen Not notwendige*]."[2]

This oracular pronouncement sounds mysterious, yet I believe Heidegger's deconstruction of education is motivated entirely by this "future need." I submit that this future need is double; like the deconstruction mobilized in its service, it contains a positive as well as a negative moment. These two moments are so important that the rest of this chapter will be devoted to their explication. Negatively, we need a critical perspective which will allow us to grasp the underlying historical logic according to which our educational institutions have developed and will continue to develop if nothing is done to alter their course. As we will see in the examination of Heidegger's ontohistorical critique, Heidegger was one of the first to diagnose correctly what a growing number of incisive critics of contemporary education have subsequently confirmed: we now stand in the midst of a historical *crisis* in higher education. Heidegger's profound understanding of the *nature* of this crisis—his insight that it can be understood as a total eclipse of Plato's original educational ideal—reveals the ontohistorical trajectory leading up to our current educational crisis and, more importantly, illuminates a path which might lead us out of it.

This is fortunate, since the gravity of Heidegger's diagnosis immediately suggests a complementary, *positive* need: We need an alternative to our contemporary understanding of education, an alternative capable of favorably resolving our educational crisis by averting the technological dissolution of the historical essence of education. Heidegger's hope is this: Since an ambiguity at the heart of Plato's original understanding of education lent itself to a historical misunderstanding in which the essence of education has been obscured and is now in danger of being forgotten, the deconstructive recovery of this long-obscured essence of education can now help us envision a way to restore substance to the increasingly formal and empty ideals guiding contemporary education. It thus makes perfect sense that this need for a positive alternative leads Heidegger back to Plato's cave. Retracing his steps in the part I have titled "Heidegger's Return to Plato's Cave," we will reconstruct "the essence of education" Heidegger seeks to recover from the shadows of history, thereby fleshing out his positive vision. In "Envisioning a University of Teachers," we will consider briefly how this re-ontologization of education might help us begin to envision a path leading beyond our contemporary educational crisis.

HEIDEGGER'S ONTOHISTORICAL CRITIQUE
OF THE TECHNOLOGIZATION OF EDUCATION

The first aspect of our "future need" is for a critical perspective which will allow us to discern the underlying logic that has long guided the historical development of our educational institutions, a perspective which will render visible the developmental trajectory these institutions continue to follow. As intimated above, Heidegger maintains that his "history of being" (*Seinsgeschichte*) provides precisely this perspective. As he puts it, "the essence of truth and the kinds of transformations it undergoes first make possible [the historical unfolding of] 'education' in its basic structures."[3] Heidegger means by this that the history of being *makes possible* the historical development of our educational institutions, although to see this we must carefully unpack this initially puzzling reference to "the essence of truth and the kinds of transformations it undergoes."

From the Essence of Truth to the History of Being

Heidegger's pronouncement that the essence of truth *transforms* sounds paradoxical; how can an essence *change*? This will seem impossible to someone like Saul Kripke, who holds that an essence is a property an entity possesses necessarily, a "rigid designator" fixing its extension across all possible worlds.[4] The paradox disappears, however, once we realize that Heidegger, too, uses "essence" (*Wesen*) as a technical term, albeit quite differently from Kripke. To understand "essence" in phrases such as "the essence of truth" and "the essence of technology," Heidegger explains, we cannot conceive of "essence" the way we have been doing since Plato, as what "*permanently* endures," for that makes it seem as if by "essence" "we mean some mythological abstraction." Instead, Heidegger insists, we need to think of "essence" as a *verb*, as the way in which things "essence" (*west*) or "remain in play" (*im Spiel bleibt*).[5] In Heidegger's usage, "essence" picks out the extension of an entity unfolding itself in historical intelligibility. Otherwise put, Heidegger understands essence in terms of being, and since being is not a predicate (as Kant showed), there is little likelihood that an entity's "essence" can be picked out by a single, fixed predicate or underlying property (as "substance" metaphysics assumes). Rather, for Heidegger *essence* simply denotes the *historical* way in which an entity comes to reveal itself ontologically and be understood by *Dasein*.[6] Accordingly, "essence" must be understood in terms of the "ek-sistence" of *Da-sein*, that is, in terms of "being set-out into the disclosedness of beings."[7]

In "On the Essence of Truth" (1929), Heidegger applies this historical understanding of "essence" to *truth*, contending famously (if no longer terribly controversially) that the original historical "essence of truth" is not simply "unforgottenness" (*Unvergessenheit*, a literal translation of the original Greek word for "truth," *a-lêtheia*, the *alpha*-privative "un-" plus *Lêthê*, the mythological "river of forgetting"), but phenomenological "unconcealedness" (*Un-verborgenheit*) more generally. Historically, "truth" first refers to *revealedness* or *phenomenological manifestation* rather than accurate representation; the "locus of truth" is not originally the correspondence of an assertion to a state of affairs, but the antecedent fact that there is something *there* to which the assertion might correspond. So conceived, the "essence of truth" is a "revealedness" fully coextensional with *Dasein*'s "existence," the basic fact of our "standing-out" (*ek-sistere*) historically into phenomenological intelligibility. "The essence of truth" thus refers to the way in which this "revealedness" takes shape historically, namely, as a series of different ontological *constellations of intelligibility*. It is not surprising, then, that Heidegger first began to elaborate his "history of being" in "On the Essence of Truth"; for him "the essence of truth" *is* "the history of being."

Of course, such strong claims about the radically historical character of our concepts (even cherished concepts like "essence," "truth," "history," "concept," and "being") tend to make philosophers nervous. When Heidegger historicizes ontology by re-rooting it in the historical existence of *Dasein*, how does his account avoid simply dissolving intelligibility into the flux of time? Heidegger's answer is surprising; the metaphysical tradition prevents intelligibility from dissolving into a pure temporal flux. Indeed, careful readers will notice that when Heidegger writes that "eksistent, disclosive *Da-sein* possesses the human being so originarily that only *it* secures for humanity that distinctive relatedness to *the totality of beings as such* which first grounds all history," he is subtly invoking his account of the way in which metaphysics grounds intelligibility.[8] Unfortunately, the complexity of Heidegger's idiosyncratic understanding of Western metaphysics as *ontotheology*, coupled with his seemingly strong antipathy to metaphysics, has tended to obscure the unparalleled pride of place he in fact assigns to metaphysics in the historical construction, contestation, and maintenance of intelligibility. Put simply, Heidegger holds that our metaphysicians' *ontological* understandings of what entities are "as such" ground intelligibility from the inside-out (as it were), while their theological understandings of the way in which the "totality" of beings exist simultaneously secure the intelligible order from the outside-in. Western history's successive constellations of intelligibility are thus "doubly grounded" in a series of ontotheologically structured understandings of "the being of beings" (*das Sein des Seienden*), understandings, that is, of both *what* and *how* beings *are*, or of "the totality of beings as such" (as Heidegger puts it above).

This account answers our worry; for although none of these ontotheological grounds has served the history of intelligibility as an unshakeable "foundation" (*Grund*), nor have any of the major ontotheologies instantly given way like a groundless "abyss" (*Abgrund*). Rather, each ontotheology has served its historical constellation of intelligibility as an *Ungrund*, "a perhaps necessary appearance of ground," that is, as that point at which ontological inquiry comes to a rest.[9] Because each ontotheology serves for a time as the point where "the spade turns" (as Ludwig

Wittgenstein put it), the history of intelligibility has taken the form of a series of relatively durable, overlapping historical "epochs" rather than either a single monolithic understanding of what-is or a formless ontological flux.[10] Thus metaphysics, by repeatedly supplying intelligibility with dual ontotheological anchors, effectively "holds-back" (*epochê*) the floodwaters of intelligibility for a time—the time of an "epoch." It is this "overlapping" historical series of ontotheologically grounded epochs that Heidegger calls *the history of being*.

The History of Being as the Ground of Education

With this philosophical background in place, we can now understand the reasoning behind Heidegger's claim that our changing historical understanding of "education" is grounded in the history of being.[11] Heidegger defends a kind of ontological *holism*: By giving shape to our historical understanding of "what *is*," metaphysics determines the most basic presuppositions of what *anything* is, including "education." As he puts it: "Western humanity, in all its comportment toward beings, and even toward itself, is in every respect sustained and guided by metaphysics."[12] The "great metaphysicians" focus and disseminate an ontotheological understanding of what and how beings *are*, thereby establishing the most basic conceptual parameters and ultimate standards of legitimacy for their historical epochs. These ontotheologies function historically like self-fulfilling prophecies, reshaping intelligibility from the ground up. For as a new ontotheological understanding of *what* and *how* beings *are* takes hold and spreads, it transforms our basic understanding of what all entities *are*.[13] Our understanding of education is "made possible" by the history of being, then, since when our understanding of what beings *are* changes historically, our understanding of what "education" *is* transforms as well.

This conclusion is crucial; not only does it answer the question which has guided us thus far, it positions us to understand what exactly Heidegger finds *objectionable* about our contemporary understanding of education (and the educational institutions which embody this understanding). For Heidegger, our changing historical understanding of what "education" *is* has its place in a historical series of ontological "epochs," holistic constellations of intelligibility which are themselves grounded in a series of ontotheological understandings of *what* and *how* beings *are*. In order fully to comprehend Heidegger's critique of contemporary education, then, we need to answer three interrelated questions: First, *what* exactly is the nature of our own ontological epoch? Second, in *which* ontotheology is our constellation of intelligibility grounded? And third, *how* has this underlying ontotheology shaped our present understanding of education? I will take these questions in order.

Heidegger's name for our contemporary constellation of intelligibility is, of course, "enframing" (*das Gestell*). Heidegger chooses this polysemic term because, by etymologically connoting a *gathering together* ("*Ge-*") of the myriad forms of *stellen* ("to set, stand, regulate, secure, ready, establish," and so on), it succinctly conveys his understanding of the way in which our present "mode of revealing"—a "setting-upon that challenges forth"—forces the "presencing" (*anwesen*) of entities into its metaphysical "stamp or mold" (*Prägung*).[14] Yet this is not simply to substitute etymology for argument, as detractors allege. Heidegger uses etymology in order to come up with an appropriate name for our contemporary "mode of revealing," but the argumentative work in his account is done by his understanding of metaphysics. This means that to really understand why Heidegger characterizes our contemporary epoch as *das Gestell*, we must take the measure of his claim that "enframing" is grounded in an ontotheology transmitted to us by Nietzsche. On Heidegger's reading, Nietzsche's staunch anti-metaphysical stance merely hides the fact that he actually philosophized on the basis of an "unthought" metaphysics. Nietzsche's *Nachlaß* clearly demonstrates that he conceptualized "the totality of beings as such" *ontotheologically*, as "eternally recurring will-to-power," that is, as an unending disaggregation and reaggregation of forces without purpose or goal.[15] This Nietzschean ontotheology not only inaugurates the "metaphysics of the atomic age," *it grounds enframing*: Our unthinking reliance on Nietzsche's ontotheology is leading us to transform all beings, ourselves included, into mere "resources" (*Bestand*), entities lacking intrinsic meaning which are thus simply optimized and disposed of with maximal efficiency.[16]

Heidegger famously characterizes enframing as a *technological* understanding of being. As a historical "mode of revealing" in which entities increasingly show up only as resources to be optimized, enframing generates a "calculative thinking" which, like the mythic touch of King Midas, quantifies all qualitative relations. This "limitless 'quantification'" which absorbs all qualitative relations (until we come to treat "quantity *as* quality") is rooted in enframing's *ontologically-reductive* mode of revealing, whereby "[o]nly what is calculable in advance counts as being." Enframing thus tends to reduce all entities to bivalent, programmable "information," digitized data, which increasingly enters into "a state of pure circulation."[17] Indeed, as Heidegger's phenomenological meditation on a highway interchange revealed to him in the 1950s—and as our "information superhighway," the Internet, now makes plain—we exhibit a growing tendency to relate to our world and ourselves merely as a "network of long distance traffic, paced as calculated for maximum yield."[18] Reading quotidian historical developments in terms of this ontohistorical logic, Heidegger believed our passage from Cartesian modernity to Nietzschean postmodernity was already visible in the transformation of employment agencies into "human resource" departments. The technological move afoot to reduce teachers and scholars to "on-line content providers" merely extends—and so clarifies—the logic whereby modern subjects transform themselves into postmodern resources by turning techniques developed for controlling nature back onto themselves.[19] Unfortunately, as this historical transformation of subjects into resources becomes more pervasive, it further eludes our critical gaze; indeed, we come to treat ourselves in the very terms which underlie our technological refashioning of the world: no longer as conscious Cartesian subjects taking control of an objective world, but rather as one more resource to be optimized, ordered, and enhanced with maximal efficiency—whether cosmetically, psychopharmacologically, or *educationally*.

Here, then, Heidegger believes he has uncovered the subterranean ontohistorical logic guiding the development of our educational institutions. But *how* does contemporary education reflect this nihilistic logic of enframing? In what sense are today's educational institutions caught up in an unlimited quantification of qualitative relations which strips beings of their intrinsic meanings, transforming them into mere resources to be optimized with maximal efficiency?

Education as Enframing

Heidegger began developing his critique of higher education in 1911 and continued elaborating it well into the 1960s, but perhaps his most direct answer to this question comes in 1929.[20] Having finally been awarded a professorship (on the basis of *Being and Time*), the thirty-nine-year-old Heidegger gives his official "Inaugural Lecture" at Freiburg University, the famous "What is Metaphysics?" He begins boldly, directing his critical attention to the university itself by emphasizing philosophy's concrete "existential" foundations (since "metaphysical questioning must be posed . . . from the essential position of the existence [*Dasein*] that questions"). Within the lifeworld of the university, Heidegger observes, "existence" (*Dasein*) is determined by *Wissenschaft*, the knowledge embodied in the humanities and natural sciences. "Our *Dasein*—in the community of researchers, teachers, and students—is determined by science or knowledge [*durch die Wissenschaft bestimmt*]."[21] Our very "being-in-the-world" is shaped by the knowledge we pursue, uncover, and embody. When Heidegger claims that existence is fundamentally shaped by *knowledge*, he is not thinking of a professoriate shifting in the winds of academic trends, nor simply arguing for a kind of pedagogical or performative consistency, according to which we should practice what we know; his intent, rather, is to emphasize a troubling sense in which it seems that we cannot help practicing what we know, since we are "always-already" implicitly shaped by our guiding metaphysical presuppositions. Heidegger's question thus becomes: What is the *ontological impact* of our unquestioned reliance on the particular metaphysical presuppositions which tacitly dominate the Academy? "What happens to us essentially, in the ground of our existence," when the *Wissenschaft* pursued in the contemporary university becomes our guiding "passion," fundamentally shaping our view of the world and of ourselves?

Heidegger's dramatic answer introduces his radical critique of the hyper-specialization and consequent fragmentation of the modern university:

> The fields of science are widely separated. Their ways of handling the objects of their inquiries differ fundamentally. Today only the technical organization of universities and faculties consolidates this multiplicity of dispersed disciplines, only through practical and instrumental goals do they maintain any meaning. The rootedness of the sciences in their essential ground has dried up and died.[22]

Here in 1929 Heidegger accurately describes the predicament of that institution which, almost half a century later, Clark Kerr would satirically label the "Multi-versity": an internally fragmented *Uni*-versity-in-name-only, where the sole communal unity stems from a common grievance about parking spaces.[23] Historically, as the modern university loses sight of the shared goals which originally justified the endeavors of the academic community as a whole (at first, the common pursuit of the unified "system" of knowledge; then the communal dedication to the formation of cultivated individuals), its members begin to look outside the university for some purpose to give meaning to lives of research. Since only those disciplines (or subdisciplines) able to produce instrumentally useful results regularly find such external support, all disciplines increasingly try to present themselves in terms of their use-value. Without a counterideal, students, too, will adopt this instrumental mentality, coming to see education merely as a means to an increased salary down the road. In this way fragmentation leads to the professionalization of the university and, eventually, its deterioration into vocationalism. At the same time, moreover, the different disciplines, lacking any shared, substantive sense of a unifying purpose or common subject matter, tend by the logic of specialization to develop internal standards appropriate to their particular object-domains. As these domains become increasingly specialized, these internal standards become ever more disparate, if not simply incommensurable. In this way, disciplinary fragmentation leaves the university without common standards—other than the now ubiquitous but entirely empty and formal ideal of *excellence*.

Following in Heidegger's footsteps, critics such as Bill Readings and Timothy Clark show how our contemporary "university of excellence," owing to "the very emptiness of the idea of excellence," is "becoming an excellent bureaucratic corporation," "geared to no higher idea than its own maximized self-perpetuation according to optimal input/output ratios."[24] Such diagnoses make clear that the development of our educational institutions continues to follow the underlying metaphysical logic of enframing, the progressive transformation of all entities into mere resources to be optimized. Unfortunately, these critics fail to recognize this underlying ontohistorical logic and, so, offer diagnoses without cures. Indeed, Readings' materialist explanation for the historical obsolescence of *Bildung* as the unifying ideal of the modern university (the result of an "implacable . . . bourgeois economic revolution") leads him to succumb to a cynicism in which future denizens of the university can hope for nothing more than "pragmatic" situational responses in an environment increasingly transformed by "the logic of consumerism."[25] While such critiques of the university convincingly extend and update aspects of Heidegger's analysis, they lack his philosophical vision for a revitalizing reunification of the university.

To see that Heidegger himself did not relinquish all hope for the future of higher education, we need only attend carefully to the performative dimension of his "Inaugural Lecture." On the surface, it may seem as if Heidegger, welcomed at last into the arms of the university, rather perversely uses his celebratory lecture to pronounce the death of the institution which has just hired him: "The rootedness of the sciences in their essential ground has dried up and died." Yet, with this deliberate provocation Heidegger is not beating a dead horse; his pronouncement that the university is dead at its roots implies that it is fated to wither and decay *unless it is revivified*, reinvigorated from the root. Heidegger uses this organic metaphor of "rootedness" (*Verwurzelung*) to put into effect what Derrida (who will restage this scene himself) recognizes as "a phoenix motif": "One burns or buries what is *already dead* so that life . . . will be reborn and regenerated from these ashes."[26] Indeed, Heidegger begins to outline his program for a *renaissance* of the university in the lecture's conclusion. Existence is determined by science, but science itself remains rooted in metaphysics, whether it realizes it or not. Since the roots of the university are metaphysical, a reinstauration of the scientific lifeworld requires a renewed attention to this underlying metaphysical dimension. "Only if science exists on the basis of metaphysics can it achieve anew its essential task, which is not to amass and classify bits of knowledge, but to disclose in ever-renewed fashion the entire expanse of truth in nature and history."[27]

What exactly is Heidegger proposing here? To understand Heidegger's vision for a rebirth of the university, we need to turn to a text he began writing the next year: "Plato's Teaching on Truth."[28] Here, tracing the on-tohistorical roots of our educational crisis back to Plato's cave, Heidegger (quite literally) *excavates* an alternative.

HEIDEGGER'S RETURN TO PLATO'S CAVE: ONTOLOGICAL EDUCATION AS THE ESSENCE OF PAIDEIA

Plato seeks to . . . show that the essence of paideia does not consist in merely pouring knowledge into the unprepared soul as if it were a container held out empty and waiting. On the contrary, real education lays hold of the soul itself and transforms it in its entirety by first of all leading us to the place of our essential being and accustoming us to it.[29]

Our contemporary educational crisis can be understood as an ontohis-torical dissolution of Plato's original conception of education, Heidegger contends, so the deconstructive recovery of this "essence of paideia" is crucial to successfully resolving the crisis. A deeply resonant Greek word, paideia means "civilization," "culture," "development," "tradi-tion," "literature," and "education"; thus it encompasses what to our ears seems to be a rather wide range of semantic frequencies.[30] Heideg-ger was deeply drawn to the word, not only because (thanks to Werner Jaeger) it served as a key term in that intersection of German academic and political life which Heidegger sought to occupy during the 1930s, but also because he had an undeniable fondness for what (with a wink to Freud) we could call the *polysemic perversity* of language, that is, the for-tuitous ambiguities and unpredictable interconnections which form the warp and weave of its semantic web. Recognizing that such rich lan-guage tends to resist the analyst's pursuit of an unambiguous exactness, Heidegger argued that "rigorous" philosophical *precision* calls instead for an attempt to do justice to this semantic richness.[31] Yet, as Hans Georg Gadamer and Derrida have shown, this demand for us to do justice to language is *aporetic*—a "necessary impossibility"—since the holism of meaning renders the attempt ultimately impossible, not only practically (for finite beings like ourselves, who cannot follow all the strands in the semantic web at once), but also in principle (despite our Borgesian dreams of a *complete hypertext* which would exhaustively represent the semantic web, a dream even the vaunted World Wide Web barely inches toward realizing). This unfulfillable call for the philosopher *to do justice to language* is, nevertheless, *ethical* in the Kantian sense; it constitutes a regulative ideal, orienting our progress while remaining unreachable, like a course-guiding star. It is also, and for Heidegger more primor-dially, "*ethos*-ical" (so to speak), since such a call can be answered "authentically" only if it is taken up existentially and embodied in an *ethos*, a way of being. In *Being and Time*, Heidegger describes the called-for comportment as *Ent-schlossenheit*, "dis-closedness or re-solve," later he will teach it as *Gelassenheit*, "releasement or letting-be."[32] *Ent-schlossenheit* and *Gelassenheit* are not, of course, simply equivalent terms; releasement evolves out of resolve through a series of intermediary formulations and notably lacks resolve's voluntarism. But both entail a responsive hermeneutic receptivity (whether existential or phenomenological) and both designate comportments whereby we embody, reflexively, an understanding of what we *are*, ontologically, namely, *Da-sein*, "being [the] there," a making intelligible of the place in which we find ourselves.

Such considerations allow us to see that we *are* the place to which Heidegger is referring—in the epigraph above this section—when he writes that "real education lays hold of the soul itself and transforms it in its entirety by first of all leading us to the place of our essential being [*Wesensort*] and accustoming [*eingewöhnt*] us to it." As this epigraph shows, Heidegger believes he has fulfilled the ethical dictate *to do justice to language* by recovering "the essence of paideia," the ontological carrier wave underlying paideia's multiple semantic frequencies. Ventriloquizing Plato, Heidegger deploys this notion of the essence of paideia in order to oppose two conceptions of education. He warns first against a "false interpretation": We cannot understand education as the transmission of "information," the filling of the *psyche* with knowledge as if inscribing a *tabula rasa* or, in more contemporary parlance, "training-up" a neural net. This understanding of education is false because (in the terms of *Being and Time*) we are "thrown" beings, "always already" shaped by a tradition we can never "get behind," and so we cannot be blank slates or "empty containers" waiting to be filled.[33] Indeed, this "reductive and atrophied" misconception of education as the transmission of information reflects the nihilistic logic of enframing, that ontohistorical trend by which intelligibility is "leveled out into the uniform storage of information."[34] Yet here again we face a situation in which as the problem gets worse we become less likely to recognize it; the "impact" of this ontological drift toward meaninglessness can "barely be noticed by contemporary humanity because they are continually covered over with the latest information."[35]

Against this self-insulating but "false interpretation" of education, Heidegger advances his conception of "real or genuine education" (*echte Bildung*), the "essence of paideia." Drawing on the allegory of the cave—which "illustrates the essence of 'education' [paideia]" (as Plato claims at the beginning of Book VII of the *Republic*)—Heidegger seeks to effect nothing less than a re-ontologizing *revolution* in our understanding of education.[36] Recall Heidegger's succinct and powerful formulation: "Real education lays hold of the soul itself and transforms it in its entirety by first of all leading us to the place of our essential being and accustoming [*eingewöhnt*] us to it." Genuine education leads us back to ourselves, to the place we *are* (the *Da* of our *Sein*), teaches us "to dwell" (*wohnen*) "there," and transforms us in the process. This transformative journey to ourselves is not a flight away from the world into thought, but a *reflexive* return to the fundamental "realm of the human sojourn" (*Aufenthaltsbezirk des Menschen*).[37] The goal of this educational odyssey is simple but literally *revolutionary*: to bring us full circle back to ourselves, first by turning us away from the world in which we are most immediately immersed, then by turning us back to this world in a more reflexive way. As Heidegger explains, "Paideia means the turning around of the whole human being in the sense of displacing them out of the region of immediate encountering and accustoming them to another realm in which beings appear."[38]

How can we accomplish such an *ontological revolution* in education? What are the pedagogical methods of this alternative conception of education? And how, finally, can this ontological conception of education help us overturn the *enframing* of education?

Ontological Education Against Enframing

In "Plato's Teaching on Truth," Heidegger's exposition is complicated by the fact that he is simultaneously explicating his own positive understanding of "education" and critiquing an important transformation in the history of "truth" inaugurated by Plato: the transition from truth understood as *alêtheia*, phenomenological "unhiddenness," to *orthotês*, the "correctness" of an assertion. From this "ambiguity in Plato's doctrine," in which "truth still is, at one and the same time, unhiddenness and correctness," the subsequent tradition will develop only the *orthotic* understanding of truth at the expense of the *alêtheiac*.[39] In so doing, we lose "the original essence of truth," the manifestation of beings themselves, and come to understand truth solely as a feature of our own representational capacities. According to Heidegger, this displacement of the locus of truth from being to human subjectivity paves the way for that *metaphysical humanism* (or *subjectivism*) in which the "essence of paideia" will be eclipsed, allowing "education" to be absorbed by enframing, becoming merely a means for "bringing 'human beings' . . . to the liberation of their possibilities, the certitude of their destination, and the securing of their 'living.'"[40]

Despite some dramatic rhetorical flourishes, however, Heidegger has not entirely given up on "education" (*Bildung*). He dismisses the modern understanding of *Bildung* (the deliberate cultivation of "subjective qualities") as a "misinterpretation to which the notion fell victim in the nineteenth century," yet maintains that once *Bildung* is "given back its original naming power," it is the word which "comes closest to capturing the [meaning of the] word paideia." *Bildung* is literally ambiguous, Heidegger tells us; its "naming force" drives in two directions:

> What *"Bildung"* expresses is twofold: first, *Bildung* means forming [*Bilden*] in the sense of impressing a character that unfolds. But at the same time this "forming" [*"Bilden"*] "forms" [*"bildet"*] (or impresses a character) by antecedently taking its measure from some measure-giving vision, which for that reason is called the pre-conception [*Vor-bild*].

"Thus," Heidegger concludes, "'education' ['*Bildung'*] means impressing a character, especially as guiding by a pre-conception."[41]

Few would quibble with the first claim: education stamps us with a character which unfolds within us. But what forms the "stamp" which forms us? *Who educates the educators?* According to Heidegger, the answer to this question is built into the very meaning of paideia; it is the second sense he "restores" to *Bildung*. To further "unfold" these two senses of "education," Heidegger immediately introduces the contrast-class: "the contrary of paideia is *apaideusia*, lack of education [*Bildunglosigkeit*], where no fundamental comportment is awakened, no measure-giving preconception established."[42] This helpfully clarifies Heidegger's first claim: It is by awakening a "fundamental comportment" that education stamps us with a character that unfolds within us. In the educational situation—a situation without pre-delimitable boundaries, indeed, a situation the boundaries of which Heidegger ceaselessly seeks to expand (for he holds that "paideia is essentially a movement of passage, from *apaideusia* to paideia"; that is, education is not something that can ever be *completed*)—the "fundamental comportment" perhaps most frequently called for is not the heroic *Ent-schlossenheit*, nor even the gentler *Gelassenheit*, but rather a more basic form of receptive spontaneity Heidegger will simply call *hearing* or *hearkening* (*hören*)—that is (as we will see), an attentive and responsive way of dwelling in one's environment. But whether the comportment implicitly guiding education is "resoluteness," "releasement," "hearing," or that anxiety-tranquilizing *hurry*, which generally characterizes contemporary life, depends on the second sense of *Bildung*, which remains puzzling: From where do we derive the measure-giving vision which implicitly informs all genuine education?

Heidegger's answer is complicated, let us recall, by the fact that he is both elaborating his own philosophy of education (as it were) and performing a critical exegesis of Plato's decisive metaphysical contribution to "the history that we *are*," the history of metaphysics. These two aims are in tension with one another because the education Heidegger seeks to impart—the fundamental attunement he would awaken in his students—is itself an attempt to awaken us *from* the ontological education that we have "always already" received from the metaphysical tradition; for this generally unnoticed antecedent measure comes to us *from metaphysics*, from the ontotheologically conceived understanding of the being of beings. In short, Heidegger seeks to educate his students *against* their preexisting ontotheological education. (He will sometimes call this educating-against-education simply "teaching.") The crucial question, then, is: *How can Heidegger's ontological education combat the metaphysical education we have always already received?*

The Pedagogy of Ontological Freedom

Heidegger's suggestions about how the ontological education he advocates can transcend enframing are surprisingly specific. Recall that in Plato's allegory, the prisoner (1) begins in captivity within the cave, (2) escapes the chains and turns around to discover the fire and objects responsible for the shadows on the wall previously taken as reality, then (3) ascends from the cave into the light of the outside world, coming to understand what is seen there as made possible by the light of the sun, and (4) finally returns to the cave, taking up the struggle to free the other prisoners (who violently resist their would-be liberator). For Heidegger, this well-known scenario suggests the pedagogy of ontological education. On his remarkable interpretation, the prisoner's "four different dwelling places" communicate the four successive stages whereby ontological education breaks students' bondage to the technological mode of revealing, freeing them to understand what-is differently.

When students' ontological educations begin, they "are engrossed in what they immediately encounter," taking the shadows cast by the fire on the wall to be the ultimate reality of things. Yet this "fire" is only "man-made"; the "confusing" light it casts represents enframing's ontologically-reductive mode of revealing. Here in this first stage, all entities show up to students merely as resources to be optimized—including the students themselves. Thus, if pressed, students will ultimately "justify" even their education itself merely as a means to making more money, getting the most out of their potentials, or some other equally empty optimization imperative. Stage two is only reached when a student's "gaze is freed from its captivity to shadows"; this happens when a student recognizes "the fire" (enframing) as the source of "the shadows" (entities understood as mere resources). In stage two, the *metaphysical* chains of enframing are thus broken. But *how* does this liberation occur? Despite the importance of this question, Heidegger answers it only in an aside: "to turn one's gaze from the shadows to entities as they show themselves within the glow of the firelight is difficult and fails."[43] His point, I take it, is that entities *do not show themselves* as they are when forced into the metaphysical mold of enframing, the ontotheology which reduces them to mere resources to be

optimized. Students can be led to this realization through a guided investigation of the being of any entity, which they will tend to understand
only as eternally recurring will-to-power, that is, as forces endlessly coming together and breaking apart. Because this metaphysical understanding dissolves being into becoming, the attempt to see entities as they *are*
in its light is doomed to failure; resources have no *being*, they are "constantly becoming" (as Nietzsche realized). With this recognition—and the
anxiety it tends to induce—students can attain a negative *freedom from* enframing.

Still, Heidegger insists that "real freedom," "effective freedom" (*wirk-
liche Freiheit*)—the positive freedom in which students realize that entities
are more than mere resources and so become *free for* understanding them
otherwise—"is attained only in stage three, in which someone who has
been unchained is . . . conveyed outside the cave 'into the open.'" (Notice
the implicit reference to someone doing the unchaining and conveying
here; for Heidegger, the educator plays a crucial role facilitating students'
passage between each of the stages.) "The open" is one of Heidegger's
names for "being as such"; that is, for "what appears antecedently in
everything that appears and . . . makes whatever appears be accessible."[44]
The attainment of—or better, comportmental *attunement to*—this "open"
is what Heidegger famously calls "dwelling."[45] With this positive *ontological freedom*, "what things are . . . no longer appear merely in the man-
made and confusing glow of the fire within the cave. The things themselves stand there in the binding force and validity of their own visible
form."[46] Ontological freedom is achieved when entities show themselves
in their full phenomenological richness. The goal of the third stage of ontological education, then, is to teach students to "dwell," to help attune
them to the *being* of entities, and thus to teach them to see that the being
of an entity—be it a book, cup, rose, or, to use a particularly salient example, *they themselves*—cannot be fully understood in the ontologically reductive terms of enframing.[47]

With the attainment of this crucial third stage, Heidegger's "genuine,"
ontological education may seem to have reached its completion, since
"the very essence of paideia consists in making the human being strong
for the clarity and constancy of insight into essence."[48] This claim that
genuine education teaches students to recognize "essences" is not merely
a Platonic conceit, but plays an absolutely crucial role in Heidegger's program for a reunification of the university (as we will see in the conclusion). Nevertheless, ontological education reaches its true culmination
only in the fourth stage, the *return to the cave*. Heidegger clearly understood his own role as a teacher in terms of just such a return, that is, as a
struggle to free ontologically anaesthetized enframers from their bondage
to a self-reifying mode of ontological revealing.[49] But his ranking of the re-

turn to the cave as the highest stage of ontological education is not merely an evangelistic call for others to adopt his vision of education as a revolution in consciousness; it also reflects his recognition that, in ontological education, *learning culminates in teaching*. We must thus ask: What is *called* "teaching"?

What Is Called Teaching?

The English "teach" comes from the same linguistic family as the German verb *zeigen*, "to point or show."[50] As this etymology suggests, *to teach is to reveal*, to point out or make manifest through words. But to reveal *what*? What does the teacher, who "points out" (or reveals) with words, point to (or indicate)?[51] What do teachers teach? The question seems to presuppose that all teaching shares a common "subject matter," not simply a shared method or goal (the inculcation of critical thinking, persuasive writing, and the like), but something more substantive: a common subject matter unifying the Uni-versity. Of course all teachers use words to disclose, but to disclose a common subject matter? How can such a supposition *not* sound absurd to we professional denizens of a postmodern polyversity, where relentless hyper-specialization continues to fragment our subjects, and even seeming counterforces like interdisciplinarity discourses thrive only in so far they open new subspecialties for a relentless vascular-to-capillary colonization of the scientific lifeworld? In such a situation, is it surprising that the Heideggerian idea of all teachers ultimately sharing a unified subject sounds absurd or, at best, like an outdated myth—albeit the myth that founded the modern university? But *is* the idea of such a shared subject matter a myth? What *do* teachers teach? Let us approach this question from what might at first seem to be another direction—attempting to *learn* its answer.

If teaching is revealing through words, then conversely, learning is experiencing what a teacher's words reveal. That is, to learn is actively to allow oneself to share in what the teacher's words disclose. But again, *what* do the teacher's words reveal? We will notice, if we read closely enough, that Heidegger answers this question in 1951, when he writes: "To learn means to make everything we do answer to whatever essentials address us at a given time."[52] Here it might sound at first as if Heidegger is simply claiming that learning, as the complement of teaching, means actively allowing oneself to share in that which the teacher's words disclose. But Wittgenstein used to say that philosophy is like a bicycle race, the point of which is to go as slowly as possible without falling off; and if we slow down, we will notice that Heidegger's words—the words of a teacher who would teach what learning means (in fact, the performative situation is even more complex)[53]—say more:

Learning means actively allowing ourselves to respond to what is essential in that which always addresses us, that which has always already claimed us.

In a sense, then, learning means responding appropriately to the solicitations of the environment. Of course, Heidegger is thinking of the *onto-logical* environment (the way in which what-is discloses itself to us), but even ontic analogs show that this capacity to respond appropriately to the environment is quite difficult to learn. We learn to respond appropriately to environmental solicitations through a long process of trial and error. We must, in other words, learn how to learn. Here problems abound, for it is not clear that learning to learn can be taught. To the logical analyst, this demand seems to lead to a regress (for if we need to learn to learn, then we need to learn to learn to learn, and so on). But logic misleads phenomenology here; for as Heidegger realized, it is simply a question of jumping into the *pedagogical circle* in the right way. This train of thought leads Heidegger to claim that if "teaching is even more difficult than learning," this is only because the teacher must be an *exemplary learner*, capable of teaching his or her students to learn, that is, capable of learning-in-public, actively responding to the emerging demands of each unique educational situation. Recall the famous passage:

> Why is teaching more difficult than learning? Not because the teacher must have a larger store of information, and have it always ready. Teaching is more difficult than learning because what teaching calls for is this: to let learn. The real teacher, in fact, lets nothing else be learned than learning. . . . The teacher is ahead of his apprentices in this alone, that he has still far more to learn than they—he has to learn to let them learn. The teacher must be capable of being more teachable than his apprentices.[54]

The teacher teaches students to learn—to respond appropriately to the solicitations of the ontological environment—*by* responding appropriately to the solicitations of his or her environment, which is, after all, the students' environment too. Learning culminates in teaching, then, because teaching is the highest form *of learning;* unlike "instructing" [*belehren*], "teaching" [*lehren*] is ultimately a "letting learn" [*lernen lassen*]. "The true teacher is ahead of the students only in that he has more to learn than they: namely, the letting learn. (To learn [means]: to bring what we do and allow into a co-respondence [or a suitable response, *Entsprechung*] with that which in each case grants itself to us as the essential.)"[55]

This last assertion should remind us of Heidegger's earlier claim that "the very essence of paideia consists in making the human being strong for the clarity and constancy of insight into essence."[56] I said previously that this claim plays a crucial role in Heidegger's program for a reunification of the university. By way of conclusion, let us briefly develop this claim and thereby further elaborate Heidegger's positive vision for the future of higher education.

Envisioning a University of Teachers

How can Heidegger's understanding of *ontological* education help us restore substance to our currently empty guiding ideal of educational "excellence," and in so doing, provide the contemporary university with a renewed sense of *unity*, not only restoring substance to our shared commitment to forming *excellent* students, but also helping us recognize the sense in which we are in fact all working on the same project? The answer is surprisingly simple: By *re-essentializing* the notion of *excellence*. Heidegger, like Aristotle, is a *perfectionist*; he argues not only that there is a distinctive human essence, but also that the *good life*, the life of "excellence" (*aretê*), is the life spent cultivating this distinctively human essence. For Heidegger, as we have seen, the human "essence" is *Dasein*, "being-there"—that is, the making-intelligible of the place in which we find ourselves, or, even more simply, *world disclosing*. For a world-disclosing being to cultivate its essence, then, is for it to recognize and develop this essence, not only acknowledging its participation in the creation and maintenance of an intelligible world, but actively embracing its ontological role in such world disclosure. The full ramifications of this seemingly simple insight are profound and revolutionary.[57] We will restrict ourselves to briefly developing the two most important implications of Heidegger's re-essentialization of excellence for the future of the university.

Heidegger's ontological conception of education would transform the existing relations between teaching and research, on the one hand, and between the now fragmented departments, on the other. In effect, Heidegger dedicates himself to finally redeeming the two central ideals which guided the formation of the modern university: that teaching and research should be harmoniously integrated, and that the university community should understand itself as committed to a common substantive task.[58] How does Heidegger think he can finally achieve such ambitions? First, his conception of "teaching" would reunite research and teaching, because when students develop the aforementioned "insight into essence," they are being taught to disclose and investigate the ontological presuppositions which underlie *all* research, in Heidegger's view. Today's academic departments are what he calls "positive sciences," that is, they all rest on ontological "posits," ontological assumptions about what the class of entities they study *are*. Biology, for example, allows us to understand the *logos* of the *bios*, the order and structure of living beings. Nevertheless, Heidegger asserts, biology proper cannot tell us what life *is*.[59]

Instead, biology takes over its implicit ontological understanding of what life *is* from the metaphysical understanding governing our Nietzschean epoch of enframing. (When contemporary philosophers of biology claim that life *is* "a self-replicating system," they have unknowingly adopted the basic ontological presupposition of Nietzsche's metaphysics, according to which life *is* ultimately the eternal recurrence of will to power, that is, sheer will-to-will, unlimited self-augmentation.)[60] Analogously, psychology can tell us a great deal about how consciousness (the *psyche*) functions, but it cannot tell us what consciousness *is*. The same holds true for the understanding of "the corporeality of bodies, the vegetable character of plants, the animality of animals, and the humanness of humanity" within physics, botany, zoology, and anthropology, respectively; these sciences all presuppose an ontological posit, a pre-understanding of the being of the class of entities they study.[61] Heidegger's ontologically reconceived notion of teaching is inextricably entwined with research, then, because ontological education teaches students to question the very ontological presuppositions which guide research, thereby opening a space for understanding the being of the entities they study otherwise than in enframing's ontologically reductive terms. Heidegger's reconceptualization of education would thus encourage revolutionary transformations in the sciences and humanities by teaching students to focus on and explicitly investigate the ontological presuppositions which implicitly guide research in each domain of knowledge.

Despite such revolutionary goals, Heidegger thought that his ontological reconceptualization of education could also restore a substantive sense of unity to the university community, if only this community could learn "to engage in [this "reflection on the essential foundations"] as reflection and to think and belong to the university *from the base of this engagement*."[62] From its founding, one of the major concerns about the modern university has been how it could maintain the unity of structure and purpose thought to be definitive of the "uni-versity" as such. German Idealists like Johann Fichte and Friedrich Schelling believed that this unity would follow organically from the *totality* of the system of knowledge. But this faith in the system proved to be far less influential on posterity than Alexander Humboldt's alternative "humanist" ideal, according to which the university's unity would come from a shared commitment to the educational formation of character. Humboldt's famous idea was to link "objective *Wissenschaft* with subjective *Bildung*"; the university would be responsible for forming fully cultivated individuals, a requirement Humboldt hoped would serve to guide and unify the new freedom of research. Historically, of course, neither the German Idealists' reliance on the unity of research nor Humboldt's emphasis on a shared commitment to the educational formation of students succeeded in unifying the university community. In effect, however, Heidegger's re-ontologization of education would *combine* (his versions of) these two strategies. The university community would be unified *both* by its shared commitment to forming *excellent* individuals (where excellence is understood in terms of the ontological perfectionism outlined above) *and* by the shared recognition on the part of this community that its members are all committed to the same substantive pursuit: the ultimately revolutionary task not simply of understanding what *is*, but of investigating the ontological presuppositions implicitly guiding all the various fields of knowledge. Heidegger thus believed that ontological education, by restoring substance to the notion of excellence and so teaching us "to disclose the essential in all things," could finally succeed in "shattering the encapsulation of the sciences in their different disciplines and bringing them back from their boundless and aimless dispersal in individual fields and corners."[63]

NOTES

An earlier version of this paper was presented to the University of New Mexico Philosophy Department, 2 February 2001; I would like to thank John Bussanich, Manfred Frings, Russell Goodman, Barbara Hannan, Joachim Oberst, Fred Schueler, and John Taber for helpful comments and criticisms. Thanks also to Bert Dreyfus for reading this piece and offering insightful suggestions and encouragement, and to Michael Peters for organizing this important volume and inviting me to contribute.

1. See Martin Heidegger, *Being and Time* trans. J. Macquarrie and E. Robinson (New York: Harper & Row, 1962), 44; and Heidegger *Sein und Zeit* (Tübingen: M. Niemeyer, 1993), 22.

2. See Martin Heidegger, "Plato's Teaching on Truth," In *Pathmarks*, ed. William McNeill (Cambridge: Cambridge University Press, 1998), 167; Martin Heidegger, *Wegmarken*, 3rd Edition (Frankfurt: V. Klostermann, 1996), 218. (On my translation of this title, see note 28 below.) I am aware that the preceding sentence ominously echoes the title of Nietzsche's politically compromised and deeply problematic early lectures "On the Future of Our Educational Institutions" (which culminate with a call for a "great *Führer*" [See Friedrich Nietzsche, *On the Future of Our Educational Institutions*, in O. Levy, ed., *The Complete Works of Friedrich Nietzsche*, ed. O. Levy, vol. 6 (Edinburgh: T. N. Foulis, 1909); Jacques Derrida, *The Ear of the Other*, ed. C. V. McDonald, trans. Kamuf and Ronell (New York: Shocken Books, 1985), 28]). I bracket such political connections here, but a complementary essay examines the darker side of Heidegger's philosophical critique of education, showing that it played a central role in his decision to join with the Nazis in the early 1930s; see my "Heidegger and the Politics of the University" (forthcoming).

3. Heidegger, "Plato's Teaching," 167; *Wegmarken*, 218.

4. See Saul Kripke, *Naming and Necessity* (Cambridge, Mass: Cambridge University Press, 1980). On Heidegger's distinctive understanding of "essence," see my "What's Wrong with Being a Technological Essentialist? A Response to Feenberg," *Inquiry* 43, 4 (October 2000): 429–44.

5. See Martin Heidegger, "The Question Concerning Technology," in *The Question Concerning Technology and Other Essays*, trans. W. Lovitt (New York: Harper & Row, 1977), 4, 30–31.

6. Cf. Andrew Feenberg's Hegelian misinterpretation of Heidegger's understanding of *essence* in "The Ontic and the Ontological in Heidegger's Philosophy of Technology: Response to Thomson," *Inquiry* 43, 4 (October 2000): 445–50.

7. See Heidegger, "On the Essence of Truth," *Pathmarks* 145; *Wegmarken* 189.

8. See Heidegger, "On the Essence of Truth," *Pathmarks* 145–46; *Wegmarken* 190 (my italics). I am of necessity simplifying Heidegger's complex account here, but see my "Ontotheology? Understanding Heidegger's *Destruktion* of Metaphysics," *International Journal of Philosophical Studies* 8, 3 (October 2000): 297–327.

9. See Martin Heidegger, *An Introduction to Metaphysics*, trans. R. Manheim (New Haven: Yale University Press, 1959), 3; *Einführung in die Metaphysik* (Tübingen: M. Niemeyer, 1953), 2.

10. See Ludwig Wittgenstein, *Philosophical Investigations*, third ed., trans. G. E. M. Anscombe (New York: The Macmillan Company, 1968), 85.

11. See also Heidegger, "Plato's Teaching," 170: "The essence of 'education' is grounded in the essence of 'truth.'"

12. See Martin Heidegger, *Nietzsche: Nihilism*, ed., David Krell, trans. F. Capuzzi (New York: Harper & Row, 1982), 205; *Nietzsche*, vol. II (Pfullingen Germany: Neske, 1961), 343.

13. Eventually, either a new ontotheology emerges (perhaps, as Thomas Kuhn suggests, out of the investigation of those "anomalous" entities which resist being understood in terms of the dominant ontotheology), or else our underlying conception of the being of *all* entities would be brought into line with this spreading ontotheology. Although this latter alternative has never yet occurred, Heidegger calls it "the greatest danger," for he is worried that our Nietzschean ontotheology could become *totalizing*, "driving out every other possibility of revealing" by overwriting *Dasein*'s "special nature," our defining capacity for world disclosure, with the "total thoughtlessness" of a merely instrumental "calculative reasoning." See Heidegger, "The Question Concerning Technology," 27; Heidegger *Discourse on Thinking*, trans. J. Anderson and E. Freund (New York: Harper & Row, 1966), 56.

14. See Heidegger, "The Question Concerning Technology," 16–20.

15. See esp. Friedrich Nietzsche, *The Will To Power*, ed. and trans. Walter Kaufmann (New York: Random House, 1967), 549–50. Here Nietzsche clearly conceives of beings *as such* as will to power and of the way the *totality* exists as eternally recurring. Nor can Heidegger's controversial reading be rejected simply by excluding this problematic "text" on the basis of its politically compromised ancestry, since Nietzsche's ontotheology can also be found in his other works.

16. See Heidegger, "Nihilism as Determined by the History of Being," *Nietzsche: Nihilism*, 199–250.

17. See Martin Heidegger, *Contributions to Philosophy (From Enowning)*, trans. P. Emad and K. Maly (Bloomington: Indiana University Press, 1999), 95; *Beiträge zur Philosophie (Vom Ereignis)*, *Gesamtausgabe*, vol. 65, ed. F.-W. von Hermann (Frankfurt: Vittorio Klostermann, 1989), 137; ibid., 94 (my emphasis); *Beiträge*, 135; Martin Heidegger, "Traditional Language and Technological Language," trans. W. Gregory, *Journal of Philosophical Research* 23 (1998): 136; Heidegger, *Discourse on*

Thinking, 46; Heidegger, "Traditional Language," 139; Jean Baudrillard, *The Transparency of Evil*, trans. J. Benedict (London: Verso, 1993), 4. Baudrillard envisions a dystopian fulfillment of this dream, a "grand delete" in which computers succeed in exhaustively representing meaning, then delete human life so as not to upset the perfectly completed equation. This dystopian vision stems from a faulty premise, however, since meaning can never be exhaustively represented. See Hubert L. Dreyfus, *What Computers Still Can't Do: A Critique of Artificial Reason* (Cambridge, Mass: MIT Press, 1992).

18. See Heidegger, "Building Dwelling Thinking," *Poetry, Language, Thought*, 152.

19. See Heidegger, "The Question Concerning Technology," 18; see also Hubert L. Dreyfus and Charles Spinosa, "Highway Bridges and Feasts: Heidegger and Borgmann on How to Affirm Technology," *Man and World* 30, 2 (1997).

20. On the historical development of Heidegger's critique of education, see my "Heidegger and the Politics of the University."

21. See Heidegger, "What is Metaphysics?" in *Pathmarks*, 82; *Wegmarken*, 103.

22. See Heidegger, "What is Metaphysics?" 82–83; *Wegmarken*, 103–104.

23. In 1962, Heidegger writes: "The university . . . is presumably the most ossified school, straggling behind in its structure. Its name 'University' trudges along only as an apparent title. . . . It can be doubted whether the talk about general education, about education as a whole, still meets the circumstances that are formed by the technological age." (See Heidegger, "Traditional Language," 130.) As Haskins explains: "Historically, the word university had no connection with the universe or the universality of learning; it denotes only the totality of a group . . . an association of masters and scholars living the common life of learning." See Charles Haskins, *The Rise of Universities* (New York: Henry Holt and Company, 1923), 14, 34.

24. See Bill Readings, *The University in Ruins* (Cambridge, Mass.: Harvard University Press, 1996), 152, 125; Timothy Clark, "Literary Force: Institutional Values," *Culture Machine* 1, no. 1 (November 1998), "http://www.culturemachine.-tees.ac.uk/Cmach/Backissues/j001/articles/art_clar.html" (21 August 2000).

25. See Readings, *Ruins*, 132, 178. Readings calls for a (recognizably Heideggerian) refusal "to submit Thought to the exclusive rule of exchange-value," but this is not a call he can justify in the materialist terms he adopts (see *Ruins*, 178, 222, note 10). Readings elegantly distinguishes three historical phases in the development of the modern university, characterizing each by reference to its guiding idea: "the university of reason," "the university of culture," and "the university of excellence." These distinctions are nice but a bit simplistic; for example, the university of reason existed for only a few fabled years at the University of Jena at the turn of the eighteenth century, where the greatest pedagogical and philosophical thinkers of the time—Fichte, Goethe, Schiller, Schelling, Schleiermacher, the Schlegel brothers, and others—developed the implications of German Idealism for education. Ironically, when this assemblage sought to formalize the principles underlying their commitment to the system of knowledge in order to inaugurate the University of Berlin, they inadvertently helped create the model of the university which succeeded their own: Humbolt's university of "culture" (or better, *Bildung*, that is, a shared commitment to the formation of cultivated individuals).

On Readings' materialist account, the industrial revolution's push toward globalization undermined the university of culture's unifying idea of serving a *national* culture, eventually generating its own successor, the contemporary "university of excellence," a university defined by its *lack* of any substantive, unifying self-conception. Despite the great merits of Readings' book, this account of the historical transition from "the university of culture" to "the university of excellence" is overly dependent on a dubious equation of *Bildung*—the formation of cultivated individuals—with *national culture*. Heidegger's account of the development of education as reflecting an ontohistorical *dissolution* of its guiding idea is much more satisfactory. Although Heidegger is critical of aspects of (what Readings calls) "the university of culture" and "the university of excellence," we will see that Heidegger's own vision for the future of the university combines ontologically resuscitated understandings of *Bildung* and of excellence.

26. See Derrida, *The Ear of the Other*, 26. For Derrida's deliberate restaging, see his "The Principle of Reason: The University Through the Eyes of its Pupils," *Diacritics* 14 (Fall 1983): 5, where he gives us "something like an inaugural address."

27. Heidegger, "What is Metaphysics?" 95; *Wegmarken*, 121.

28. Published in 1940, Heidegger's *Platons Lehre von der Wahrheit* summarizes and extends themes from a 1930–31 lecture course on Plato. I translate the title as "Plato's Teaching on Truth" (rather than McNeill's "Plato's Doctrine of Truth") to preserve Heidegger's reference to *teaching* and the title's dual implication that (1) education is grounded in (the history of) truth, as we have seen, and that (2) Plato's own doctrine concerning truth covers over and so obscures truth's historically earlier and ontologically more basic meaning, as we will see.

29. See Heidegger, "Plato's Teaching," 167; *Wegmarken*, 217.

30. See Werner Jaeger, *Paideia: The Ideals of Greek Culture*, trans. G. Highet (New York: Oxford University Press, 1965). Contending that "paideia, the shaping of the Greek character," best explains "the unique educational genius which is the secret of the undying influence of Greece on all subsequent ages," Jaeger pitches his work in terms that harmonize only too well with the growing Nazi currents (vitalism, the breeding of the Nietzschean "higher man," race, the community, the leader, the state, etc.), for example: "Every nation which has reached a certain stage of development is instinctively impelled to practice education. Education is the process by which a community preserves and transmits its physical character. For the individual passes away, but the type remains. . . . Education, as practiced by man, is inspired by the same creative and directive vital force which impels every natural species to maintain and preserve its own type" (*Paideia*, xiii).

31. See Martin Heidegger, *What is Called Thinking?*, trans. J. G. Gray (New York: Harper & Row, 1968), 71; *Was Heißt Denken?* (Tübingen: M. Niemeyer, 1984), 68: "Polysemy is no objection against the rigorousness of what is thought thereby. For all genuine thinking remains in its essence thoughtfully . . . polysemic [*mehrdeutig*]. . . . Polysemy is the element in which all thinking must itself be underway in order to be rigorous."

32. Heidegger writes "*Entschlossenheit*" ("resoluteness" or "decisiveness") as "*Ent-schlossenheit*" ("un-closedness") in order to emphasize that the existential "resoluteness" whereby *Dasein* finds a way to authentically choose the commitments which define it (after having been radically individualized in being-toward-

death) does not entail deciding on a particular course of action ahead of time and obstinately sticking to one's guns come what may, but rather requires an "openness" whereby we continue to be responsive to the emerging solicitations of our particular existential "situation." The existential situation in general is thus not unlike a living puzzle we must continually "re-solve." The later notion of *Gelassenheit* (or *Gelassenheit zu den Dingen*) names a comportment in which we maintain our sensitivity to several interconnected ways in which things show themselves to us— namely, as grounded, as mattering, as taking place within a horizon of possibilities, and as showing themselves to finite beings who disclose a world through language—four phenomenological modalities of "presencing" that Heidegger (in a *détournement* of Hölderlin) calls "earth," "heavens," "divinities," and "mortals." See Heidegger, "The Thing," *Poetry, Language, Thought*, trans. A. Hofstadter (New York: Harper & Row, 1971), 165–86.

33. The increasingly dominant *metaphor*, too often literalized, of the brain as a computer forgets (to paraphrase a line from Heidegger's 1942–43 lectures, *Parmenides*) that we do not think *because* we have a brain; we *have* a brain because we can *think*.

34. Heidegger, "Preface" to *Pathmarks*, xiii.

35. Heidegger, "Traditional Language and Technological Language," 140, 142.

36. Heidegger, "Plato's Teaching," 167.

37. Heidegger, "Plato's Teaching," 168; *Wegmarken* 219. See also John A. Taber, *Transformative Philosophy: A Study of Sankara, Fichte, and Heidegger* (Honolulu: University of Hawaii Press, 1983), esp. 104–15. *Aufenthalte* ("odyssey, abidance, sojourn, stay, or stop-over") is an important term of art for the later Heidegger; it connotes the journey through intelligibility definitive of human existence. Since it is the title Heidegger gave to the journal in which he recorded his thoughts during his first trip to Greece in the spring of 1962 (see Heidegger, *Aufenthalte* [Frankfurt: Vittorio Klostermann, 1989]), it could be rendered as an "odyssey" to emphasize Heidegger's engagement with the Homeric heritage. The idea of a journey between nothingnesses adds a more poetic—and tragic— dimension to Heidegger's etymological emphasis on "existence" as the "standing-out" (*ek-sistere*) into intelligibility. Yet, like the Hebrew *gêr*, the "sojourn" of the non-Israelite in Israel (Exod. 12:19; Isa. 16:4; Jer. 42:15), *Aufenthalte* clearly also connotes the "home-coming through alterity" which Heidegger powerfully elaborates in 1942's *Hölderlin's Hymn "The Ister,"* trans. W. McNeill and J. Davis (Bloomington: Indiana University Press, 1996), and is thus properly polysemic (or "jewgreek," as Lyotard puts it—borrowing Joyce's provocative expression).

38. See Heidegger, "Plato's Teaching," 167; *Wegmarken* 218.

39. See Heidegger, "Plato's Teaching,"177–78.

40. See Heidegger, "Plato's Teaching,"181; *Wegmarken* 236.

41. See Heidegger, "Plato's Teaching,"166–67; *Wegmarken* 217. The English *education* harbors a similar ambiguity; "education" comes from the Latin *educare*, "to rear or bring up," which is closely related to *educere*, "to lead forth." Indeed, "education" seems to have absorbed the Latin *educere*, for it means not only "bringing up" (in the sense of *training*) but also "bringing forth" (in the sense of actualizing); these two meanings come together in the modern conception of education as a *training* which develops certain desirable *aptitudes*.

42. See Heidegger, "Plato's Teaching," 167; *Wegmarken*, 217.

43. See Heidegger, "Plato's Teaching," 170; *Wegmarken*, 222.

44. "The open," Heidegger explains, "does not mean the unboundedness of some wide-open space; rather, the open sets boundaries to things." See Heidegger, "Plato's Teaching," 170.

45. See, for example, Heidegger, "Building Dwelling Thinking," in *Poetry, Language, Thought*, 145–61.

46. See Heidegger, "Plato's Teaching," 168–72.

47. Metaphysics forgets that the condition of its own possibility—namely, the "presencing" (*anwesen*) of entities, their preconceptual phenomenological givenness—is also the condition of metaphysics' impossibility. For the phenomenological presencing which elicits conceptualization can never be entirely captured by the yoke of our metaphysical concepts; it always partially defies conceptualization, lingering behind as an extraconceptual phenomenological excess.

48. See Heidegger, "Plato's Teaching," 176.

49. Heidegger knew from personal experience that this is no easy task; someone who has been taught to "dwell" in a mode of revealing other than enframing "no longer knows his or her way around the cave and risks the danger of succumbing to the overwhelming power of the kind of truth that is normative there, the danger of being overcome by the claim of the common reality to be the only reality." Heidegger, "Plato's Teaching," 171.

50. The etymology of "teach" goes back through the Old English *tæcan* or *tæcean*. One of the first recorded uses of the word in English can be found in *The Blickling Homilies*, 971 AD: "*Him tæcean lifes weg.*" Heidegger would have appreciated the fortuitous ambiguity of *weg* or "way" here, which, like the Greek *hodos*, means both *path* and *manner*. For Heidegger too, the teacher teaches two different "ways," both *what* and *how*, subject and method. The Old English *tæcean* has near cognates in Old Teutonic (*taikjan*), Gothic (*taikns*), Old Spanish (*tekan*), and Old High German (*zeihhan*). This family can itself be traced back to the pre-Teutonic *deik-*, the Sanskrit *diç-*, and the Greek *deik-nunai, deigma*. *Deik*, the Greek root, means to bring to light, display, or exhibit, hence to *show* by words. (I rely here on *The Oxford English Dictionary* and George Liddel and Robert Scott's *Greek-English Lexicon*.)

51. Agamben traces this important ambiguity between *demonstration* and *indication* back to Aristotle's distinction between "primary and secondary substance." See Giorgio Agamben, *Language and Death: The Place of Negativity*, trans. K. Pinkus and M. Hardt (Minneapolis: University of Minnesota Press, 1991), 16–18. In "Ontotheology?" I show that Aristotle's formalization of this distinction constitutes the inaugural *unification* of metaphysics as ontotheology (although its elements go back much further).

52. "*Lernen heißt: das Tun und Lassen zu dem in die Entsprechung bringen, was sich jeweils an wesenhaftem uns zuspricht.*" Heidegger, *What is Called Thinking?*, 14; *Was Heißt Denken?*, 49. See also James F. Ward, *Heidegger's Political Thinking* (Amherst: University of Massachusetts Press, 1995), 177.

53. Concerning the performative situation, remember that Heidegger had been banned from teaching by the University of Freiburg's "de-Nazification" hearings in 1946, a decision reached in large part on the basis of Karl Jasper's judgment that

Heidegger's teaching was dictatorial, mystagogic, and in its essence unfree, and thus a danger to the youth. Here Heidegger treads a tightrope over this political abyss, seeking unapologetically to articulate and defend his earlier pedagogical method (although with the charges of corrupting the youth and of mysticism ringing in his ears, it is hard not to read his text as a kind of *apology*). See Rüdiger Safranski, *Martin Heidegger: Between Good and Evil*, trans. E. Osers (Cambridge, Mass.: Harvard University Press, 1998), 332–52.

54. See Heidegger, *What is Called Thinking?* 15; *Was Heißt Denken?*, 50.

55. See Heidegger, "Traditional Language," 129–30.

56. See Heidegger, "Plato's Teaching," 176.

57. See the groundbreaking development of this insight by Charles Spinosa, Fernando Flores, and Hubert L. Dreyfus in *Disclosing New Worlds* (Cambridge: MIT Press, 1997), a book Dreyfus has since described as "a revolutionary manifesto for business and politics" (and for higher education as well, see esp. 151–61). See Hubert L. Dreyfus, "Responses," in *Heidegger, Coping, and Cognitive Science* ed. Mark Wrathall and Jeff Malpas (Cambridge: MIT Press, 2000), 347.

58. Recall that on the medieval model of the university, the task of higher education was to transmit a relatively fixed body of knowledge. The French preserved something of this view; universities taught the supposedly established doctrines, while research took place outside the university in non-teaching academies. The French model was appropriated by the German universities which preceded Kant, in which the state-sponsored "higher faculties" of law, medicine, and theology were separated from the more independent, "lower" faculty of philosophy. Kant personally experienced *The Conflict of the Faculties* of philosophy and theology (after publishing *Religion within the Limits of Reason Alone*), and his subsequent argument that it is in the best long-term interests of the state for the "philosophy faculty" to be "conceived as free and subject only to laws given by reason" helped inspire Fichte's philosophical elaboration of a German alternative to the French model. At the heart of Fichte's idea for the new University of Berlin, which Humboldt institutionalized in 1809, was the "scientific" view of research as a dynamic, open-ended endeavor. Research and teaching would now be combined into a single institution of higher learning, with philosophy at the center of a new proliferation of academic pursuits. See Immanuel Kant, *The Conflict of the Faculties*, trans. M. J. Gregor (Lincoln: University of Nebraska Press, 1992), 43; Haskins, *The Rise of Universities*; Theodore Ziolkowski, *German Romanticism and Its Institutions* (Princeton: Princeton University Press, 1990), 218–308; Stephen Galt Crowell, "Philosophy as a Vocation: Heidegger and University Reform in the Early Interwar Years," *History of Philosophy Quarterly* 14:2 (1997), 257–59; Wilhelm von Humboldt, *Die Idee der deutschen Universität* (Darmstadt: Hermann Gentner Verlag, 1956), 377; and Jacques Derrida, "The University in the Eyes of Its Pupils."

59. See Heidegger, "Phenomenology and Theology," in *Pathmarks*, 41; *Wegmarken* 48.

60. It is alarming to thus find philosophers of biology unknowingly extending the logic of Nietzschean metaphysics so far as to inadvertently grant "life" to the computer virus, the cybernetic entity *par excellence*.

61. See Heidegger, "The Age of the World Picture," in *The Question Concerning Technology*, 118.

62. See Heidegger, "The Rectorate 1933/34: Facts and Thoughts," in *Martin Heidegger and National Socialism: Questions and Answers*, ed.Gunther Neske and Emil Kettering (New York: Paragon House, 1990), 16.

63. Heidegger, "The Self-Assertion of the German University," in *Martin Heidegger and National Socialism*, 9. It may seem provocative to end with a quote from Heidegger's notorious "Rectoral Address," but see my "Heidegger and the Politics of the University," which focuses on the political dimension of Heidegger's philosophical views on education and critically investigates the plausibility of his program for a reunification of the university.

7

Essential Heidegger:
Poetics of the Unsaid

Paul Standish

> The knowledge that comes from the sciences usually is expressed in propositions and is laid before us in the form of conclusions that we can grasp and put to use. But the "doctrine" of the thinker is that which, within what is said, remains unsaid, that to which we are exposed so that we might expend ourselves on it.
>
> —Heidegger, "Plato's Doctrine of Truth"

WHAT ARE POETS FOR?

In his essay, "Heidegger on Ontological Education, or How We Become What We Are" (this volume), Iain Thomson discusses Heidegger's conception of education in terms of the allegory of the cave. Heidegger maintains that, while aspects of Plato's founding pedagogical vision of *paideia* have exerted unparalleled influence on our subsequent understandings of "education," more profound dimensions of that vision have been forgotten. Thomson traces Heidegger's excavation of these forgotten aspects, especially in the significance in the original myth of the *return* to the cave. At the end of the myth, after the ascent towards the light, the possibility that the emancipated person should go back down into the cave is raised. Having grown accustomed to the light such a person would find his eyes filled with darkness; he would be ridiculed; his very life might be threatened. Heidegger, drawing attention to the way that the essence of *paideia* must be understood in terms of the constant overcoming of the lack of education, describes the situation as follows:

> Hence the telling of the story does not end, as is often supposed, with the description of the highest level attained in the ascent out of the cave. On the contrary, the "allegory" includes the story of the descent of the freed person back into the cave, back to those who are still in chains. The one who has been freed is supposed to lead these people too away from what is unhidden for them and to bring them face to face with the most unhidden. But the would-be liberator no longer knows his or her way around the cave and risks the danger of succumbing to the overwhelming power of the kind of truth that is normative there, the Danger of being overcome by the claim of the common "reality" to be the only reality. The liberator is threatened with the possibility of being put to death, a possibility that become a reality in the fate of Socrates, who was Plato's "teacher." (Heidegger 1998, 171)

In the return to the cave there is a need once again to turn around one's head and to readjust one's eyes to the lack of light therein. This is the condition for seeing what is the case there. Hence there is here the danger not only of one's sliding back into acceptance of the norms that prevail there, but also of a recasting of truth: it is this that is Heidegger's overriding concern. For while the truth that is contemplated in the ascent from the cave is to be understood in terms of the progressive revealing of what has been hidden, the possibility of seeing in the return to the cave is understood first in terms of correctness, understood in terms of the criteria that prevail amongst the cave dwellers. This is then to find in the allegory an instantiation of what Heidegger sees as a decline in the conception of truth, from aletheia to representation. The allegory, it is his further claim, provides a glimpse of what is happening in the history of humanity: "Taking the essence of truth as the correctness of the representation, one thinks of all beings according to 'ideas' and evaluates all reality according to 'values'" (Heidegger 1998, 182). Put simply, this involves a kind of finessing of any authentic consideration of value and its genesis or of the nature of the emergence of ideas. Alternatively, and in Heideggerian terms more germane to the present discussion, it screens out the possibility of any ontological awareness or inquiry.

Thomson's account of Heidegger's reading of the allegory draws attention to the second stage of the emancipation from the cave, the interim stage between captivity and emergence into the light of the outside world. In this second stage, the prisoner escapes the chains and turns around to discover the fire and objects at the mouth of the cave that create the shadows that have thus far absorbed attention. To see the fire and these objects is still not to see the most real because both are the products of human endeavor and hence artificial in some sense. That is to say, they are partial and restrictive in the possibilities of knowledge they offer. But the breakthrough here is the realization that what have been seen on the wall of the cave are shadows, that these are flickering semblances of those human constructions (the fire and the objects at the mouth of the cave) and so fatefully limited by them. To understand the way that these shadows are produced is then tantamount—at least in terms of the epoch that is our present concern—to understanding the nature of "enframing," the pervasive characteristic of technology. It is to understand the way that technology has led us to come to see things and people in terms of mere resources. This stage then constitutes a negative freedom from enframing. It is a (relative) freedom from illusion on the path to a positive freedom to contemplate the true and the good. But while conditions for correctness can be satisfied in terms of negation, the nature of truth that is realized in the third stage depends on the objects of contemplation being themselves true: that is, real as opposed to fake; that is, *alethes* as opposed to *pseudos*. For the Greeks, and still in Aristotle, Heidegger says in the lecture course of 1942–43 published as *Parmenides*, "*aletheia* is a character of the beings of beings and not a character of the perceiving of beings and of assertions about them" (Heidegger 1992, 34). Contemplation of the true at this stage must involve affirmation, and this affirmation can never spring from negation: a positive of this kind cannot be derived from the negation of a negation. Nor can such affirmation be detached or neutral: the objects of knowledge are objects of love.

Yet the relations here are not well considered simply as oppositions, and the picture is more complicated than these words imply: it is necessary to see a dynamism in the stages through which the learner moves on the path to understanding. As Heidegger's exploration of the idea of the *pseudos* shows, this path is to be understood in terms of modes of hiddenness and forgetting. The *pseudos* is not necessarily the fake. The pseudonym "Johannes de Silentio" adopted sometimes by Kierkegaard is not exactly a fake name; it is not one that sets out to deceive (Heidegger 1992, 36ff.). Dissembling takes different forms and hides in subtly modulated ways. In a sense, moreover, Heidegger, wants to say, the opposite of aletheia is to be found through the removal of the privative prefix: it is to be found in the forgetfulness of *lethe* itself. And forgetting itself takes different forms, including, as Heidegger is prepared to recognize, the kind of oblivion where the very forgetting is itself forgotten. These are themes to which we shall need to return. But first let us consider an initial response to the problems of the university to which Heidegger's account of the passage towards aletheia might lead.

Thomson acknowledges the way that critics such as Bill Readings have followed in Heidegger's footsteps to identify the degeneration of education—specifically the university, specifically its instrumentaliza-tion and its fragmentation in hyper-specialization—as a result of the ni-hilistic logic of enframing. But he finds the conclusion of Readings' *The University in Ruins* (1996) bleak and mistaken. In Readings' view the University of Excellence has become "excellent" in virtue of its excel-lence above all as a bureaucratic corporation—that is, an excellence char-acterized by no substantive values and hence a perpetuation of nihilism. Heidegger's view, in contrast, according to Thomson, is to be under-stood as a reaffirmation of the unity of the university, quite simply through a re-essentializing of the notion of excellence. This is to be achieved in two ways. First, there must be a shared commitment to "forming *excellent* individuals." Excellence is to be understood in terms of the cultivation of the essence of *Dasein*—that is, its making-intelligible of the place in which we find ourselves, or, even more simply, *world dis-closing*. For a world-disclosing being to cultivate its essence, then, is for it to recognize and develop this essence, not only acknowledging its par-ticipation in the creation and maintenance of an intelligible world, but actively embracing its ontological role in such world disclosure (Thom-son 2001, 260–261).

The second way in which unity is to be achieved is through its common pursuit of the understanding not only of what is, the *posits* of the different sciences, but of the ontological *presuppositions* of those various modes of inquiry themselves.

The University of Excellence, of Readings' dystopian description, con-tributes to and thrives on the flickering images at the back of the cave. It is in tranquilized, busy, largely unwitting collusion with these images that students, teachers, and administrators fill their time. There is no need here to illustrate the nihilistic tendencies of such an institution—in its performativity, its instrumentalism, in the way that the substance of education disappears in proceduralism.[1] In what follows, I shall concen-trate rather on the kinds of resource that the enlightened teacher might be thought to bring back to the cave, bearing in mind that the path of that student must be toward that same light. In the University of Excellence such a person is an alien. How is this teacher to turn the heads of those who are taught? The implications here are not confined to higher educa-tion.

The nature of the turn that is considered here is not to be understood without reference to the celebrated "turn" in Heidegger's own thinking—specifically in what has sometimes been called his turn from philosophy to poetry. The turn also constitutes an attempt to move away from the an-thropocentrism of *Being and Time*, and this is achieved in part through a move away from the central concern with the elaboration of *Dasein* to-ward a realization of the pervasive importance of language—toward the significant reversal of "Language Speaks" (Heidegger 1971a, 189ff.). While language figures importantly in the elaboration of *Dasein*, it does not there have the supreme status that Heidegger comes to attach to it in writings from the 1930s onwards. The degeneration he associates with technology is then progressively understood as tied essentially to language, while the possibility of a resistance to technology's totalizing effects is seen especially in the nature of the poetic itself.

In *Being and Time* this is foreshadowed most clearly perhaps in the account of "idle talk" (*Gerede*). The use of this term, the translation of which is perhaps a little unfortunate, is not intended to be disparaging. Rather it connotes a mode of *Dasein's* everydayness, one in which it is uprooted existentially, cut off from its primordial relationships of being-in-the-world. And yet this is the most common form of everydayness; it constitutes *Dasein's* "most stubborn 'Reality'" (Heidegger 1962, 214). Idle talk, characteristic idiom of the They, busies itself with passing on information, with hearsay; it is floating and unattached. It is in its contrast with, and to some extent its standing in the way of, authenticity that its foreshadowing of the problems of enframing can perhaps be seen.

A number of points need to be made about Heidegger's turn to the poetic and the reasons why this offers the resistance to the logic of enframing that is needed. What does Heidegger mean by the poetic? It must be recognized from the outset that language is not a tool at man's disposal or simply a means of communication. So too the poetic is not to be understood in terms of a kind of ornamental accompaniment to existence. Thus, and in contrast to the circulation of idle talk, language is poetic to the extent that it is a kind of *poiesis*. This refers to its producing or bringing into being, its instituting of things and possibilities for us and for our world. This is seen most readily, though perhaps in a way that is not initially transparent, in the naming of things. As Heidegger puts this in his 1936 address "Hölderlin and the Essence of Poetry,"

> The poet names all things with respect to what they are. This naming does not merely come about when something already previously known is furnished with a name; rather, by speaking the essential word, the poet's naming first nominates the beings as what they are. Thus they become *as* beings. Poetry is the founding of being in the word. (Heidegger 2000, 59)

Man is precisely he who attests to his own existence, to his belonging to the earth as the "inheritor, and the learner of all things" in what Hölderlin calls their "intimacy" (Heidegger 2000, 54). Man's bearing witness to his belonging among things occurs as history. Not only is this possible through language alone; language guarantees man's historicality. Moreover, this cannot be realized without others: the ground of our existence is conversation. Our speaking together makes possible our naming of the highest and the most lowly.

It is clear, however, that while the poetic is a general possibility of language where this does not degenerate under the impress of enframing or in the vacuity of idle talk, it is seen especially in the work of great poets. In the 1946 lecture "What Are Poets For?" Heidegger raises explicitly the relationship between the destitution of the time, in Hölderlin's phrase, and the potential of the poet to uncover the trace of the holy by examining a poet whose work explicitly addresses the question of the effects of technology. The reason that the time is destitute is that "it lacks the unconcealedness of the nature of pain, death, and love" (Heidegger 1971a, 97). Heidegger ponders Rainer Maria Rilke's dwelling on the nature of money as a metonym for this degeneration. In Rilke's *Book of Pilgrimage* (1901) he sees the metal from which money is made as debased by its "congealing"—a Marxian motif (Marx 1886, 106)—in coin and the wheels of industry. He imagines the metal becoming homesick: it "uncongeals" and flows back to the open mountain vein, over which the mountain closes again. The object character of technological dominion spreads over things and over people to reduce them to the terms of the calculable. Man is particularly vulnerable under these circumstances in that self-assertion is such that it extends the realm of the danger that he will turn himself over to the realm of unconditional production: thus the menace that threatens man's nature arises from that nature itself (Heidegger 2000, 115). In this sometimes less than oblique (though surely mistaken) attack on Nietzsche's will to power, Heidegger goes further: "Self-assertive man, whether or not he knows and wills it as an individual, is the functionary of technology" (Heidegger 2000, 116). This is the apotheosis of willing and it reaches a kind of fulfillment in the peacefulness of a tranquility in which all of nature is channeled and stored as resource, as standing-reserve.

In such a world the gods have withdrawn. Yet the poets can realize their absence, as Rilke's words demonstrate. In their acknowledgment of this, at the heart of this negativity, they make possible a kind of recovery or renewal. In Heidegger's 1943 lecture on Hölderlin's "Homecoming/To Kindred Ones" it is said that the poet must "remain near to the god's absence, and wait long enough in this prepared nearness to the absence till out of the nearness to the absent god there is granted an originative word to name the high one" (Heidegger 2000, 46–47). In "Hölderlin and the Essence of Poetry" the poet is said to be the one who has been "cast out——out into that *between*, between gods and men," to bring together the hints of the gods and the voice of the people (Heidegger 2000, 65). And in 1939, his address on the poem "As When On A Holiday . . ." speaks of the way that the poet co-responds to the wonderful all-present, to the "powerful, divinely beautiful" (Heidegger 2000, 76). "Nature" becomes an inadequate word for what Hölderlin calls the "all-creative" and the "all-living"; as *physis* it is fire and flame (Heidegger 2000, 79); for the poet who names things, it is inspiration (Heidegger 2000, 82). This intimates the broad metaphysical structure of the mutual appropriation of man and world through language. Thus, the turn to Hölderlin is aligned with the turn to the pre-Socratics, towards a unity of *logos* and *physis*.

The poet leads the way from the shadows of the cave by drawing attention to the way they are projected. This thematization becomes possible especially through a reflection on the nature of poetry itself. This is a reflection on the productive nature of *poiesis*, on the apophantic nature of language, on the way that it lets things appear. For the ascent to the second stage, it will be recalled, involves coming to understand how the language of enframing has enabled a certain kind of appearing. Heidegger writes about Hölderlin because the latter is centrally concerned in his writing with the nature of poetry, with its essence ("Hölderlin and the Essence of Poetry," Heidegger 2000, 52). This is a kind of ontological inquiry, one in which saying, destining, and essence progressively coalesce.

Recognition of the institutive power that such poetic thinking has, however, involves the acknowledgment of the possibility of danger. If it is only through language that man is exposed to something manifest, then this "most innocent" thing also creates the possibility of danger: "The word as word never offers any immediate guarantee as to whether it is an essential word or a deception. . . . This language must constantly place itself into the illusion which it engenders by itself, and so endanger what is most its own, genuine utterance" (Heidegger 2000, 55). The dangers of technology itself will not be recognized if they are not seen in these terms. It is the precariousness into which language pitches us that must be understood if the promise of education and the vices to which it is prone are to become apparent.

In later writings, particularly in the 1951 lectures "Building Dwelling Thinking" and in "Poetically Man Dwells," Heidegger brings these themes together in his linking of the poetic to the very possibility of building and dwelling. Naming, it will be recalled, was always more than the furnishing of an already existing thing with a name. It here comes to be understood in connection with measure-taking, without which there can be neither building, as is plain, nor dwelling, as is less plain but as can be seen in the way that in our learning we must gradually come to be able to take the measure of things, extending that measuring in new and unforeseen ways. (As Ludwig Wittgenstein might say, this is a matter of learning to follow a rule.) This measure-taking is to be understood less as the application of a preexisting measure to an already existing thing, than as an instituting of the very possibility of measuring. To ask how our measure-taking gets going is akin to the familiar question of how our language gets going. In important respects these are indeed the same thing:

> This measure-taking is itself an authentic measure-taking, no mere gauging with ready-made measuring rods to the making of buildings. But poetry, as the authentic gauging of the dimension of dwelling, is the primal form of building. Poetry first of all admits man's dwelling into its very nature, its presencing being. Poetry is the original admission of dwelling. (Heidegger 1971a, 227)

It is not just the nature of our measuring, of what is to count as criteria for us, but the very possibility of such criteria that is the heart of the matter here. The house of being that such a poetic thinking constructs must also be the institution of education, its building and instauration of our world. Poetry is, as we saw, the "founding of being in the word."

We have seen then how the account of the poetic as *poiesis*, and of language as apophantic, is critical not only for the kind of world and education that there is to be but for a necessary and integrally related ontological reflection on the very possibilities of that *poiesis*. Of course, Heidegger's work is to be celebrated in education for its power to reveal the totalizing effects of technology on our practice. Performativity is the most pervasive and the most pressing threat to education today. But the valuable negative critique that this supplies needs to be seen in relation to the immense richness of Heidegger's affirmation of value, realized in the account of the poetic. The restoring of the sense of truth as tied to the intrinsic worth, the reality, of the objects of knowledge, as opposed to the understanding of truth as a property of propositions, should be at the heart of the overcoming of nihilism. This indicates something of the task that besets the teacher. The force of the German word *Dichte*, with its connotations of spiritual leader and teacher, is then particularly significant in the scenario of the return to the cave. Given the nature of the ascent toward the truth and Heidegger's account of the essential nature of the poetic, such a figure must model what good teaching must be. The *Dichte* leads the way also by being able to institute practices: in finding the measure of things, through realizing criteria of what is to count, by edification, where this, as the word tells us (*aedificare*), is simultaneously building.

Notwithstanding Heidegger's account of the poetic, there are notorious problems here. These are difficulties and failures that his own texts sometimes hint at—in spite of himself, in spite of his denials, as it were, or so at least it would appear to be. In turning to these now I shall highlight especially Heidegger's relation to what is not said. This applies not only to the substantive question of what cannot be said but also to his relation to sources upon which he draws. I shall use this to lay the way for some un-Heideggarian questioning of the themes of interpretation and forgetting.

The purpose here is not directly to address familiar questions concerning his silence about his political actions and beliefs but to uncover more subtle aspects of his relation to the unsaid that cast light on his conception of the poetic and of essence.

It is clear that there is a close, indeed an essential, connection between ideas of essence and the poetic in Heidegger's thought. As Thomson emphasizes, essence should not be thought of in terms of the Platonic notion of what permanently endures but should be taken rather, as Heidegger says, as a verb (Thomson 2001, 246ff.). "Essence" denotes the historical way in which entities are revealed and come to be understood by *Dasein*. It is to be understood in terms of a historical series of constellations of intelligibility that each provide the necessary appearance of a ground, supporting that way of thinking from the inside out, as it were. These ontotheologies function historically like "self-fulfilling prophecies, reshaping intelligibility from the ground up" (Thomson 2001, 248). Historical changes in the understanding of what beings are transform our understanding of what education is. Our current education, it is Heidegger's plain lament, is shaped by enframing. That this is a technological understanding of being is clear enough. That it is the product of Nietzsche's thought—the eternally recurring will to power—seems gravely mistaken.[2]

While these remarks, and especially the point concerning the "verbal" nature of "essence," are sufficient to show that Heidegger's thought cannot be simply mapped onto the metaphysical picture commonly understood to be implied by the cave allegory,[3] it is not clear how far they can be reconciled with Heidegger's understanding of the poetic and his reading of poets. Two points about this should be made. In the first place, the nature and understanding of interpretation needs to be understood in connection with his conception of destiny and with the recurrence of a particular vocabulary in his essays. In the second, the turn in Heidegger's thought can be related to the prominence of the theme of the home; this in turn is suggestive of the aspects of mourning and nostalgia in his thought. Ironically, the verbal dynamism that Heidegger finds in the idea of essence is far more vividly apparent in the dionysian elements of Nietzsche's thought.

DISCLOSURE AND INTERPRETATION

Hermes is the divine messenger. He brings the message of destiny; *hermeneuein* is that exposition which brings tidings because it can listen to a message.   —Heidegger, "A Dialogue on Language"

In the first place it is worth paying attention to some possible influences on Heidegger's thought. Powerful, rich, and immensely important though

Heidegger's notion of the poetic undoubtedly is, it is perhaps less wholly original than has sometimes been assumed. For example, in important respects Ralph Waldo Emerson's "The Poet" adumbrates a conception of the poetic not remote from Heidegger's own. In his 1844 essay "The Poet," Emerson writes: "Every one has some interest in the advent of the poet, and no one knows how much it may concern him. We know that the secret of the world is profound but who or what shall be our interpreter, we know not" (Emerson 1982, 264). It is not meters but a metre-making argument that makes a poem.[4] The poet's role is to announce and to affirm. For what nature offers is to be understood not as something fixed or permanent—in terms of raw data or sensory impressions; rather it is to be seen semiologically: "Nature offers all her creatures to him as a picture-language. Being used as a type, a second wonderful value appears in the object, far better than its old value; as the carpenter's cord, if you hold your ear close enough, is musical in the breeze" (Emerson 1982, 266). And in the essay "Nature," Emerson writes: "The world is emblematic. Parts of speech are metaphors, because the whole of nature is a metaphor of the human mind. . . . The axioms of physics translate the laws of ethics" (Emerson 1982, 53).

There is a founding of being in the word such as to reflect an intimacy of language and world, or, as Stanley Cavell puts this, to underwrite ordinary language philosophy (Cavell 1989, 80ff.). Cavell's thought here turns around the Emersonian theme of "finding as founding," the title of Cavell's essay, laying the way for his examination of Emerson's preoccupation, so it seems, with the very idea of *condition* itself. It is the *dict*ation and *con*formity compressed in this term that Emerson addresses. The words that I must inherit, my very means of expression, can impel me towards conformity,. Otherwise put, if thinking is a handicraft, as Heidegger says (Heidegger 1968, 16ff.), this implies not only its fruitful, practical work but also its tendency towards prehensility, say, its violence towards things; so too Emerson in his essay "Experience," as Cavell shows, takes the way that objects slip through our hands as we grasp at them to be the "most unhandsome part of our condition" (Emerson 1982, 288). And otherwise again, this is a matter of the criteria of my culture, which must be convened for me, supplying the conditions in terms of which or against which I must extend my freedom[5]—the alternative being a dull conformity, a congealing of my life's blood.

The poet then exemplifies a possibility of handsome thinking. In words that both anticipate Heidegger but that also might be taken to be salutary for him, Emerson emphasises the fluidity of the poet's constructive writing:

> But the quality of the imagination is to flow, and not to freeze. The poet did not stop at the color of the form, but read their meaning; neither may he rest in this meaning, but he makes the same objects exponents of his new

thought. Here is the difference between the poet and the mystic, that the last nails a symbol to one sense, which was a true sense for a moment, but soon becomes old and false. For all symbols are old and fluxional; all language is vehicular and transitive, and is good, as ferries and horses are, for conveyance, not as farms and houses are, for homestead. (Emerson 1982, 279)

The thought that is carried in this conveyance, which is not a house, is salutary in its indication of something other than settlement or turning back home: this thinking looks for new ways to actualize its energy. It is a releasing and a realizing of new intensities of experience. Such a man, Emerson says, is "the conductor of the whole river of electricity" (Emerson 1982, 283). There is here an intimation of the dionysian in Nietzsche, something that in part he learns from Emerson. This is a world apart from Heidegger's egocentric interpretation of the will to power. Yet the views expressed in Emerson's essay resonate sufficiently with Heidegger's conception of the poetic to make some influence seem likely, however misconstrued Heidegger's conception of the passage of such thoughts through Nietzsche may be.

In the case of the relationship with Eastern sources, the influence is more direct, and, though eagerly sought, it often remained unacknowledged. Conversely, in Japan there was widespread interest in Heidegger's work: a number of scholars visited Heidegger, and several translations of *Sein und Zeit* were undertaken.[6] Tezuka Tomio, in his brief account of his meeting with Heidegger, makes clear the strong sense of affinity that was felt by the two men. He shared with Heidegger the sense of the importance of poetry and also the conviction that this comes into closest touch with the time and the tasks of the time at points where the contact goes unnoticed ("An Hour with Heidegger", in May 1996: 64). The "doctrine" of the thinker, it will be recalled from the epigraph to the present essay, is "that which, within what is said, remains unsaid." Reinhard May's careful discussion of East Asian influences draws the conclusion that Heidegger frequently adopted ideas and modes of language that he was to leave largely unacknowledged, especially from the poet Chuang Tzu, whose work he encountered in Martin Buber's (1910) translation. Perhaps the poet is not expected to cite sources, especially where this might compromise the effects of what is said—or so at least the pretext might run. The role of *Dichte* then had a certain convenience for Heidegger in this respect. Moreover the assumption of a poetic idiom in relation to the reading of such texts leaves very much in question the extent to which the thought emanating from the nonmetaphysical traditions of China, for example, can be compatible with Heidegger's conception of the history of being. Can nonmetaphysical thought of the nothing be reconciled with this history of ontological settlements without a return of metaphysics. The fact that it is out of, or in relation to, this history that Heidegger determines the nature of the nothing may lay the way for the critique of the metaphysics of presence, but it can scarcely reflect well those aspects of Eastern thought that are most concerned with silence or the unsaid. There is something self-defeating here about Heidegger's project, however much he tries to avoid this. In contrast, a text such as "A Dialogue on Language" may reveal a degree of sensitivity on Heidegger's part to these problems. In response to the Inquirer's question concerning the mystery of saying, and the attempt to say this unsayable, the Japanese responds: "A mystery is a mystery only when it does not even come out *that* mystery is at work" (Heidegger 1971b, 50).

To turn more directly to the poets that have been under discussion in this essay it is worth attending to the detailed study of Heidegger's poets by Véronique Fóti. She calls attention to the ways in which his readings tend to draw the texts toward points of concentration or convergence. Sometimes this is against, or in excess of, what the poems actually say. For example, in the work of Georg Trakl the "gathering point" is in fact typically indicated but never reached; it remains "dislocated in the unsaid" (Fóti 1992, 15). Heidegger's reading amounts to an "appropriative invasion and deformation of the poetry"; it "masks the rupture and negativity in Trakl's poetry, particularly in his thematization of estrangement" (Fóti 1992, 15–16). The figure of the stranger in Trakl's poetry is read by Heidegger as a motif for ascent through spiritual darkness towards the holy; yet far from being the romanticization of solitude that Heidegger tries to make it, the stranger is a disruptive element in Trakl's poetry, symbolizing affliction and exile (Fóti 1992, 18).

Fóti makes similar points about the reading of Hölderlin. Heidegger explicitly states that his own work is divorced from the practices and purposes of literary scholarship. Instead it understands its object (and itself) in terms of a destinal transformation that brings to fruition the promise of early Greek thought (Fóti 1992, 61); this much would of course be part of the historically instituting and founding work of the poet and thinker, the *Dichte* that Heidegger has become. This destinal thinking guides Heidegger's approach in such matters as his identification of, and mantra-like recursion to, significant words such as "greeting" and "festivity," an approach reflected in the incantation in his own writing of "essence," "destiny," and their cognates. The reading resists heterology and plurivocity. It fails adequately to register the differences between poems, and between genres of poems, moving everything toward its unified, essential interpretation, bringing tidings because it uniquely can listen to the message. When Hölderlin, in "Mnemosyne," speaks of the death of remembrance, or the failure of poetic communication, Heidegger misses this, and he misses also the appalling destruction implied by the imagery of fire, interpreting the text as referring instead to the "abyssal failure of ground experienced by the poets" (Fóti 1992, 68). He misses the destructive aspect of fire, as Jacques Derrida shows, even as his ponderings of spirit, in the politically fateful years from 1933–53, lead him to see this itself in terms of "fire, flame, burning, conflagration" (Derrida 1989, 83). Perhaps most significantly, his interpretation is oblivious to the unreadability of some of the texts—their resistance to reading, their disruption of totalizing thought. For, however tendentious Heidegger's interpretation may in fact be, the recurrent tone is of a sustained affirmation of the coherence of his attunement to the destinal words that speak through these poets: it realizes the essence of the poem.

Such is Heidegger's confidence in his own interpretation—and so much is this predicated on a tacit presumption in favor of, on a determined impetus toward, univocity of interpretation—that he is incapable of recognizing the significance of certain kinds of silence. Silence "appears" in Heidegger's texts, it is true, but only to be aestheticized, emblem of the fate of the political in his thought. Véronique Fóti raises Theodor Adorno's question and Edmond Jabès' response: Can one no longer write poetry after Auschwitz? Or is it the case that one must? (Fóti 1992, 74) In Heidegger this unsaid, the impossibility of even asking these questions, reflects his inability to think the immemorial, as Jean-François Lyotard has amply shown (Lyotard 1990).[7] There is little need to advert to Heidegger's "silence" about his political activities in the 1930s in order to realize that this is a question that he could scarcely have been capable of hearing. His poetics becomes a politics of the unsaid.

Finally, the limitations and omissions in Heidegger's interpretation and understanding of the poetic need to be situated in the broader context of a general incapacity that is evident in his thought. The failure to respond adequately to the figure of the stranger in Trakl is symptomatic of a more pervasive failure of acknowledgment and hospitality in his thinking, apparent especially in his eulogy of home and destiny. Those within a community are absorbed into a communal sharing (*Miteinandersein, miteinanderteilen*) that muffles the voice of the other, while other-regarding virtue is turned not to (other, different) people but to a piety toward being—or toward the fourfold or toward language itself. In what follows it will be my concern in part to retrieve something of this regard for the other from these limitations.

Before proceeding, however, it is worth adverting to two interrelated patterns in the imagery that converges in the above texts around the idea of the poetic and the nature of education. One pattern includes the tropes of home, settlement, conveyance, movement, and return. Its poles are the (backward-looking) nostalgia for home that is sometimes prevalent in Heidegger's texts, and the (forward-looking) electric intensity found in Emerson and the dionysian Nietzsche. The other pattern brings together money, coins, currency, freeze and flow, with its poles of "congealing" and "uncongealing." In Rilke these two patterns are found together. In a letter quoted by Heidegger, he recalls how long ago, in the fourteenth century, "money was still gold, still metal, a beautiful thing, the handsomest, most comprehensible of all" (Heidegger 1971a, 113–114). The "vibrations" that this currency came to acquire in the modern world are a degeneration, in response to which he envisions its real energy flowing back into the stillness and hiddenness of the rock from which it came.

So too our words are a kind of currency that stands in danger of becoming dull in their circulation and exchange. So too our thinking can remain static; it can look back, closing off possibilities. In contrast, our poetic language, or, better, our language to the extent that it is poetic, gives the possibility of coining new words, not, ridiculously, by the contriving of neologisms, but by finding new ways of expressing the way things are for us, by finding a language that points forward in multiple ways. Indeed this possibility is our responsibility, and this above all in education.

EDUCATION OTHERWISE

What light has the above shown on Heidegger's significance for education? It is time to draw a number of conclusions. First, Heidegger's account of the enframing of technology is of great value, there is no doubt, in understanding the contemporary world, and the world of education in particular. Second, his account of the poetic is immensely rich, presenting a conception of language that is of critical importance if these enframing tendencies are to be resisted. Third, that account is less original than Heidegger implies (cf. Emerson, Nietzsche). Fourth, Heidegger's reading of texts gravitates towards a univocal mode of interpretation. This distorts and restricts even (perhaps especially) those texts that he most cherishes. It arrests and essentializes the poetic. Fifth, Heidegger fails to acknowledge some of his sources. His "forgetting" of certain influences and sources is of a piece both with his forgetting of aberrations in his political life and with his inability to think the immemorial. (This in turn distorts his appropriation of Eastern thought.) Sixth, and as a result of the above, his aestheticization of the political is the outcome of his ultimately metaphysical piety of thought, his prioritization and aestheticization of ontology itself.

In the light of this it is appropriate to return briefly to the implication for higher education that Thomson finds in Heidegger's thought: the reessentialization of the idea of excellence. This is taken to involve, first, the shared commitment to "forming *excellent* individuals," and second, the common questioning of the ontological *presuppositions* of the various subjects studied. There is surely a close connection between these two aims. While the perfectionist form of excellence is understood in terms of the human being's distinctive essence as world-disclosing, the ontological commitment incumbent upon all forms of inquiry is itself a reflection upon the nature and manner of that disclosure. Reflection upon disclosure must itself be a kind of disclosure. Welcome though such commitments in education in many respects are, these are somewhat abstract and formal outcomes from Thomson's enquiry. It is not clear how far they address the problems that beset higher education today. There is, moreover, a lingering doubt as to how far they escape the return of metaphysics that threatens Heidegger's best thought.

My own inclination is to see the best implications of that thought, not only in its exposure (negatively) of technology, as indicated above, but in its revealing (positively) of the following truth: that the kind of language we use is critical for the kind of education we have. Why do we lack a sensible and rich language to talk about education? Why don't educated people ask this question more? However much Heidegger's account of the poetic may ultimately be compromised, it has the potential to reveal the nature of the contemporary frustration of education and the possibility of a way beyond this. It is necessary to find a language for education that is not trapped in the destitution of performativity. This, as was said at the outset, is the most urgent problem of education today.

Nevertheless, while Heidegger's extensive thoughts on these matters are richly thought-provoking, I have tried to show something of their shortcomings. They are apt to subside into a negativity and nostalgia, turning back the energy they would otherwise release. Their unsaid bears witness not to the immemorial but to repression. They aestheticize ontology where things are of most pressing ethical concern. And in their destinal bringing of tidings, they cover over the disseminative power of our language and lives. In contrast to these tendencies towards negativity, though on the strength of a similar understanding of the poetic, Emerson points toward an intensity of thought and being, and lays the way for Nietzsche's dionysian thought.[8]

An illustration of the significance of such an appropriately sensitive language is to be found in its relevance to the central question of standards in education. The jargon of standards and quality control that now prevails reflects the mechanistic and behavioristic character of current practices in all their spurious rigor. This is a counterfeit currency, or at best one where the sense of worth that standards should otherwise sustain has worn dull. The sustaining of standards cannot be simply a matter of reading off assessments from a pre-given scale ("a mere gauging with ready-made measuring rods"). Our criteria stand in need of application, that is, judgment, and in our judgments we exercise our words.

True rigor in such matters requires "authentic gauging," the meter-making argument of the poetic, of *poiesis*. Without such a responsibility to language there can be no raising of standards (where a standard is to be remembered to be a flag that we might raise and march behind).

There is, however, a further way in which the present argument leads towards a redirecting of the significance of Heidegger's thought for education. This involves a return to the theme of the stranger, for in many respects this brings together problems that beset his understanding of the poetic. In numerous texts Emmanuel Levinas shows the ways that Heidegger's preoccupation with ontology prevents him from understanding, or accounting adequately for, the relation to the human other. In Heidegger, this relation is little more than a *Miteinandersein*, with the appalling limitations of vision that this permits. In *Totality and Infinity* Levinas writes of the figure of "the Stranger who disturbs the being at home with oneself" (Levinas 1969, 39). Ultimately this lack in Heidegger undermines his ontological project itself; his piety towards being becomes aestheticised and depleted. It founders toward a kind of nihilism. For Levinas, in contrast, reverence attaches essentially to the asymmetrical relation to the other human being (the Other).

In order to retrieve the regard for the other in Heidegger's thought, jeopardized as it is, I want to consider the attempt by John Llewelyn to extend to other others the asymmetry of the relation to the human other. In a lyrical, difficult, richly allusive passage, the source and sense of which I elaborate below, Llewelyn gestures towards the play in Heidegger's later thought around the poetic, the ordinary, response, and responsibility:

> The ordinary mortal shares with the poet who is "struck by Apollo" and whose "eye too many" is dazzled by the fire of the sky the responsibility of loyally remembering the extraordinariness of ordinary beings, whether they be human beings or not: "the jug and the bench, the footbridge and the plough . . . tree and pond too . . . brook and hill . . . heron and roe deer, horse and bull . . . mirror and clasp, book and picture, crown and cross," where the book may be the Book or may not, its word the word of the prophet or the word of the poet, where the cross may be the cross of the Word, of the Trinity, or may not, because the cross of the word ~~Being~~, the quaternity, and the burden of ontological responsibility it carries with it, are prior to theistic and atheistic faith as well as to rational onto-theology and onto-atheology. (Llewelyn 1991, 141)

The poetic is implied here to have consequences that affect our ordinary lives—and that is, let us make no mistake, the morality of our ordinary lives. But the sensibility or response in question in these words has less to do with a heightened sense of *being* than with the *responsibility* of remembering the extraordinariness of ordinary things—of their otherness to us and ultimate unfathomability even as they are part of our ordinary world. These particular things—"the jug and the bench . . ."—Llewelyn finds in the closing paragraphs of Heidegger's essay "The Thing" (in Heidegger 1971a). Such things are discovered, Heidegger shows us, not as items amongst the innumerable "objects" in the world, or amidst the "measureless mass of men as living beings." They depend upon a dwelling with things. And this dwelling is characterized by a reverence for things that is poetic in kind, where the poetic implies something both about language itself (and the dangers of an excessive emphasis on the indicative or representational), and about the *poiesis* of bringing things forth into being. With Heidegger's turn from the project of fundamental ontology, the notion of being is displaced by the fourfold of earth, sky, gods, and mortals—a quaternity graphically gestured by the four points of this cross. These are the dimensions of the world in which our lives are lived out. They are dimensions without which things as things cannot be understood. For what is (something so simple as) a jug? Is it a three-dimensional object, inert matter, of a certain weight and shape? This is how the jug is understood in abstraction, by way of a reduction of language that can, if it is imagined to be somehow fundamental, obscure more than it reveals. This is not the jug of lived experience. For that jug holds the water that slakes the thirst after the day's work; it pours the wine shared at the family meal. The jug focuses a practice in such a way that what it means must be something more than the physical description offered above can possibly convey: that physical description effects a kind of etiolation of the thing. What the jug means, the way it is understood, is tied to the practices of which it is a part, in all their fourfold richness. In contrast to the reductiveness that threatens to deny this richness, the language of poet and prophet, in proximity here, suggests a way of thinking beyond rational ontology or rational theology, beyond also the idolatrous deification of Being, in that a responsibility is realized to what cannot be directly named or represented: this is a responsibility to what *may be*, to a way of being that is *always still to come*.

The richness of Heidegger's thought here is the way it makes vivid the possibilities of a receptivity—in *Gehörenlassen*, *Seinlassen*, and *Gelassenheit*. These are other-regarding virtues that are necessary to the mirroring relationship between the fourfold: "The round dance of the world" constitutes the "ringing mirror-play" from which "the thinging of the thing takes place" (Heidegger 1971a, 180). For Emerson there is music in the carpenter's cord caught in the breeze. If the verb-making of the thing echoes the sense of "essence" as a verb, it recalls also Emerson's insistence that the poetic must not arrest or freeze but must be a means of conveyance of thought. The practice of teacher and learner then must be to read meaning but not to rest in it—to make the same objects exponents of new thought.

What is new in Heidegger's reading of the allegory of the cave is its emphasis on the return of the one who has ascended towards the light. This is the teacher's return. Is it possible to read this pattern as something other than the return of the bearer of tidings with the message of destiny? The teacher cannot come back to the darkness simply pre-armed with truth for its bright light will blind him to the "overwhelming power of the kind of truth that is normative" there, the common "reality" of the cave. The teacher would be lost in the face of the illusions that make up the student's world. Can the pattern be read then as the repeated return that the teacher must make—finding new words, finding as founding, to return only to start again? The receptivity and responsibility that this implies might retrieve, or wrest, from Heidegger a fitting response for our condition, a poetics for education otherwise.

NOTES

1. For a more thorough account of these problems, see Blake et al. (1998) and Standish (2001). For a critical discussion of Readings' *The University in Ruins* see Standish (1999).

2. For an exploration of Nietzsche's relevance to a critique of the dominance of the contemporary technological understanding of education, see Blake et al. (2000).

3. It is surely the case, however, that in that common understanding the function of the poetic in Plato's own account has been insufficiently recognized. This has a bearing on the way his metaphysics is understood. It is a reflection on the ambivalence of the relation to the poetic, to art, in such a text.

4. Emerson writes: "For it is not metres, but a metre-making argument that makes a poem,—a thought so passionate and alive that like the spirit of a plant or an animal it has an architecture of its own, and adorns nature with a new thing" (Emerson 1982, 263–264).

5. In *The Claim of Reason* Cavell writes: "What I require is a convening of my culture's criteria, in order to confront them with my words and life as I pursue them and as I may imagine them; and at the same time to confront my words and life as I pursue them with the life my culture's words may imagine for me: to confront the culture with itself along the lines in which it meets in me" (Cavell 1979, 125). Later in this text, when Cavell speaks of "the simultaneous tolerance and intolerance of words," the double genitive indicates something of the tensions and the potential in this relationship (186).

6. See especially Yasuo Yuasa's "The Encounter of Modern Japanese Philosophy with Heidegger" (in Parkes 1987, 155–174).

7. Eschewing the sensationalism of many inquiries into Heidegger's political acitivities, Lyotard subtly reveals the embeddedness of Heidegger's actions and

silence in his thought as a whole. For a discussion of this text in relation to this educational aspects of this theme see Standish (2001).

8. The different, and differently Emersonian, possibilities for education in Nietzsche's thought are explored in Blake *et al.*, 2000, especially chapters 7 and 9. For a dazzling account of dionysian intensity inspired by Nietzsche and Lyotard, see Gordon Bearn's "Pointlessness and the University of Beauty" (in Dhillon and Standish, 2000).

REFERENCES

Blake, N., P, Smeyers, R. Smith, and P. Standish 2000 *Education in an Age of Nihilism*. London: Routledge.

Blake, N., R. Smith, and :P. Standish, 1998 *The Universities We Need: Higher Education after Dearing*. London: Kogan Page.

Buber, M. 1910. *Reden und Gilichnisse des Tschuang-Tse*. Trans and ed. Leipzig.

Cavell, S. 1979. *The Claim of Reason:Wittgenstein, Skepticism, Morality, and Tragedy*. New York: Oxford University Press.

Cavell, S. 1989. *This New Yet Unapproachable America: Lectures after Emerson after Wittgenstein*. Albuquerque: Living Batch Press.

Derrida, J. 1983. "The Principle of Sufficient Reason: The University in the Eyes of Its Pupils." *Diacritics* (Fall).

Derrida, J. 1987 *Of Spirit: Heidegger and the Question*. Chicago: University of Chicago Press.

Dhillon, P. and P. Standish, eds. 2000. *Lyotard: Just Education*. London: Routledge.

Emerson, R. W. 1982. *Selected Essays*, Harmondsworth: Penguin.

Fóti, V. 1992. *Heidegger and the Poets: poiesis/sophia/techne*. New Jersey: Humanities Press.

Heidegger, M. 1962. *Being and Time*. Trans. J. Macquarrie and E. Robinson. Oxford: Blackwell.

Heidegger M. 1966. *Discourse on Thinking* Trans. John M. Anderson and E. Hans Freund. New York: Harper & Row.

Heidegger, M. 1968. *What is Called Thinking?* Trans. J. Glenn Gray New York: Harper & Row.

Heidegger, M. 1971a. *Poetry, Language, Thought*. Trans. A. Hofstadter. London: Harper & Row.

Heidegger, M. 1971b. *On the Way to Language*. Trans. P. Hertz. London: Harper & Row.

Heidegger, M. 1977. *The Question Concerning Technology and Other Essays* Trans. William Lovitt. New York: Harper & Row.

Heidegger, M. 1991. *The Principle of Reason*. Trans. Reginald Lilly Bloomington: Indiana University Press.

Heidegger, M. 1992. *Parmenides*. Trans. A Schuwer and R. Rojcewicz. Bloomington: Indiana University Press.

Heidegger, M. 1998 *Pathmarks*. Trans. W. McNeill. Cambridge: Cambridge University Press.

Heidegger, M. 2000. *Elucidations of Hölderlin's Poetry*. Trans. K. Hoeller. Amherst, N.Y.: Prometheseus Books.

Levinas, E. 1969. *Totality and Infinity: An Essay on Exteriority*. Trans. A. Lingis. Pittsburgh, PA: Duquesne University Press.

Llewelyn, J. 1991. *The Middle Voice of Ecological Conscience: A Chiasmic Reading of Responsibility in the Neighbourhood of Levinas, Heidegger and Others*. London: Macmillan.

Llewelyn, J. 2000. *The HypoCritical Imagination:Between Kant and Levinas*. London: Routledge.

Lyotard, J-F. 1990. *Heidegger and "the Jews."* Trans. A. Michel, Minneapolis: University of Minnesota Press.

Lyotard, J-F. 1991. *The Inhuman: Reflections on Time*. Trans. G. Bennington and R. Bowlby. Stanford, Calif.: Stanford University Press.

Marx, K. 1886. *Capital: A Critical Analysis of Capitalist Production*. London: William Glaisher, Limited.

May, R. 1996. *Heidegger's Hidden Sources: East Asian Influences on His Work*. Trans. with a complementary essay by G. Parkes, London: Routledge.

Parkes, G. 1987. *Heidegger and Asian Thought*. Honolulu: University of Hawaii Press.

Readings, B. 1996. *The University in Ruins*. Cambridge.: Harvard University Press.

Standish, P. 1999. "Centre Without Substance: cultural capital and *The University in Ruins*." *Jahrbuch der Erzieungswissenschaft*, 83–104.

Standish, P. 2000b. "In Freedom's Grip." In: *Lyotard: Just Education*, ed. P. Dhillon and P. Standish. London: Rouledge.

Standish, P. 2001. "Disciplining the Profession: Subjects Subject to Procedure." *Educational Philosophy and Theory*, 34: 1, 5–23.

Thomson, I. 2001. "Heidegger on Ontological Education, or: How We Become What We Are." *Inquiry* 44: 243–268.

8

Enframing Education

Patrick Fitzsimons

Our flight from the mystery toward what is readily available . . . this is erring . . .

—Martin Heidegger, *On the Essence of Truth*, 1930

The question of whether modern technology has been beneficial or detrimental to human beings is perhaps one of the most important questions for society. This question clearly also refers to education. In his introduction to a speech by the controversial German philosopher Martin Heidegger entitled *The Question Concerning Technology*, David Farrell Krell asserts that on this question "hinges nothing less than the survival of the species man and the planet earth" (1977, 308). Therefore, the work of Heidegger on the essence of modern technology is bound to be of considerable interest. Accordingly, the chapter begins by explaining Heidegger's (1977) idea of *Enframing* (*Gestell*) as the current technological understanding of the world. It then distinguishes between the essences of ancient and modern technology. Next, Heidegger's view that *Enframing* is our present mode of being is discussed. Some implications of the question for *Enframed* education are then addressed. The chapter concludes that because *Enframing* is only one way of Being other possibilities should be entertained.

WHAT IS THE QUESTION?

The question concerns the problem for education of what Heidegger termed *Enframing* that has occurred as a result of modern technology which is best addressed by viewing Heidegger's work in its historical context. In 1949 Heidegger delivered four lectures to the Bremen club under the general title "Insight into What Is" (cf. Krell 1977, 308). Each lecture had its own title, one of which, *"Das Gestell"* (*"The Enframing"*), Caputo (1993, 132) (in a revision of this own thinking) describes as notorious. Heidegger's speech was later expanded and retitled *The Question Concerning Technology* when he presented it to the Bavarian Academy of Arts in 1953. It was delivered as a contribution to the debate on modern technology, a debate which he assessed as hopelessly inadequate. The debate had not addressed the *essence* (where essence is the manner in which technology *comes to presence*) of technology involved in the atom bomb. This atomic weapon, in Heidegger's opinion, represented a fundamental technological rupture with the past; it was not merely dangerous but it was also vastly different from any previous technology. It was different in kind, precisely because, although human beings had always been able to kill on a mass scale, this atomic weapon (brought into presence by modern technology) for the first time in history made the extinction of the human species conceivable. This technological development was occuring in conjunction with the total mobilization of nation-state economies, a process that lent new intensity to the debate. Under nation-states, war had been industrialised through the mobilization of all resources, including the redefinition of citizens themselves as resources. The extent of the danger can be illustrated with reference to the destruction brought about by the two world wars of the twentieth century, which were sufficient testimony to the dangers of such industrialization.

According to Michael Zimmerman (1990, 55), it was Heidegger's fellow countryman, Ernst Junger, who promoted a positive view of the development of the nation-state as a technological machine under total mobilization. In fact, Junger went so far as to claim that "technology is the real metaphysics of the twentieth century" (Ellul 1964, ix). Junger made no distinction between civil society and war society because, following Von Clauswitz the Prussian military strategist, he claimed that war can be continued by other means, such as with the power of civil diplomacy; diplomacy and war were cast as merely different means to the same end. Although opposed to the view that society was a machine, and "increasingly convinced that Junger's vision would be fulfilled after all, Heidegger could not avert his eyes from the horrific 'prescencing' of entities in the technological era" (Zimmerman 1990, 83). Unlike Jungev, however, Heidegger did not see as positive the idea of society as a machine, because even as he affirmed technology, the awesome nature of nuclear activity threatened to destroy the world. For Heidegger, then, the affirmation of technology was important, but it was also dangerous.

Heidegger was posing a new challenge for theories of technology. Andrew Feenberg (1991) suggests that theories of technology fall into two major categories—instrumental and substantive. Instrumental theories offer the most widely accepted explanations of technology based on the view that technologies are tools for human purposes, neutral in value, universally applicable, and with their only problem being the use to which they are put. This theory is also referred to as the anthropological explanation. In this view, the only price for resistance to technology on environmental, religious, or cultural grounds, is reduced efficiency. In other words, because of an infatuation with technology's efficiency and instrumental rationale, substantive issues do not arise. Standing in contrast to instrumental theories are substantive ones. The substantive theories of technology hold that technology is anything but neutral; rather it has a substantive value bias and through this bias transforms what it is to be human. To put it another way, we might ask how we do things technologically determines our identity? The substantive criticism is that technology constitutes a new cultural system that restructures the entire social world as an object of control. For example, through the atom bomb, technology has had an impact on the substance of our world. According to Heidegger, this impact is the subjugation of human beings; modern technology subjugates humanity to its own essence. In this view, the more we become affected by technology, paradoxically, the less of life is under our control and we are controlled by it. Substantive theories contradict the commonly held view that technology frees us from the ravages of nature; they suggest, rather, that our current condition is actually produced by technology.

In an almost prophetic sense, Marshall McLuhan even went as far as suggesting that eventually technology may control everything except the reproduction of humans, because, as he put it rather dramatically, technology has reduced us to the "sex organs of the machine world" (1964, 46). But technology has since infiltrated us further. If, for example, under conditions of artificial intellegence machines can author each other, this human sexual reproduction function will be of no consequence in the machine world; we simply will not be needed. This point is highlighted by Jean-François Lyotard, who when wondering if thought could go on without a body, comments that even to a lay person like himself "the combined forces of nuclear physics, electronics, photonics and information science open up a possibility of constructing technical objects, with a capacity that's not just physical but also cognitive, which 'extract' (that is select, process, and distribute) energies these objects need in order to function from forms generally found everywhere in the cosmos" (1991, 14). If this level of technological invasion were to be a common effect across cultures, the cultural variety in the reception and appropriation of technology would be a non-event because difference would disappear and we would, as Gilles Deleuze (1995) suggests, become nodes on a network ("dividuals"), or maybe even disappear altogether. Although we cannot live without technology, in terms of human agency, we are put at risk by it, all the more so when it becomes our primary means of communication and consequently transforms, or even becomes, us. If we extend this view, as technology "progresses" it will affect more and more of social life, and less and less of life will remain free to constitute a cultural difference. Human agency would thus be reduced, perhaps even extinguished. Under this condition, agency would inhere within the technological system where its expression would be confined to technological production; humans would no longer be required.

   The Question Concerning Technology addresses this dehumanized "darkening of the world" where technology enters into the inmost reaches of human existence, transforming the way we know, live, and will. As technology develops into more sophisticated forms such as cyberspace, cyborgs, or genetic categories, it will, in effect, become a mode of human existence[1]. Heidegger's analysis shows technology with a determinate existence of its own—a notion of a "will to will" beyond what Nietzsche (1968) called the "will to power." If Heidegger is correct, contrary to Enlightenment expectations and certain religious ideals, human existence is not guaranteed and its progress is merely an idea and a modern one at that, not a fact of life. Nietzsche says that mankind does not show any evolution toward better or stronger or higher levels, as these terms are understood today—"only too often I shall have occasion to show the reverse" (1968, 211). And reflecting Lyotard's (1991) concern about a takeover by technology, Richard Schacht argues that even our very survival as a species, as well as that of nature, is problematic. He writes that Nietzsche thought that "while the eventual outcome is still very much in doubt, nature is making a unique experiment in us. In our social and conscious life, a complex alternative to the general kind of instinct structure operative in other forms of life has emerged. Indeed, he considers certain aspects of the conditions imposed upon us by our social life to have played an important role in breaking down of our former instinct structure, as well as in the filling of the resulting void" (1995, 217).

WHAT IS TECHNOLOGY?

B. Foltz argues that there is good reason to believe that Heidegger "came to regard technology as *the issue* . . . for any contemporary attempt to think seriously and honestly" (1995, 84). Heidegger himself argues that, as an idea, technology is problematic, and questions regarding it often escape our ordinary thinking because "technology is normally defined anthropologically or as an instrumental means to the realisation of human ends" (1977, 4–5). He says that this is not so much a false as a misleading explanation of technology because it unnessarily limits our thinking[2]. As a corrective, he makes three points when comparing the instrumental and substantive views of technology. First, the instrumental definition encourages the view that there is no fundamental difference in kind concerning technology from various epochs in history. As he puts it rather critically, "the merely correct is not yet true. . . . the correct instrumental definition of technology still does not show us technology's essence" (Heidegger 1977, 6). There is a discernable difference, he suggests, between the technology involved in traditional handcraft and the technology involved in modern industrial production. Second, he argues that focusing on instrumental theories makes technology seem neutral; but the essence of technology is by no means anything technological. As he puts it, "thus we shall never experience our relationship to the essence of technology so long as we merely conceive and push forward the technological, put up with it, or evade it. Everywhere we remain unfree and chained to technology . . . we are delivered over to it in the worst possible way" (Heidegger 1977, 4). Instrumental thinking leads us to the conclusion that there is neither good nor bad technology, merely ends. According to Heidegger, this single-minded focus on ends is a sinister phenomenon of modern life. Third, the instrumental definition makes the problem of technology seem to be only a problem of mastering it. As he says, "everything depends on our manipulating technology in the proper manner as a means. . . . The will to mastery becomes all the more urgent the more technology threatens to slip from human control" (Heidegger 1977, 5). He argues that the way to address this threat is not through developing better technology, but rather in identifying that the problem is concerned with the *Enframing* that sets up the very conditions that blind us to that threat. Technology *per se* is not the problem; the problem is with our thought, Heidegger concludes.

Heidegger's view is not without its critics. In a revision of his own thinking, John Caputo, for example, saw Heidegger's reduction to "thought" in the face of major human problems as a scandal. Caputo sees the scandal in Heidgger's refusal to distinguish between the production of corpses in concentration camps and the production of other inert commodities in factories (1993, 132). Heidegger asserts that it is *Enframing* that stops us from seeing what we are doing, but strangely he does not distinguish between these types of activities. Caputo has it that Heidegger's position was that we lack thought of the right kind (1993, 136). For Heidegger, it was more that we have got the thinking wrong rather than any particular lack of housing or care (e.g., of the Jews)—bad and all as he admitted these things were. If we get the thinking right, suggests Heidegger, we would address the essense of issues such as technology and not make the mistakes we do.

In order to highlight the *Enframed* essence of modern technology, Heidegger contrasts it with ancient technology. Heidegger rejected modern explanations that devalue ancient technology merely because of its simplicity and lack of instrumental function. For him, these devaluations are not explanatory; the instrumental understanding of cause and effect as not linear is wrong because "the end in keeping with which the kind of means to be used is determined is also considered a cause" (Heidegger 1977, 6). Another way of putting this is to examine the logic of cause and effect. In that logic, we say that B was caused by A. But we could just as properly say that A may well have been caused by, say, Z, which makes A an effect, not a cause. There may also be many other "causes" that we do not, or perhaps cannot, know about. The truth is that, because of the complexity of the world, we may not know what causes what—ordinarily we simply attribute a cause. In fact, Heidegger does not separate out cause and effect this way at all.

To illustrate this problem of cause and effect, Heidegger draws a distinction between ancient craft and modern technology with an explanation of the doctrine of the four causes that he traced back to Aristotle. With this tracing, he wants to highlight what he means by efficient cause. As he writes:

> For centuries philosophy has taught that there are four causes: (1) the *causa materialis*, the material, the matter out of which, for example, a silver chalice is made; (2) the *causa formlis*, the form, the shape into which the material enters; (3) the *causa finalis*, the end, for example, the sacrificial rite in relation to which the chalice required is determined as to its form and matter; (4) the *causa efficiens*, which brings about the effect that is the finished, actual chalice, in this instance, the silversmith. What technology is, when represented as a means, discloses itself when we trace instrumentally back to fourfold causality. (Heidegger 1977, 6)

In contrast, to simply focus on efficient cause (*causa efficiens*) limits our understanding of technology in that it denies human agency in which the means is also a cause. In the case of the ancient craft technology involved in the making of the silver chalice, there are four causes, of which human agency is but one. When "[t]he silversmith considers carefully and gathers together the three aforementioned ways of being responsible and indebted (Heidegger 1977, 8), there is more to these life events than rational human control. It is, after all, religion that turns the cup into the chalice, or the table into an altar, with sacred value. Efficiency does not value cultural signification that gives meaning to ancient technology. Instead, modern tools destruct ancient craft because they limit Aristotle's first three causes that are essential to it. Under conditons of modern production, technology is limited to *causa efficiens*. If, for example, the modern factory is characterized as *causa efficiens*, it could be seen as merely an artifact or finished product or work of art with the manager as artist and in which the workers could be seen as mere equipment (i.e., as resources for an artist's painting, or, as Heidegger has it, "standing reserve"—*bestand*). In this picture of the factory as an artifact of *causa efficiens*, Aristotle's other three causes are not acknowledged. Insofar as human agency is involved, this picture suggests that modern technology is limited to *causa efficiens*. The contribution of the agent is limited to a matter of bringing about the effect—the production. The other three causes are not acknowledged. Herein lies an explanation for humans as mere resources brought about by modern technology.

In contrast to modern technology, the essence of ancient technology (*techne*) was the bringing forth (aletheia) grounded in revealing in which the other three causes were included.

> Bringing forth, indeed, gathers within itself the four modes of occasioning—causality—and rules them throughout. Within its domain belongs ends and means, belongs instrumental characteristic of technology. If we enquire, step by step, into what technology, represented as means, actually is, then we shall arrive at revealing. The possibility of all productive manufacturing lies in revealing. . . . Technology is therefore no mere means. Technology is a way of revealing . . . the truth. (Heidegger 1977, 12)

Prior to Plato, the word *techne* was linked with the word *episteme*. Both words are names for knowing in the widest sense, and indicate what it means to be entirely at home in something, to understand and be expert in it. Such knowing provides an opening up, "a revealing" (Heidegger 1977, 13); in terms of revealing, technology is our way of knowing our world. Through the notion of poetry, or *poiesis*,[3] the ancient Greeks understood their techne as a way of knowing the world. Since techne aids nature to "bring forth," the essence of ancient technology is in the revealing. This is a very different kind of technology from modern technology that challenges and demands from nature, and stores the ouput as standing reserve.

At the heart of Heidegger's explanation of modern technology are two important concepts—*essence* and *Enframing*. In German, the prefix *ge-* denotes a totalizing and *stell* indicates a position; *Gestell*, therefore, denotes a totalizing position. Heidegger also draws on the noun *stellen*, meaning to set upon or hunt down, thereby giving *Gestell* a sense of agency. *Gestell*, then, is an active framework that both constitutes and institues order. This technology is by no means neutral, because its essence is to hunt down and draw into itself all that is not already in the framework. This function is not revealed to the human components of the system. In modern technology, the agency of revealing lies in the framework as a whole. That means the status of the human components of a modern technological system would remain persistently hidden from them. The essence of ancient technology, then, is revealed through "bringing forth" that which is within nature, whereas, in absolute contrast, the essence of modern technology is revealed in "challenging," or "demanding from," nature. Modern technology is "something completely different and therefore new" (Heidegger 1977, 5).

Enframing is employed by Heidegger in an unfamiliar way to refer to the particular mode of revelation of Being in our modern epoch in the form of modern technology, which "gathers man thither to order the self-revealing as standing-reserve" (Heidgger 1977, 19). *Enframing* is the historical stamping which compels humanity to disclose everything in one dimension, as standing reserve; it is a problem in that it imposes upon everything to the degree that nothing is allowed to appear as it is in itself. Under this imposition, things are not regarded as objects because their importance is confined to their readiness for human control; that is, they do not exist for their own sake. Heidegger makes clear that exploitation and control are not the product of human agency, and that the subject never was anything but an effect of other forces when he says that "man becomes the subject and the world the object, is a consequence of technology establishing itself, and not the other way around" (Heidegger 1977, 112). The problem is the *Enframing* essence of modern technology, not technology itself; technology has always been with us, but not in its current mode.

The direction of technological practices that flow from such an *Enframing* is towards order for its own sake as "everywhere everything is ordered to stand by, to be immediately at hand, indeed to stand there just so that it may be on call for a further ordering" (Heidegger 1977, 17). In other words, the treatment of everything as resource is to be ever more efficiently and flexibly ordered—an "ordering of ordering"—where nature has become "a system of information" (Heidegger 1977, 23). As an example of *Enframing*, he points out that a modern airliner is not the object we ordinarily perceive it to be at all; it is a flexible and efficient cog in the transportation system and passengers are presumably not subjects but rather resources to fill the planes, thereby enabling the ordering of the system. Here the subject (the passenger) becomes the object (a resource to enable the system) and, therefore, it could be argued that the distinction between subject and object collapses. With no human subjectivity, that is, merely as a resource, there is no human agency. Our systemic ordering and control produce a very bleak picture indeed and the very opposite of what airline marketing would signify in their celebratory publicity about "freedom" and "self determination" that they say arises from deciding to travel to wherever one wants and to be able to choose from whatever exotic images have been advertised as fitting such travel. Whatever else it does, such travel and adoption of the relevant imagery primarily enables the transportation system. In this modern age we celebrate our ability to get everything under control. "Thus the current paradigms that hold up to us what our culture is dedicated to, and is good at, are examples of flexibility and efficiency, not for the sake of some further end, but just for the sake of flexibility and efficiency themselves" (Dreyfus 1993, 310). Modern science is another example because it reveals everything as equipment; the world is merely a collection of subatomic particles that comprise that equipment. This also suggests that science as an enframed entity is produced by modern technology and not the other way around as is commonly thought. Such *Enframing* does not present itself as merely a helpful representation among many possibilities, but rather, as the only view. This intolerance to other views is the defining characteristic of *Enframing*. *Enframing* is not simply a framework, it is also an ordering that puts into a configuration everything it brings forth through an ordering for use that it is continuously restructuring. Although technological activity responds to the calling forth in the modern age, it never comprises *Enframing* itself, or brings it about.

Heidegger's mystical leanings emerge when he suggests that although human beings respond to what is revealed, they do not have control over the self-revealing of the real—the unconcealment—itself. There is a puzzle here. If modern technology is a mode of revealing, how does the concealment, that is, the *Enframing*, continue? His answer is that individuals or groups do not bring unconcealment about, nor can it be removed by their own unaided efforts. *Enframing*, therefore, is outside human agency. It is sent to us by the "real" or that which genuinely is, that is, Being. This results in a fundamentally undifferentiated supply of what is available. The revealing never ceases because modern humanity "puts to nature the unreasonable demand" (Heidegger 1977: 14) that it supply energy which can be not only extracted, but stored as well. Modern technology, for example, extracts energy from water, coal, or uranium, stores that energy for future use, and distributes it at will. To illustrate, Heidegger compares and contrasts four things from a previous technological era; the windmill, the peasant planting seeds, the old wooden bridge and the hydroelectric dam across the stream. "The windmill does not unlock energy from the air currents in order to store it" (Heidegger 1977, 14). "The work of the peasant does not challenge the soil of the field" (Heidegger 1977, 15). "The old wooden bridge . . . joined bank with bank for hundreds of years" (Heidegger 1977, 16). Taken together these characterizations provide an image of ancient technology that does not challenge or demand from nature. Modern technology by contrast, is a "setting-upon that challenges the energies of nature as an expenditure, and in two ways" (Heidegger 1977, 15). First, "it unlocks and exposes," and second, it stockpiles for use. The modern technology of the windmill not only unlocks the energy for immediate use but also stockpiles the energy, so unlocked, for future use. Unlocking is the antithesis of *bringing forth* and, in the sense of demanding, does not see nature as a self-revealing Being. "[T]he revealing never simply comes to an end" (Heidegger 1977, 16).

Heidegger's view that the technological age compulsively discloses things as raw material to be transformed into products by the most efficient technical means was similar to the views of the early Critical Theorists of the Frankfurt School of Critical Theory. The ultraefficient instrumental production of self in everyday life that now prevails was despised as a distortion of culture by the Critical Theorists who, in the words of two of its most prominent writers, thought that "the inflection on the telephone or in the most intimate situation, the choice of words in a conversation, and the whole inner life as classified by the now somewhat devalued depth psychology, bear witness to man's attempt to make himself a proficient apparatus, similar (even in emotions) to the model served up by the culture industry" (Adorno and Horkheimer 1973, 167). However, Heidegger is critical of those (like the Frankfurt School) who think that technology is dangerous merely because it embodies instrumental reason. Capitalism, with its limited instrumental view of people in the production process, is, for the Marxist theory of the Frankfurt School, a byproduct of human agency and therefore, removable. If instead we follow Heidegger's logic, such an attempt at removal is dialectical and therefore technological because it is in itself a further attempt to control and rationalize the world. In the Hegelian dialectic the antithesis is itself as further intensification of Enframing. There is simply no way out of this problem through the dialectic, in Heidegger's view. And as the technologization of the world intensifies, research programs such as Critical Theory illustrate the futility of using technology to overcome technology, an imperative where "[t]he will to mastery becomes all the more urgent the more technology threatens to slip from human control" (Heidegger 1977, 5).

WHAT IS THE DANGER?

Heidegger thought that modern technology was the major danger for humanity not because technology might destroy the world, but because "technology reduces humanity to the status of a clever animal with no insight into its own authentic possibility and obligation: to disclose things and to shelter their being" (Zimmerman 1990, 221). Because of *Enframing*, then, we cannot look after ourselves in that we cannot shelter our being; rather, through it we destroy our dwelling. Heidegger maintains that the problem with modern technology is that there is a "sense of purposeful self assertion in everything" (1971, 116) and it is this very belief in human agency without sensing that this belief is *Enframed*. (Critical theory, for example, promotes this belief.) He argues that it would be threatening to the very survival of the human species if technology, under the command of human agency, solved all our problems because what threatens man is the "willed view that man, by the peaceful release, transformation, storage, and channelling of the energies of physical nature, could render the human condition, man's being, tolerable for everybody and happy in all respects" (Heidegger 1971, 116). The attempt to provide a total solution at the same time intensifies the essence of modern technology. More challenging, setting upon, and extraction is involved to produce the things required for that solution.

In addition, whatever the human condition, because of belief in the technological solution as the road to happiness, intolerable conditions would be made more tolerable. In other words, technology would become an apology for inhospitable totalitarian conditions, and we could become ever more tolerant without ever changing those conditions. With this toleration we would be making a virtue out of suffering—the very thing Nietzsche (1989), in his polemic against Christianity, warned us against (i.e., his idea that suffering and sadness do not have inherent value, and that the valorization of the "sad passions" is an invertion of value for a full life). Walter Benjamin, who is regarded as the founder of the Frankfurt School of Critical Theory, maintained that the Nazi regime in Germany of the 1930s believed that the unruly proletarian masses would gain (nonrevolutionary) satisfaction by being provided with new ways of expressing themselves. Like the Roman emperors who employed the practice of "bread and circuses" to distract the masses from whatever problem could not be solved, the Nazis thought that the provision of a spectacle would quiet protest; satisfaction could be brought about by the *Volk* taking part in massive technologically based public displays designed to help them feel they belonged to something important. "In fascism, then, politics used modern technology to transform politics into an artistic event, one which would mystify and conceal the fact that property relations went unchanged despite 'revolutionary' events" (Zimmerman 1990, 103). The ideological fashions in Germany after 1936 praised technology as "the very expression of the *Volksgeist*" (Zimmerman 1990, 104). The movement of Futurism also "praised war as an aesthetic movement, which brought forth new forms of architecture, shiny tanks, the geometrical flights of soaring airplanes, and the "smoke spirals from burning villages." Hitler increasingly embodied this fascination with the shiny machinery of modern technology as he sped around Germany in his Mercedes convertible, or flew place to place in his airplane—"descending like a god from the skies" (Zimmerman 1990, 104). Such imagery raised the possiblity that technology would eventually provide a positive future for the Third Riech (which, of course, it did not). Today another utopian future is attributed to the promise of hope provided by current versions of electronic technology and its associated "Knowledge Economy" by Western governments.

Nevertheless, Heidegger thinks it would be foolish to attack technology blindly. "We depend on technological devices; they even challenge us to ever greater advances" (Dreyfus 1993, 306). What we might do instead, he suggests, is to find ways of employing technological devices but somehow avoid the technological understanding of Being. Heidegger argues that the greatest danger is that "the approaching tide of technological revolution . . . calculative thinking may someday come to be accepted and practice *as the only way* of thinking" (quoted in Dreyfus 1993, 305).

WHAT CAN WE DO?

We need, suggests Heidegger, "some shared meaningful concerns that grip us that can give our culture a focus and enable us to resist acquiescence to a state that has no higher goal than to provide material welfare for all" (Dreyfus 1993, 312). Hubert Dreyfus is alluding to the status of our felt concerns because Heidegger's account of *Enframing* illustrates that human agency is not the sole source of value in the world. Heidegger is critical of the Cartesian idea of a self-transparent subject and the related Kantian ideal of autonomous agency, and although he does not deny the importance of human freedom, he opposes the claim that a person's relation to the world must necessarily be mediated by human agency. As he says "[t]he idea of a subject which has intentional experiences . . . encapsulated within itself is an absurdity which misconstrues the basic ontological structure of the being that we ourselves are" (Heidegger 1982, 63–64). With this sublime understanding of the so-called *apriori* human agency, we might be tempted to think that we can prevent the destruction of the world through efficiency in its control (as *Enframing* demands). But, since Being cannot be mastered through human agency, such control is not available. The manifestation of such control would be merely a furtherance of the technological condition of Being; the very attempt at control is an example of *Enframing*. If we actually ever did arrive at a technological solution to all human problems, that would indicate that *Enframing* had allowed us to forget completely that we are receivers of Being. If this happened, technology would have achieved what most religions and philosophies have aspired to. For Heidegger, the achievement of this aspiration would represent the ultimate nihilism; *Enframing* would signify the end of history.

Instead Heidegger wants us to pay attention to what remains of the different, the local, and the recalcitrant in our current practices, what Borgman (1984, 196–197) calls "focal practices." Heidegger calls this function "earth" which he says "shatters every attempt to penetrate into it" (Heidegger 1971, 47). Although Heidegger's "earthy" marginal practices such as tramping in the hills, "getting back to nature" and celebrating our heroes, may provide individual insights, they offer little social resistance to *Enframing*. Heidegger wants us to resist with such "little things." Yet, against the forces of global attempts at an integrated, economic, rationalist world order, marginal practices—however enjoyable—are more than problematic as a social mode of resistance. As a first step, Zimmerman argues, we might be better to accept our paradoxical condition. Thus

[i]nstead of trying to "solve" the problem of modern technology by furious actions and schemes produced by the rational ego, then, Heidegger counselled that people learn that there is no exit from that "problem". We are cast into the technological world. Insight into the fact that there is no exit from it may, in and of itself, help to free us from the compulsion that characterises all attempts to become "masters" of technology—for technology cannot be mastered. Instead, it is the destiny of the West. We are "released" from its grip only to the extent that we recognise that we are in its grip—this is the paradox. (1990, 220)

WHAT IS THE QUESTION FOR EDUCATION?

The literature of globalization as an integrated world economic order has it that education is vital to the production of correspondingly appropriate subjectivities. The OECD and the World Bank, for example, have stressed the significance of education as the key to participation in the development of human resources and for the production of research and scientific knowledge. One OECD (1997a) report on education argues that the radical changes introduced over recent years to the economy in response to globalization, will be "severe and disturbing to many established values and procedures" (7). Their view is that educational institutions must embrace and adjust to these changes through structural reform and identity reformation. Another OECD (1997b) report on higher education, argues that "internationalism should be seen as a preparation for twenty-first century capitalism" (11) and is "a means to improve the quality of education" (8). These two reports indicate that the focus on education as a cultural and economic instrument of capitalism is to be intensified. Under these economic definitions, education is becoming technologized, in the sense of introducing computers and other electronic communication equip-ment. In schools, for example, systemic targets are set for the use of computers by all teachers and students across the whole curriculum. The belief is that this type of curriculum will enable children to join the "techno-future" as productive "e-workers." And that may even be a useful way of conducting education. But Heidegger's troubling question of *Enframing* remains. He takes issue not with these "things" as things-in-themselves; the real problem, according to Heidegger, is that we are destined to understand things—including education (and ourselves)—primarily as exploitable objects. Contrary to liberal humanist Enlightenment traditions, we cannot liberate ourselves from this Will to Power (cf. Nietzsche 1968) which impels us toward the total mobilization of all things. In order to explain the problem of *Enframing,* we should not attack technology or even the redefiniton of education as a technology for economic development. For Heidegger, it is the essence of our technological way of being rather than mere equipment that is the problem. What we need to do instead is to understand the *essence* of the education framework in its *Enframed* state.

When we take education primarily as a technology for national economic development, that "technology" is focused on some predetermined goal, itself already evaluated as of value. Education so configured does not suggest or ask about education's purpose. The process to the ends is purely to produce the predetermined ends, and the human is part of that structure. For example, just as in industry, the student (as consumer) supplies the consumption, the government supplies the capital, and the teacher supplies the product. All parts of the framework depend on the regulation of all other parts; it is the system and not the individual that reveals. Foltz (1995, 100) suggests that under the condition of modern technology the agency of revealing lies in the framework as a whole. If this is the case, the *Enframing* of education conceals the state of beings from themselves. What is revealed instead is an educational framework for constituting and instituting order (*Gestell*). Such education demands, sets upon, engages, but does not entertain any other mode of revealing. This is an educational process in which whatever threatens to get out of order is reinstalled into the framework. Thus education provides a framework that demands a constant supply of resources—whether that be knowledge, people, or financial capital assets.

In this educational framework of total regulation, entities are "set in place," "set upon," "interrupted," and so on, precisely because they must be—always and already—"in supply." This is an imperative of modern technology. A rocket on its way into space, for example, must have ready and available at all times all entities and systems it needs to complete its mission as there is no compelling alternative. Manufacturing, similarily, requires a constant supply of materials and systems in place with clearly understood variations in supply. And again, governments must have totally reliable supplies of vaccines and qualified professionals to administer them properly or face questions about their legitimacy to govern. Everything in the system, including human beings, then, are resources; resources that must be available as a stockpile in reserve, or, as the new managerialism would have it, be available for supply in the "just in time" production process in what David Harvey (1989) calls flexible accumulation. In *Enframed* education there must be continual supply and constant improvement in value. "Extraction," "provocation," "forcing out," are the modern ways of revealing. Any tendency towards self-emergence is thus overruled and absorbed into forced production. We see, for example, the rising power of managerialism and its human resource function in universities, where the human is a resource to have value added, and education is primarily about the production of that added value of those resources. In fact human resource departments now conduct self-improvement courses for academics. One could similarily view the campaigns for social justice for those who have been classified as marginal; not simply as appeals to social justice or to altruism, but to the avoidance of waste through the efficient use of all resources. This efficiency includes the productivity of all those who had previously been excluded—such is the logic of efficiency. To be sure, those who were previously classified as marginal or excluded, as well as those who classify them as such, may well find the current surface rhetoric focused on equity subtly comforting. Under *Enframing*, however, what individuals believe is not the point, what matters is the increase in efficiency. A similar analysis can be applied to a range of Western government policy initiatives that promote, for example, inclusive education, increased participation rates, increased certification, lifelong learning (defined by Deleuze [1990] as perpetual training), the knowledge society, special needs, systems of behavior mangement, counseling, the proliferation of narratives about educating the "whole child," and so on. Such educational activity is directed increasingly toward the development and subsequent "discovery" of small openings, niches, and crevices, that can be filled with more and more highly sophisticated and differentiated services. Whether there is new knowledge generated about the world or not is not the point. What matters is the "more and more" that produces the Enlightenment illusion of progress and a further search for "more and more" again. Because progress is a notion that has no limits, there is no end to this demand—progress promotes itself, all the more so because it is generally valued. Some notable (and, understandably, probably unnoticed) effects are the "need" for more and more research, or reform, and consequent occupational positions to govern and implement it. It is the *acceleration* of research, knowledge, implementations, and occupations, and not the *content*, that is the major effect. This explanation is not normally available because *Enframing* conceals its essence. Such an explanation of education invokes images of a metaphysics of presence, a sense of its condition being absolute. No trace of absence, self-revelation, or bringing forth as in *techne* is available. The mere hint of absence or of a "less than best performance" or productive effort is a stimulus for further demands in order to bring the aberration into order. The "bringing to order" invokes a varied repertoire of practices such as motivation strategies, counseling, self-improvement, and attitude adjustments, commissions of inquiry, and further research, all of which enter into education discourse.

In this world, there is no shelter and no dwelling outside the system from where self-revealing might emerge. The very hint of a deviation or possible self-emergence from, or outside, the system is a signal that activates pressures to draw that deviation into the system. In fact the very *possibility* of a deviation is one of the reasons for the development of auditing and accreditation systems that order the ordering of the system. Any deviations that might (heaven forbid!) occur are not defined as moral or psychological matters; rather they are merely a stimulus for accelerating the development and implementation of increasing effective systems of control. These systems of control are articulated through such discourses as total quality management, total quality control, accreditation, and auditing. All thinking is dedicated to "improvement" toward ends, not to thinking about essences or purposes. Educational authority relations that depend on morality or psychological manipulation are probably going to melt down under this reconfiguration of education because they simply have no meaning in that system.

With no self-emergence, no dwelling outside the framework, and with the imperative of continuous production, no place is available that is not productive. It is as if the whole world has become a treadmill that exists primarily to accelerate itself rather than produce anything material *per se*. It is a world in which workers have learned to willingly adopt the ethos of efficiency as a personal moral respsonsibility; it seems that a functional subjectivity is required. And with no place from which to view the framework, all is concealed. With total concealment, all resources, including human ones, are a mute indifferent stockpile with no condition of self-generative renewal. It is important to emphasize the mute condition of the human resources. There is no inner depth of self-sufficiency; all we have is the opportunity for using resources, including our own. The result is an available, consumable, and replaceable inventory. What might loosely be termed a traditional, liberal, humanist perspective would perhaps interpret this explanation of education as "heartless" or even "inhuman" because it does not theorize agency as inherent in the individual. However, following Heidegger, the type of education emerging that mobilizes all entities is better explained in terms of *Enframing*.

WHAT CAN WE HOPE FOR?

To alert us to at least the idea of other possibilities, Heidegger advances *poiesis*—another mode of revealing—that inherently contains the idea that there are infinite possibilities for Being. Only the sense of the world as awesome as in a poetic understanding makes that world sacred, never able to be mastered, and therefore an object of reverence. Only to the extent that the world is understood as poetic or magic is it a world in which man can dwell, a world in which, as Heidegger writes, "poetically dwells man upon this earth" (1977, 34). Dwelling requires the sustained integration of man with nature and it will diminish to the extent that resources are depleted through *Enframing* of the world that desecrates the sacred. This is the problem with modern technology's *Enframed* efficiency—there is no mystery, nothing sacred, and, therefore, man cannot dwell there. It is the sense of the sacred that is required, not the destruction wrought under modern technology. Yet, we do not see this, because *Enframing* blocks *poiesis* as an alternative understanding of Being; *poiesis* as an ontology admits to alternatives, *Enframing* does not. *Poiesis* allows for humans as equipment but also allows for much more—including the idea that life is ultimately a mystery (as the celebration of life in Greek tragedies so clearly illustrates). The error of modern technology's *Enframed* negation of life as a mystery is referred to in the epigraph at the begining of this chapter where Heidegger says "[o]ur flight from the mystery toward what is readily available . . . this is erring" (1930). Because of its incapacity to allow other views, *Enframing* is a first order of understanding whereas *Poiesis* (because it can) is a second order of understanding and conceptually a more powerful one precisely because of it.

Today education has been appropriated as the key technology for globalization in the attempt at a new integrated world economic order—a kind of rational universal condition. But if technology is viewed as a "rational universal," then culture—a kind of particular—would be reduced to the spaces uncontrolled by technology, that is, small, nontechnical, symbolic domains. Technology would cross epistemological boundaries but would only pose a problem in these small, insignificant cultural domains. In the light of technological progress under globalization, these spaces are fast diminishing. An extension of this process would be homogeneity, the end of culture, and therefore, the end of difference—that is, the end of history and cultural difference would become an interesting historical artifact. Such a technologically determined world depends on theorizing technology as a rational universal that would push societies toward an identical model. On the other hand, to show that cultural difference has significance, we would need to argue that the cultural appropriation of technology is also of the essence of technology, not only symbolically but technically as well. This would be a considerable move away from *Enframing* as the essence of technology. If the essence of technology has such a cultural dimension, then we could expect difference to continue both symbolically and technically. If so, hopefully, we can dwell poetically on the earth.

Dreyfus and Baruch Spinosa have argued that "a tendency towards one unified world would impede the gathering of local worlds (and that) in a late seminar, Heidegger abandoned . . . the notion of a single understanding of being . . . the only comprehensiveness we can hope to achieve is our openness to dwelling in many worlds and the capacity to move among them" (1997, 12). This, they suggest, "will allow us to accept Heidegger's and Borgman's criticisms of technology and still have Heidegger's genuinely positive relationship to technological things" (Dreyfus and Spinosa 1997, 12). That view of cultural diversity would allow us to conceive of the technological future as indeterminate without trying to split the technological from the ontological. Diversity can, of course, be found in the local where "marginal" practices or counternarratives have been suggested as ways of clearing *Enframing*. If *Enframing* depends on its concealment, one significant way in which it might be revealed is to speak of it as a concept rather than to try to undo it or, even more erroneously, oppose technology. The danger of not speaking is that, as Ludwig Wittgenstein signalled, "what we cannot speak about we must pass over in silence" (1961, 74), we might be tempted to pass over *Enframing* into silence. The question is whether we can speak about *Enframing*—on Heidegger's record, it seems we can. More than that, of *Enframing* we must speak, because without a voice, we lose our existence as we know it. So if we accept that words "speak us into existence"—and we wish to live—in the face of *Enframing* we cannot remain silent. To speak we need a language community within which to "stand still," and within which a "clearing" might reveal Being itself to us poetically. The promotion of suitable educational language communities in many cultural worlds is the purpose of this chapter.

NOTES

1. According to Haraway (1991), this is already under way with Cyborgs that are the osmotic flows between the technological and the natural. Cyborgs name

the relationship between biology and cybernetic organisms. "The term 'Cyborg' was coined by Manfred Clynes and Nathan Kline to refer to the enhanced man (sic) who could survive in extra-territorial environment" (Haraway 1995, xv).

2. For examples of the latest trend in Western governments to define economy under knowledge, see the following websites:

http://www.oecd.org/dsti/sti/it/infosoc/prod/online.htm
http://www.morst.govt.nz/foresight/front.html
http://www.worldbank.org/html/extdr/extme/jssp012799a.htm

3. There are two sorts of *poiesis*: (1) aided, which involves human agency; and (2) unaided, which brings itself to fruition, for example, a bulb brings itself forth into a flower. Nature is unaided, *physis*. There is a difference in ancient Greek and modern understandings of nature. Modern nature is thought of in Kantian/Newtonian physics terms, whereas an ancient Greek view of nature is thought of in terms of a pre-Socratic self-revealing of Being. Ancient nature was thought of as the "fire of the gods" that was more feared than controllable. The flames of the fire of the gods, for example, were not explained (as they are for us) scientifically, but thought of as a manifestation of a universal concept of "flameness." With flameness there is the sublime, which is awesome and not controllable.

Model of Poiesis

	Poiesis (poetry—bringing forth)	
techne' (aided)		*physis (unaided)*
craft	art	nature

REFERENCES

Adorno, T and M. Horkeheimer. 1979. *Dialectic of Enlightenment*. Trans. J. Cumming. London: Verso.

Borgman, A. 1984. *Technology and the Character of Contemporary Life: A Philosophical Inquiry*. Chicago: University of Chicago Press.

Caputo, J. 1993. *Demythologizing Heidegger*. Bloomington: Indiana University Press.

Deleuze, G. 1995 "Postscript on Control Societies." In *Negotiations: 1972–1990*, New York: Columbia University Press.

Dreyfus, H. 1993. "Heidegger on the connection between nihilism, art, technology, and politics," in *The Cambridge Companion to Heidegger*. Ed. C. Guignon. Cambridge: Cambridge University Press.

Dreyfus, H. and C. Spinosa. 1997. *Highway Bridges and Feasts: Heidegger and Borgaman on How to Affirm Technology*. http://focussing.org/dreyfus.html

Ellul, J. 1964. *The Technological Society*. Trans. J. Wilkinson. New York: Vintage Books.

Feenberg, A. 1991. *Critical Theory of Technology*. New York: Oxford University Press.

Foltz, B. 1995. *Inhabiting the Earth: Heidegger, Environmental Ethics, and the Meta-physics of Nature.* New Jersey: New Humanities Press.

Haraway, D. J. 1991. *Simians, Cyborgs, and Women: The Reinvention of Nature.* London: Free Association Press.

Heidegger, M. 1971. *Poetry, Language, Thought.* Trans. A. Hofstadter. New York: Harper & Row.

Heidegger, M. 1977. *The Question Concerning Technology and Other Essays.* Trans. W. Lovitt. New York: Harper & Row.

Heidegger, M. 1982. *The Basic Problems of Phenomenology.* Bloomington: Indiana University Press.

Krell, D., ed. 1977. *Basic Writings: Martin Heidegger.* London: Routeldge.

Lyotard, J-F. 1984. *The Postmodern Condition: A Report on Knowledge. Vol. 10 of Theory and History of Literature.* Minneapolis: University of Minnesota Press.

Lyotard, J-F. 1991. *The Inhuman: Reflections on Time.* Trans. G. Bennington & R. Bowlby. Oxford: Polity Press.

McLuhan, M. 1964. *Understanding Media.* New York: McGraw Hill.

Nietzsche, F. 1956. *The Birth of Tragedy.* Trans. F. Golffing. New York: Doubleday.

Nietzsche, F. 1989. *On the Genealogy of Morals.* Trans. W. Kaufmann & R. Hollingdale. New York: Vintage Press.

Organisation for Economic Co-operation and Development. 1997a. *Thematic Review of the First Years of Tertiary Education.* Paris: Directorate for Education, Employment, Labour and Social Affairs, 26 February.

Organisation for Economic Co-operation and Development. 1997b. *Internationalisation of Higher Education.* Paris: Centre for Educational Research and Innovation.

Schacht, R. 1995. *Making Sense of Nietzsche: Reflections Timely and Untimely.* Chicago: University of Illinois Press.

Wittgenstein, L. 1961. *Tractatus Logico-Philosophicus.* Trans. D. Pears & B. McGuinness. London: Routledge.

Zimmerman, M. 1990. *Heidegger's Confrontation with Modernity: Technology, Politics, Art.* Bloomington: Indiana University Press.

9

Heidegger and Nietzsche: Nihilism and the Question of Value in Relation to Education

F. Ruth Irwin

Recently the debates over "values education" have heated up. The neoliberal emphasis on vocationalism and commodification has been perceived as inadequate to describe the scope of the role of education in society. As the West emerges from several decades of neoliberal, self-centerd and competitive individualism, a dissonance arises in the classroom for an ethical and meaningful approach to life. Is it enough though, to simply revisit the existing debate with historical arguments, such as the role of schools in creating informed citizens capable of making critical decisions as a basis of democracy, or the redemptive do-gooder ethics of non-violence— or are new contours to the debate required? The issue of environmental damage has changed the scope of ethical concerns in general and educative ethics in particular. The traditional anthropocentric relation of humanity to, as Kant puts it, "the manifold" cannot continue without irreversibly destroying our habitat—in the same fashion as a deadly virus kills its host. Unfortunately, unlike Kim Stanley Robinson's trilogy *Red Mars, Blue Mars* and *Green Mars*, there are currently no alternative host planets available for terraforming and recolonizing, and so the peril of environmental devastation looms large on the horizon of worldwide social organization. There is a tendency to offer technological fixes to what are perceived as technical environmental problems—such as bringing the extinct Tasmanian Devil to life through a combination of genetically engineering the DNA and emplanting the embryo in another related species. Counterpointing the reductionism of technological "fixes" is the Judeo-Christian crisis response of redemptive ethics. Heidegger tends towards the latter. What he is arguing for is a reconfiguring of the relationship between humanity and the world and he conceptualizes this through the special significance of the ability of *Dasein* to apprehend Being. Heidegger relegates the problem of nihilism to the corrosion of the originary force of this relationship into a rigid representation of the language as *logos*. He describes nihilism as the stagnation of our awareness of Being in an anthropocentric table of *values*. Preempting the neoliberal takeover of liberal terminology, we might take him to argue that it is this slippage into monetarist terms such as "value," "importance," and "weight," rather than "care" and "openness," that inevitably produces a logic of consumerism between humanity and beings-as-a-whole.

The issue envelops forms of political organization and the style of struggle between peoples. It is the subject that has long been the focus of philosophical attention—the relation between humanity and existence itself. The role of education in the exploration of values is important. Consciously opening up the interpretation of existing values about the relationship between people and the planet repositions the educational project as the means to reimagining human society.

This chapter is a philosophical analysis of Heidegger and Nietzsche's approach to metaphysics and the associated problem of nihilism. Heidegger sums up the history of Western metaphysics in a way that challenges common sense approaches to values education. Through close attention to language, Heidegger argues that Nietzsche inverts the Platonic-Christian tradition but retains the anthropocentric *imposition* of "values." I have used Nietzsche's theory to suggest a slightly different definition of metaphysics and nihilism which draws attention to the ontological parameters of human truths as a struggle between competing sets of conflicting or contradictory values (perspectives) and opens space for rethinking and reeducating human possibilities. How this openness will show up in educational theory and practice is only beginning to be evoked. The two philosophers indicate an approach to issues of morality, decision making, and knowledge production that may surprise and disconcert traditional views. As the forefathers of poststructuralist thinking, Nietzsche and Heidegger offer a critique of Humanism while retaining the Renaissance tradition of positioning education as the wellspring of values in society. The institutions of education, in theory if not in practice, are somewhat protected from exposure to the dynamics of consumerism, at least to a greater extent than other realms of civil society. The role of universities as the "critic and conscience of society" gives us the unique opportunity and responsibility to imagine alternative ways of living. It is through the generation of new knowledges, the development of critique, and the nurturing of character that society reformulates itself in relation to the earth. The ethical evaluation of these new forms of knowledge is crucial to the creative and caring regeneration of the human environment, as opposed to the corrosive adoption of consumerism and usury.

In his text *An Introduction to Metaphysics*, Heidegger outlines his theory of Being. He distinguishes a significant relationship between apprehension of Being by *Dasein* from the nothingness of mere existence. He takes an ontological position reminiscent in many ways of the emphasis Aristotle places on primary substance. Being is not an abstract Ideal but "shows up" in the ordinary activity of particular beings. In contrast to the traditional view of Being underlying the changing differentials of individuals and groups like a static "ground," Heidegger conceptualizes Being as a dynamic "event ontology." The significance of *Dasein* is the "passion for questioning" which "wrests" Being from concealment.

Heidegger argues that there was a historical shift in ancient Greek thought in the concept of Being from *physis* to *ousia* and then to the Roman translation "substance." He argues that this shift is a decline in the originary force of human awareness and ability to make Being manifest. Plato began the "decline" by positioning Being "beyond" the "World of Appearance" and at a remove from particular beings. Aristotle redressed this problem to some extent but his reliance on categorical statements of the *logos* in, for example, *The Categories,* produced a stale representation rather than a poetic, forceful "wresting" of Being from concealment. This corruption has resulted in a degeneration and complacency of society and history.

Clearly Heidegger requires language to do more work than classify or designate logical routes of deduction. He regards the significance of humanity as lying in the reciprocal relation between *Dasein* and Being. His theory of the significance of *Dasein* as a questioner is important, if anthropocentric, because it defines the most important role of humanity as being open to Being rather than developing new ways of utilizing the world as a resource. The educational concern of inquiry lies at the heart of human characteristics. Heidegger's ideas about the function of language, logic, and values have important consequences for the emphasis we place on different fields of human endeavor. In sharp contrast to liberal faith in the "sciences of the State," which elevates positivist technology and economics, Heidegger relegates science to "busyness" and argues that works of art constitute the best way of reconfiguring culture and opening up original aspects of Being. Thus, Heidegger (and Nietzsche) calls into question the elevation of a technicist enframing of educational disciplines at the expense of the vital functions of the arts and humanities. He remains within the modern framework in his Renaissance-like interest in the ideas of classical antiquity and his faith that home and hearth will solve the contemporary problems of consumerism and the nihilist attitude of society. It is his focus on *questioning* and reconfigurement in terms of the relationship between humanity and the environment that gives us a vital indication of the potential role and motivation for education.

LIFE-WORLD

The issue at stake between Heidegger and Nietzsche's theory lies in their distinctively different philosophical attitudes to the environment, based on either the solipsistic notion of "world" or a wider, force-driven concept of "life." Nietzsche's upbringing and later rejection of Christianity produces a radical emphasis on "Life" and a subsequent re-evaluation of the relative importance of humanity. Nietzsche's definition of metaphysics is the unquestioned faith in an absolute truth, either as an ontological "ground," such as the concept of "substance," or a theological "beyond," such as the Christian God, or the Platonic "Good." Truths define the moral laws of society and as such are necessary components constituting the conditions for activity we define as "human." Thus 'faith' in truths is not to be entirely abandoned—Nietzsche simply explores the parameters of perception, interpretation, and knowledge. By doing so, he situates the busy purposefulness of many forms of social organization as productive within the limited field of human intelligence. He contextualizes the nihilism of metaphysics as an unsubstantiated call to the "beyond" of nothingness, or the void. Drawing up the parameters of meaning, truth, knowledge, and purpose emphasizes that nihilism is a meager way of understanding human life. It is based on an inflated sense of our own importance. Once we have our status in perspective, the daily existence of life is valuable for its own sake.

Heidegger, on the other hand, also echoes Schopenhauer, by defining metaphysics as the inquiry into the relation between the universal and the plurality, or Being and beings. Heidegger clearly delineates the legitimate field of inquiry of Being into that which can be ascertained by *Dasein*—rather than extraneous, "busy" alien existence, which he defines as nothingness. Following Parmenides and, in a way, Nietzsche, Heidegger is wary of nothingness. He understands nothingness as nihilism which is a road leading to loss, annihilation, or as he puts it, the forgetting of Being. He argues that instead of overcoming nihilism, Nietzsche brings about the culmination of metaphysics by inverting the Platonic and Christian "beyond" in a dualistic opposition that does not transform the problem of Being's obscurity.

Michael Peters argues that Heidegger sets forth "a deepening of humanism, but a deepening that, at the same time, recognises forces somehow beyond 'Man'."[1] Beyond Man is Heidegger's concept of the unique quality of

Dasein as the ability to ascertain the nature of Being without relying on a rationalist or positivist position of control "over" nature. Heidegger puts emphasis on the hubris of Humanism, which he argues, "forgets" the unique ability of *Dasein* to apprehend Being. He writes, "Humanism is opposed because it does not set the *humanitas* of man high enough."[2]

BEING

The framework Heidegger finds at the source of Western metaphysics, in the earliest fragments of Greek philosophy, is the question: "what is Being?" The mode of questioning is vital. Its etymology and grammar will only get us so far, Heidegger argues. Instead of first asking this question— what is Being? we need initially to find a mode of inquiry that will be fruitful. Logically, the more comprehensive a term, "the more indeterminate and empty is its content."[3] The term "Being" is so huge and all-encompassing that Nietzsche argues that its meaning has become "empty" and "vaporous." Thus, Heidegger says it is easy for the question "What is Being?" to become "merely a mechanical repetition of the question about the Being as such." What is required is an engagement with Being which allows its "appropriate unfolding."[4] Heidegger advocates poetry as making the term "strange" and thereby enabling a discerning and fresh revealing of the Being of beings. Plato assumed that the Ideal nature of Being was *a priori* and inaccessible to the temporality of a human. But this is not a limitation that Heidegger takes seriously, because the *questioning* is only viable through a peculiarly human ability to apprehend the ground from which Being springs. As Peters argues, in this way Heidegger is advocating a deepening of Humanism, not a rejection of it.[5]

In his book *An Introduction to Metaphysics* (1935), Heidegger looks to the poetry of the early Greeks—Parmenides, Heraclitus, and Sophocles—as an originating experience of Being. He documents the shift from these vital and "originary" authors to the nihilistic "degradation" of Being by Plato and, to a lesser extent, Aristotle, and consequently the metaphysical tradition up until and including Nietzsche. As Charles Guignon puts it, in the foreground of the book is "the dawn of metaphysics in ancient Greece, its decline and calcification up to the present, and the prospects for rejuvenation today."[6]

NOTHINGNESS

Heidegger accepts the traditional dualism between Being and Nothingness. He does not expound at any length on nothingness, except to say it is indescribable and, again, best approximated through poetry rather than philosophy: "Authentic speaking about nothing always remains extraordinary. It cannot be vulgarised. It dissolves if it is placed in the cheap acid of a merely logical intelligence."[7] His notion of nothingness does not appear to rest significantly on "the void," or "madness," or even outer space, which might be juxtaposed with Being, but rather on not-being, which is the removal of the once-being, such as the absence of the cup from the bench or death. The question for Heidegger here is—"Why are there beings rather than nothing?"[8] Being elicits the possibility of nothing—and in that possibility reveals itself.[9] He says that nothingness coalesces with being because it "*is* nothing." His analysis begs the question—is nothingness conflatable with Being? That appears to be an entire thesis on its own. A question, perhaps, best left open at this stage.

Heidegger distinguishes though, between "existence" and (non)Being in a manner that is surprising.

> Nonbeing means accordingly to depart from such generated permanence: *existasthai*, "existence," "to exist," meant for the Greeks nonbeing. The thoughtless habit of using the words "existence" and "exist" as designations for Being is one more indication of our estrangement both from Being and from radical, forceful, and definite exegesis of Being.[10]

The term "existence" for Heidegger, then, is an exit, as I understand it, a kind of "exit-ence" from the now. Anything lost or forgotten might qualify as long as it was truly gone, and not simply operating in a hidden or obscured manner. To be comprehended by other animals (for example) is not a qualification for entering the peculiarly reflective human language of Being; "existence" departs from *Dasein's* co-representation of Being. The previous short passage is all that Heidegger devotes to existence as non-Being, but in view of his anthropocentric version of Being, which only "shows" itself apprehendable to human thought, the notion that existence as nonbeing exits from the encircling of Being is important. Nonbeing is slightly, but profoundly, different from "concealment" because where Being is "concealed" it is still there, simply obscured from view. Nonbeing is partly not-present, but primarily not-present to human apprehension. Thus a corpse might be literally present, but Being is inapprehendable in its being. However, it is a mistake to think that Being means Life (in either a biological or Nietzschean sense). Many aspects of life abound in a manner that humans are completely oblivious to and this is *existence*, not Being. Indeed, Heidegger argues that expanding the boundaries of human comprehension in regard to the natural environment simply results in "busyness" rather than increased access to the truth of Being.

Nietzsche talks about "life" rather than Being or existence. His theory of the Will to Power attributes perspectives to other forms of existence that are outside the parameters of human comprehension. The concept is anorganic rather than being limited to breathing, "living" things. He regards each mode of being as having its own perspective and thus its own "world."

EVENT ONTOLOGY

For Heidegger, the boundaries of Being, and the manner in which Being is discernible through beings, are interesting. On the one hand, the relationship of *das Seiende*, "Being" to "beings" is fundamental, because "thinking Being in abstraction from being is artificial."[11] The aspect of human apprehension in relation to Being, and through beings, is vital because Being presents to a view, in other words, oblivion is a poverty of viewing. Our apprehension of Being is limited to its appearance in examples of being. *Dasein* is a German word commonly designated to mean general "existence." For Heidegger *Dasein* is a very specific technical term which he uses to refer to humans (and conceivably other beings which *care* about "being as a whole"). Without apprehension by *Dasein*, the Being in beings could not shine forth, and all would be nothing.

The parameters of apprehension are also set by the mode in which *Dasein* questions. What is important is the relation between the duality of beings and Being. This relation is not based on beings *participating* in Being, such as Plato argued in the *Sophist*, but rather on a more Aristotelian notion of beings *ascending* towards Being.[12] *Dasein* moves from ascertaining a particular and transient being to comprehending the enduringness of Being. Thus, the essential concepts are Being and *time*.

In the philosophical tradition, "Being" has a static feel to it, as in "ground." Being is usually associated with "substance ontology"; *it* "is" a *thing* that endures, rests, and has weight and importance. Guignon explains Heidegger's conceptual shift from the static to the dynamic; "Heidegger conceives of human existence not as a thing or object, but rather as an *event*, the unfolding realization of a life story as a whole."[13] There is an obvious and long-standing contrast in the philosophical tradition, between Being and the dynamism of "becoming." Being shows up in beings, states Heidegger, which bears a relation to Kant's notion that the universal thing-in-itself shows an aspect in each individual object, or being. It seems that there is a connection between Heidegger's focus on the relation between Being and beings, and Schopenhauer's concept of the Will as the One and as plurality. Heidegger's theory is that Being has no external universal truth independent of the beings it exhibits itself *as*. Being does not change location as it does for Plato.[14] Being is not a description of the substance ontology of the philosophical tradition, and not quite the force that Schopenhauer's

Will connotes, but rather an unfolding event. Thus, Being is concerned with becoming, or in a manner of speaking, which is Schopenhauer's rather than Heidegger's terminology; the "One" *is* the plurality. Heidegger explains Being as the Greek *physis* that is the power of emerging and holding sway;

> In this power rest and motion are opened out of original unity. This power is the overpowering presence that is not yet mastered (*bewältigt*) in thought, wherein that which is present manifests itself as a (being). But this power first issues from concealment i.e. in Greek *aletheia* (unconcealment) when the power accomplishes itself as a world.[15]

Guignon describes the significant shift from substance to event ontology as a "retrieval" of an early Greek "pre-metaphysical" experience of Being.

> What this retrieval is supposed to provide is a way of replacing the dominant substance ontology in the Western world with an alternative understanding of Being, an understanding that emphasizes the way beings show up in (and as) an unfolding *happening* or *event.*[16]

DAS DASEIN

The "potential" and "fruition" of Being has been strongly influenced by Aristotle's notion of essence—which "causes" the substance to be formed in a way that shows what it *is*. Guignon argues that Heidegger distinguished himself from Aristotle because neither Being nor *Dasein* has an inevitable telos. Taking a Nietzschean stance, the subject, *das Dasein* "styles" her/himself by projecting towards the future (promising), and recouping the past in a process that looks at one's life as a whole, and as an ongoing becoming. But the future is not linear, as it is for Aristotle. There is no precise goal in this collation of our finite life as a whole. Similarly to Nietzsche, there is no determinant end point, no Ideal of the "good" or heaven to guide or complete a life. Any faith resides in "life," and "fate" for Nietzsche, and in Being for Heidegger. Thus, as an entity, humans are an example of how Being exhibits itself. More than this though, Heidegger argues that humans have a unique relation to Being, because unlike any other animal, vegetable, or mineral, we are open to comprehending the appearance of Being which "shines forth" from beings; a privileged, unique relation arises between (beings as a whole) and the act of questioning. For through this questioning beings as a whole are for the first time opened up *as such* with a view to its possible ground, and in the act of questioning it is kept open.[17]

On the one hand, Heidegger recognizes that humans are insignificant in the scale of the history of the earth, let alone the universe. "What is the temporal extension of a human life amid all the millions of years?"[18] On the other hand, Heidegger has developed Kant's theory of time, such that time is not simply *a priori* to subjectivity but emerges commensurately with *human* subjectivity.

> There is the pure possibility that man might not be at all. After all there was a time when man was not. But strictly speaking we cannot say: There was a time when man *was* not. At all *times* man was and is and will be, because time produces itself only insofar as man is. There is no time when man was not, not because man was from all eternity and will be for all eternity but because time is not eternity and time fashions itself into a time only as a human, historical being-there [*Dasein*].[19]

The term *Dasein* was invented in the 19th century as a Germanic transliteration of "existence."[20] Heidegger has limited the term into a technical designation for an inquiring relation with the "world." *Das Dasein* is a play on words. On the one hand, *Dasein* translates as *"das,"* "the" and *"ein"* or "one"; "the one" or "any one." Although *Dasein* relates to the world solispsistically in a certain sense, "any one" is a nod towards community; that any individual can question the openness of Being. It echoes his theory of the relation between being as an entity and the enduringness of Being. Heidegger enlarges his concept of *Dasein* from an individual consciousness to include a group of consciousness in his later writing. Alternatively *"Da"* means "there" and *"sein"* is "being"; "being-there." Anyone being *there* projects *Dasein* away from "here" toward a future. Being-there is the movement of potentiality. According to Manheim "he means man's conscious, historical existence in the world, which is always projected into a there beyond its here."[21] Being needs to be in relation to the future directed being-there of *Dasein*. *Dasein* must face the anxiety of her/his own "finitude," in what Heidegger calls being-toward-death. The uniqueness of each individual is that they must face their own death alone. This finitude offers the chance to comprehend their life, past, present, and future, as a whole. While constrained by the historical conditions and possibilities into which they are "thrown," *Dasein* can take a stand and, from the perspective of finitude, style an authentic life.[22] The finitude of being-toward-death is the condition in which thinking happens as an openness and receptivity which projects "there" and apprehends Being. For *Dasein*, the here and now clouds or conceals the present state of affairs because the environment is so familiar it is invisible.

Das Dasein is "thrown" into an 'always already' public environment. For *das Dasein*, its own environment is a completely familiar "world," undifferentiated from the self. Guignon explains, "Heidegger's 'phe-nomenological' approach to understanding the human starts by de-scribing our lives as they unfold in familiar, everyday contexts of ac-tion, prior to theorizing and reflection."[23] Heidegger called this transparent integration the "clearing," whose characteristic is that it is too normal and everyday to be overtly noticeable. Consciousness is analogous with the tip of an iceberg—for the bulk of our lives we are "objects amongst objects," and are indistinguishable from our environ-ment. This amounts to knowing and reacting to the lived environment so "organically" or unconsciously that we no longer "think" about a large proportion of our activities.

During the 1930s Heidegger expanded the concept of *Dasein* to encom-pass *das Volk*, the people: "Even to speak of our capacity for *selfhood* 'does not mean that man [insofar as he is Dasein] is primarily an 'I' and an in-dividual . . . any more than he is a We and a community.'"[24] The public as-pect of *Dasein* is important for overcoming the individual solipsism in-herent in Idealism. 'The world' is no longer constituted by the subject (and no longer expires with the death of the subject). Guignon explains that Heidegger's concept *Dasein*,

> (r)efers to the fact *that* there is a (finite) understanding of Being. On the as-sumption that humans are the only beings with an understanding of Being, Dasein appears in, or at least arises only where there are humans. Having an understanding of Being (i.e. being the opening in which beings can show up) is humanity's most essential trait.[25]

Being is codependent with *Dasein*. It is not conditioned by *Dasein* (as in humanism) nor is it independent (as in existence), but it retains a certain Idealist mega-solipsism on the part of human kind (*das Volk*) rather than human individuals.

STRUGGLE; BEING AND BECOMING

Heidegger specifically rejects the historical presumption that Being is a static mode of existence. He finds evidence of the dynamism involved in Being in three ways: through the coming to presence of Being through be-ings, the growth and fulfilment of potential, or "form," and finally through the active grammar of language. The dynamism of Being is not achieved strictly through human apprehension and language though. Change is the precondition, the "nature" of Being and it is only when our expectations stagnate and ossify into "statements" rather than an attitude of inquiry, respect, and awe, that we fail to find it.

Perhaps one of the most important, and the most underworked aspects of Heidegger's theory is this precondition of change. It shows up in his exploration of Heraclitus and the concept of strife. Heidegger cites Heraclitus as the first to "think" of Being as conflict and the "becoming" of flux: "In the conflict (*Aus-einandersetzung*, setting-apart) a world comes into being. (Conflict does not split, much less destroy unity. It constitutes unity, it is a binding-together, *logos*.)"[26]

Being has an affinity with beings and has a particular relation to *Dasein*, but its *origin* is in struggle that Heidegger finds in fragment 53 of Heraclitus. Heidegger's translation reads,

> Conflict is for all (that is present) the creator that causes to emerge, but (also) for all the dominant preserver. For it makes some to appear as gods, others as men; it creates (shows) some as slaves, others as freemen.[27]

Struggle initiates rank (gods, men, slaves), and "sets forth their Being."[28]

The traditional view of the concept of struggle is to conflate it with violence. Violence is a form of evil that causes suffering and must be righted through retribution. The struggles and conflict over comparative rank and the competition for resources is a significant component of the field of ethics. It is important to be wary of a conception of Being that is anthropocentrically ranked (like Darwin's Great Chain of Being for example). The ordering of chaotic existence into hierarchical rank inevitably brings with it conflicts of interest. Ethics will continue to grapple with these problems but could leave behind the utopian ideal of a world without struggle. The subtle shift is, as Guignon deduces, that gods or men do not initiate (an ordered) "world"; struggle itself does. Heidegger explains the manner in which struggle "works" to order chaos,

> Against the overwhelming chaos they set the barrier of their work, and in their work they capture the world thus opened up. It is with these works that the elemental power, the *physis* first comes to stand. Only now does the being become being as such. This world-building is history in the authentic sense. . . . Where struggle ceases, the being does not vanish, but the world turns away. The being is no longer asserted (i.e. preserved as such). Now it is merely found ready-made, it is datum.[29]

This insight from Heraclitus along with Nietzsche's concept of the will to power as the driving force of Life initiates the rethinking of strife and power in poststructuralist thought. Deleuze has generated a theory that strife produces a positive distribution of difference rather than an oppressive negation of the "other," and similarly, Foucault has developed a more positive evaluation of the effects of power that is in the process of shifting the ground of ethics and educational issues.

On the face of it, at the root of Greek thought, Parmenides' exposition on Being as ultimate and enduring appears to oppose Heraclitus saying *"panta rhei,"* everything is in flux. Accordingly, the traditional interpretation of Heraclitus is that there is no Being: everything "is" becoming.[30] But through emphasis on "is," the flux of becoming is subsumed in the endurance of Being. Heidegger brings Parmenides' Being to bear on Heraclitus' flux, arguing that they are both essentially talking about the same thing. Becoming is an engagement of Being with the existence of beings. At the center of this engagement is dynamic struggle.

BEING AND APPEARANCE

Briefly, Heidegger's argument is that Plato began the stagnation of the ability of *Dasein* to apprehend Being from the earlier Greek thinkers' forceful and originary insights. Plato placed the universal Being beyond the mundane daily shifts and changes of Becoming and appearance, beginning the slide of inquiry into statement and finally the forgetting of Being. The initial assumption of the Platonic dichotomy between Being as an abstract enduring ideal and appearance as the mundane and transitory episodes of daily living is that it is similar to the metaphysical distinction between Being and becoming; Being is assumed to be permanence, whereas appearance is a semblance, it is deceptive, unstable, temporal, emerging, and vanishing again. In a new move, Heidegger conflates Being and becoming by drawing out three aspects of appearance that are based on the "shining" forth of Being. The German term for appearance is *Schein*, and it has an interpretive range, firstly as "radiance" or glow, secondly as "appearing" or coming to light, and thirdly, as "mere appearance" or semblance.[31] At one end of the range, appearance divulges Being by letting it radiate from beings. At the other end, the variation of the subjective view of the appearance of the being is (in Platonic terms), a deviation, a copy, or even an illusion of Being. Heidegger argues that the shining forth of Being has to be "wrested" from the being, by refusing complacently to accept a view as correctitude. Heidegger admonishes us to ignore "subjective," "objective," "realistic," or idealistic" as the mode of questioning Being. *"Schein"* in its fulcrum as coming to light, both of the radiance of Being and the semblance of Being, offers the opportunity for Being to be apprehended by *Dasein* through beings. Thus, appearing is the means by which Being emerges from unconcealment. Heidegger argues, "Appearing is the very essence of Being."[32] *Dasein* apprehends the truth of Being through both manifest appearance and the enduring sway of becoming. *Dasein* can look at the visual semblance of the appearance and also, by "being-there," partake in the unconcealed radiance of the Being as it is manifested in being.

Being as *Physis* was divided at this early point in Greek thought into three aspects; firstly as emerging, secondly, becoming as presencing, and finally, the appearance as manifesting. The Sophists and Plato "degraded" the distinction between appearance and Being by hardening the difference between concealment and distortion (appearance) as opposed to unconcealment (Being). Heidegger describes Plato as the culmination of the beginning of philosophy,[33] and as such is a "falling away" from the question of Being as it is best explicated by Parmenides. Plato emphasized the *mimesis* of the appearance, which implies that being is a replica and Being the original, that which re-presents itself as an appearance, or simulacra of the original Being. Furthermore, the Platonic notion of the *eidos*, or idea is derived from *ousia*, or enduring manifestation. We can see here how the notion of *ousia* is not simply the more static half of the notion of *physis;* the degradation from *physis* to *ousia* becomes a divorce in terms. The permanence of Being is juxtaposed against the temporal limits of beings. The Idea is in opposition to the illusion, the deficiency of appearance. Being shifts to a model that transcends the mere apprehension of transient objects. The theory of apprehension changes—"it becomes a correctness of vision, of apprehension as representation."[34]

Furthermore, Heidegger argues that the Being of *logos* as statement is "always already" unconcealed in relation to appearance. It no longer has the ability to inquire into the ground of Being because *logos* cannot "wrest" Being from unconcealment. Statements discern in-cidents, but logic is a stale form of inquiry. For Plato, *physis* has congealed with *logos* so that the emerging radiance, which up until Plato was described as complete unto itself as Being, can only be made apparent as a surface appearance that occupies a place. Logos describes the being's quidity—its *whatness*—and appearance designates its quodity—or *thatness*. Being can be *represented* as having different properties, such as magnitude and extension. Aristotle's categories derive from statements as *logos*, thus, unconcealment has been shifted to correctness. The idea and statement has taken over the possibility of finding the truth of Being in its ground.[35] Christianity and modernity, Heidegger admonishes, adheres to the metaphysical traditions' "paralysis of all passion for questioning."[36]

Clearly, it is here that the role of education is most vital. According to a Heideggerian reading, the ethical task of education is to inspire a psychology of awe. To *care* about Being as such. As teachers know, in the moments when we do achieve this, as opposed to the long hours where students are struggling not to fall asleep, real learning and thinking occurs.

The crucial point of Heidegger's argument in relation to Nietzsche is the "degradation" of the inquiry into Being by Plato, then Aristotle and the tradition of Western metaphysics. Through the reworking of the Idea, Being is reserved as the model of beings for Plato. The appearance is the semblance or simulacra of Being which, through an always-already existing language, thinking can "correctly" ascertain. Becoming also changes from the viewpoint of *logos*. It is no longer the enduring presence that occupied a place, but is instead the calculable magnitude and movement of space and time. Becoming shifts its emphasis to movement and away from permanent presence, its velocity being calculable as distance divided by time. For Parmenides, Being is *a priori* both appearance and becoming. But because Being has lost its "ground" in beings, it is susceptible to Plato's transcending it with "the good." Values impose an "ought" upon Being, and so it no longer intrinsically "is" in a radiant unconcealment through beings. Heidegger argues that the usurpation of Being by values is the beginning of nihilism. Here the human imprint takes over Being; there is no longer a reciprocal relationship where thinking both "is" and at the same time apprehends Being. The staleness of the *logos* intercedes with the replica or representation rather than wresting Being originally and forcefully from beings. Philosophy remains captured by the *logos* of values and statements.

Heidegger argues that Nietzsche's thought is fundamentally the inversion of the Platonic Idea.[37] Well before Heidegger was writing, Nietzsche wrote in his notes for *The Will to Power*,

> The great concepts "good" and "just" are divorced from the first principles of which they form a part, and, as "ideas" *become free*, degenerate into subjects for discussion. A certain truth is sought behind them; they are regarded as entities or as symbols of entities: a world is *invented* where they are "at home," and from which they are supposed to hail. *In short:* the scandal reaches its apotheosis in Plato.[38]

Heidegger argues that Nietzsche wishes to "naturalise" humanity and "deify" the appearance rather than the "otherworldly" value of the "good." He argues that Nietzsche's revaluation of the highest values does not transcend the dichotomy between the World of Appearance and the World of Ideas. It is only inverted, and thus, *preserved*.

NIETZSCHE

Nietzsche's critique emerges from his revelation that "God is dead." With this flash of insight the entire edifice of Western metaphysics with its faith in universal truth collapses. Nietzsche talks instead in terms of the "will to power" which generates a particular constellation of perspective(s) and constitutes a "ground" from which a person or group will understand their world.

Nietzsche describes the will to *nothingness*, at the end of *Towards a Genealogy of Morals*, as nihilism. Many of the values that are entrenched in the will to power of people who are dominated by reactive *ressentiment* values are defensive and aimed at retribution. They insist on striving for an overarching universal purpose and meaning at the expense of merely living in the incomprehensible and often mundane daily world. Nietzsche's argument centers upon a reclaiming of the genuine importance, the ecstatic moment of existing in the here and now, rather than some abstracted heavenly "beyond." He describes this simply as "life." Effectively he has rejected the dualism between God and nature, or come down on the side of nature rather than God. Nietzsche argues that the *ressentiment* form of will to knowledge promulgates a purpose which is life-denying and, therefore, nihilistic.

Nietzsche himself has often been accused of being a nihilist. And in a restricted sense this has some validity. In *The Will to Power* notes, Nietzsche explains that the disillusionment with the belief in God has resulted in a loss of meaningfulness; "And thus the belief in the utter immorality of nature, and in the absence of all purpose and sense . . . as though there were no meaning in existence at all, as though everything were in vain." But he does not abandon thinking or decision making in this void. Nietzsche argues that the significance of human life is the ability to be creative and inquire about our environment and ourselves. These inquiries have no recourse to the authority of God, or Being, or the legitimacy of the State, or less still the pragmatic paramount importance of the "good of the greatest number." Knowledge is contestable at every level. It is constantly in a state of flux. It is the differentiation, as Deleuze puts it, that produces a dynamic democratic "rhizome" of links, overlays, missed connections, and multiplications of meaning. The will to power of different perspectives generates institutions, communities, and modes of social organization, rather than relying upon rigid societal structures as a source of legitimation.

Heidegger has a subtly different concept of nihilism to Nietzsche. Heidegger describes nihilism as the *forgetting* of Being. "Nothingness" is simply existence for Heidegger, which is outside the scope of *Dasein's* openness to Being. Nothingness is a false path of inquiry—it is simply irrelevant. He follows Nietzsche's lead and associates metaphysics with nihilism, for rigidly fixing truth and "forgetting" Being. In the last chapter of *An Introduction to Metaphysics*, Heidegger describes the Platonic concept of the "Idea" as historically deriving from the original form of Being as *physis* or emerging and *ousia*, or enduring presence, with its associated appearance, which is apprehendable by thinking. The "Idea" consolidates appearance into the simulacra, that is, the being is a limited copy of Being. Furthermore, Aristotle's development of *logos* into logical discourse, or statement, brings the apprehension of the appearance into an always-already developed language. The idea can only be *represented* by *logos*. It is repeatable, and communicable, as correctness, but *logos* loses the capability of truly apprehending Being.

Being retreats into the inaccessible Ideal and becomes conceptualized as the model which beings simulate. The model of Being itself loses validity through the loss of its ground. Thus, argues Heidegger, Plato conceived of the "Ought" which transcends Being as an *a priori* supreme model of the "good." It is at this point that values are prioritized and imposed on Being. Following Plato, the discourse of values arrived, through *logos*, at Aristotle's Categories. Values and categories are a trap which philosophy has been unable to disengage from, and they effectively cloud the relationship of humans to the question of Being. This is nihilism for Heidegger, and he believed that Nietzsche was also caught up in the "trap" of reducing Being to values, or the will to power as a reevaluating force.

In contrast, Nietzsche posits nihilism as a psychological phenomenon, a phase of disillusionment which humanity must pass through, deriving meaning, as we do, from an ethos of purpose. Nihilism is a crucial part of a cycle of decision making as we rid ourselves of outdated moral truth concepts that have become life degenerating rather than life enhancing. Nihilism is something to be overcome through willing, choosing values to motivate our own actions, in the knowledge, however, that these motivations will also be subject to question and the disorientation of disillusionment. Whereas for Heidegger nihilism takes a different form; nihilism negates being as a whole (which is determined by Being) and, therefore, Being is nothing. For over a generation, Modernity finds itself struggling without a nobility of purpose. Neoliberal marketization as a metaphor for all aspects of society, including education, has exacerbated the danger and the disillusionment of the self-serving degeneration of a civil society that has no regard for the other living beings, the biosphere, the world's poor, or even our own future generations. This fall into depravation and the unease it generates in all thinking people is, for Nietzsche, a necessary precondition for the creation of new values that will reshape society into an entirely new, ethical configuration. Not that we should imagine all problems will be solved, for struggle and change will show up in differently arranged distributions of difference. Education has potentially a central role to play in this metamorphosis of the relationship between human society and the environment we live with.

The tone of redemption is not absent from either Nietzsche or Heidegger's accounts of nihilism or its nemesis. But present at the core of their work is a recognition that strife generates life itself. In the form of suffering, strife is not something we can eliminate or return in kind, explain or redeem. Strife is *how* differentiation occurs. No two items are ever identical. Differences generate the flux of positions that create identifiable perspectives and meaning. Strife is not *why* life is unbearable or meaningless, it is simply the powerful, chaotic generation of movement and change.

Although I disagree with Heidegger about Nietzsche's position as the culmination of western metaphysics, in some ways Heidegger too has a genuine point. By focusing on the significance of the relationship between *Dasein* and Being, he has avoided the technological minimalization of scientific, site-specific "fixits" to problems such as pollution and human-caused extinction. Nietzsche was taken up by the Nazis in precisely this manner; the Nazi will to power sought to technologically "solve" the "Jew problem."[39] Technology is not merely a neutral tool with which we can affect the environment. Heidegger's analysis of the technological frame within which we find ourselves has no field of vision "outside" of itself. Every attitude we have, Luddite or scientific, is a response to the technological world. Attention to language, a refusal to fall into the "stale representation" of the *logos*, and an awareness of the creative possibilities of all knowledge as means to a vital, life enhancing culture is the massive task of humanity in general, and education in particular.

Values education will have to deal with these issues of scope and the relationship between humanity and the environment at the same time as we analyze our modes of social organization and issues of equity and difference. This constitutes a new framework for ethics. It is not a return to liberal justifications for vocationalism or critical democratic participation, nor is it a mode of redemption. The debate over educational values is having to engage with the shift in relationship between humanity and life such that consumerism gives way to an ethic of care and coexistence.

NOTES

1. Peters, 2000, p. 214.
2. Heidegger, 1996, pp. 233–234.
3. Heidegger, 1973a, p. 40.
4. Heidegger, 1973a, p. 17.
5. Peters, 2000.
6. Guignon, 2001, p. 39.
7. Heidegger, 1973a, p. 26.
8. Heidegger, 1973a, p. 2.
9. Heidegger, 1973a, p. 29.
10. Heidegger, 1973a, p. 64.
11. Heidegger, 1973a, p. 32.
12. Heidegger, 1968, pp. 222–223.
13. Guignon, 2000, p. 67.
14. Heidegger, 1968, p. 227.

15. Heidegger, 1973a, p. 61.
16. Guignon, 2001, p. 38.
17. Heidegger, 1973a, p. 4.
18. Heidegger, 1973a, p. 4.
19. Heidegger, 1973a, p. 84.
20. Guignon, private communication.
21. Manheim's note in Heidegger, 1973a, p. 9.
22. Guignon, private communication, 1999.
23. Guignon, 2000, p. 67.
24. Guignon, 2001, footnote 5, including a quote from Heidegger 1959, p. 156.
25. Guignon, 2001, footnote 5, including a quote from Heidegger 1959, p. 156.
26. Heidegger, 1973a, p. 62.
27. Heidegger, 1973a, pp. 61–62.
28. Guignon, 2001, p. 43, quoting Heidegger, 1973a, p. 157.
29. Heidegger, 1973a, p. 62.
30. Heidegger, 1973a, p. 97.
31. Heidegger, 1973a, p. 100.
32. Heidegger, 1973a, p. 101.
33. Heidegger, 1973a, p. 180.
34. Heidegger, 1973a, p. 185.
35. Heidegger, 1973a, pp. 186–188.
36. Heidegger, 1973a, p. 142.
37. Heidegger, 1982, p. 171.
38. Nietzsche, 1909a, vol. 1, no. 430, p.351.
39. There is a large body of literature on both Nietzsche and Heidegger's connections with the Nazis. I do not have the space to contribute to this debate in this paper.

REFERENCES

Aristotle. 1972. *The Works of Aristotle, Vol. VIII, Metaphysica.* Oxford: Clarendon Press.

Deleuze, Gilles. 1962. *Nietzsche & Philosophy.* Trans. Hugh Tomlinson. New York: Columbia University Press.

Dreyfus, Hubert. 1998a. "Being and Power: Heidegger and Foucault." Unpublished.

Dreyfus, Herbert. 1998b. "Heidegger and Foucault on the Subject, Agency and Practices." Unpublished.

Dreyfus, Hubert & Harrison Hall, eds. 1992. *Heidegger; A Critical Reader.* Oxford: Blackwell.

Foucault, Michel. 1983. "The Subject and Power." in *Michel Foucault: Beyond Structuralism and Hermeneutics.* Ed. Hubert Dreyfus and Paul Rabinow. Chicago: University of Chicago Press.

Foucault, Michel. 1980. *Power/Knowledge: Selected Interviews and Other Writings 1972–1977.* Ed. Colin Gordon. Brighton: Harvester Press.

Foucault, Michel. 1980b. "Truth and Power." In *Power/Knowledge: Selected Interviews and other writings 1972–1977.* Pantheon Books: New York.

Foucault, Michel. 1977. "Nietzsche, Genealogy, History." In *Language, Counter-Memory, Practice*. Ed. Donald Bouchard, Trans. Donald Bouchard and Sherry Simon. New York: Cornell University Press.

Guignon, Charles 1999. "Philosophy and Authenticity: Heidegger's Search for a Ground for Philosphizing." In *Heidegger, Authenticity, and Modernity*. Eds. Mark Wrathall and Jeffrey Malpas. Camridge, Mass.: The M.I.T. Press.

Guignon, Charles. 2000. "Authenticity and Integrity; A Heidggerian Perspective." In *The Psychology of Mature Spirituality: Integrity, Wisdom and Transcendence*. Eds. Polly Young-Eisendrath and Melvin Miller. London: Routledge.

Guignon, Charles. 2001. "Being as Appearing: Retrieving the Greek Experience of Phusis." In *A companion to Heidegger's Introduction to Metaphysics*. Eds. Gregory Fried and Richard Polt. New Haven: Yale University Press.

Heidegger, Martin. 1996. "Letter on Humanism." In *Basic Writings, From Being and Time* (1927) to The Task of Thinking (1964). Trans. and introduction by David Farrell Krell. London: Routledge: 213–266.

Heidegger, Martin.1982. *Nietzsche*, vols. I–IV. Ed. Farrell Krell. Trans. Frank A. Capuzzi. San Francisco: Harper & Row.

Heidegger, Martin.1977. *The Question Concerning Technology and Other Essays*. Trans. William Lovitt. New York: Harper & Row.

Heidegger, Martin. 1973a, *The End of Philosophy*. Trans. Joan Stambaugh. New York: Harper & Row. (Originally published in 1954.)

Heidegger, Martin. 1973b. *An Introduction to Metaphysics*. Trans. Ralph Manheim in 1959. Massachusetts: Yale University Press. (Originally published in 1953.)

Heidegger, Martin. 1969. *Identity and Difference*. Trans. Joan Stambaugh. New York: Harper & Row. (Originally published in 1957.)

Heidegger, Martin. 1968. *What is Called Thinking?* Trans. J. Glenn Gray. New York: Harper & Row.

Irwin, Ruth. 2000. "Nietzsche: Deleuze, Foucault, and Genealogy as a Method for Education." In *Past and Present Values: Nietzsche's Legacy for Education*. Ed. Michael Peters, James Marshall, and Paul Smeyers. Westport, Conn.: Bergin and Garvey.

Marshall, James. 2000a. "Nietzsche's New Philosopher: The Arts and the Self." In *Past and Present Values: Nietzsche's Legacy for Education*. Ed. Michael Peters, James Marshall, and Paul Smeyers, Westport, Conn.: Bergin and Garvey, forthcoming.

Marshall, James. 2000b. "Electronic Writing and the Wrapping of Language." *Journal of Philosophy of Education* 34(1): 135–149.

Marshall, James. 1998. "Information on Information: Recent Curriculum Reform." *Studies in Philosophy and Education* 17(4): 313–321.

Marshall, James. 1997. "The New Vocationalism." In *Education Policy in New Zealand: The 1990s and Beyond*. Ed. Mark Olssen and Kay Morris Matthews. Palmerston North NZ: Dunmore Press.

Nietzsche, Friedrich. 1989, *On the Genealogy of Morals and Ecce Homo*. Ed. Kaufmann Walter. Trans. RJ Hollingdale. New York: Vintage Books. (Originally published: 1887 and 1899.)

Nietzsche, Friedrich. 1986. *Human, All Too Human*. Trans. K. J. Hollingdale.Cambridge: Cambridge University Press. (Originally published in 1880.)

Nietzsche, Friedrich. 1985. *Twilight of the Idols* and *The Anti-Christ*. Trans. R. J. Hollingdale. Middlesex: Penguin. (originally publ. 1889/1895)

Nietzsche, Friedrich. 1982. "Thus Spoke Zarathustra." In *Portable Nietzsche*. Ed. and Trans. Walter Kaufmann in 1954. New York: Penguin.

Nietzsche, Friedrich. 1979. *Ecce Homo; How One Becomes What One Is*. Trans. R. J. Hollingdale. Penguin: Harmondsworth.

Nietzsche, Friedrich. 1974. *The Gay Science*. Trans. Walter Kaufman. New York: Random House. (Originally published in 1887.)

Nietzsche, Friedrich. 1966. *Beyond Good and Evil; Prelude to a Philosophy of the Future*. Trans. Walter Kaufman, New York: Random House.

Nietzsche, Friedrich. 1909a. *The Will to Power; An Attempted Transvaluation of all Values*. Vol. 2, Books 3 and 4. Ed. Dr. Oscar Levy, Trans. Anthony Ludovici. London: T. N. Foulis.

Nietzsche, Friedrich. 1909b. "On The Future Of Our Educational Institutions." In *The Complete Works of Nietzsche*. Ed. Dr. Oscar Levy. Trans. J. M. Kennedy. Edinburgh: Foulis. (original publ. 1872)

Peters, Michael. 2000. "Nietzsche, Nihilism and the Critique of Modernity." In *Past and Present Values: Nietzsche's Legacy for Education*. Ed. Michael Peters, James Marshall, and Paul Smeyers. Westport, Conn.: Bergin and Garvey, forthcoming.

Peters, Michael. 1999. "Humanism and Education: Heidegger, Derrida and the New Humanities." Auckland University: (unpublished paper).

Peters, Michael. 1998. *Naming the Multiple: Post-structuralism and Education*. Westport, Conn.: Bergin and Garvey.

Peters, Michael. 1997. "Neoliberalism, Welfare Dependency and the Moral Construction of Poverty in Aotearoa/ NZ." *NZ. Sociology* 12, no. 1: 1–34.

Peters, Michael. 1996a. "Poststructuralism and the Philosophy of the Subject: The Games of the Will to Power against the Labor of the Dialectic." In *Poststructuralism, Politics and Education*. Westport: Conn.: Bergin and Garvey.

Peters, Michael. 1996b. "What is Poststructuralism? The French Reception of Nietzsche." in *Political Theory Newsletter* 8: 39–55.

Peters, Michael. 1995. "After Auschwitz: Ethics and Educational Policy." *Discourse: Studies in the Cultural Politics of Education* 16, no. 2: 237–251.

10

Learning as Leavetaking and Homecoming

Pádraig Hogan

We all still need an education in thinking, and first of all, before that, Knowledge of what being educated and uneducated in thinking means.

—Heidegger, *The End of Philosophy and the Task of Thinking*

CONFRONTATIONS ON HEIDEGGER'S PATHS

There is little by way of explicit treatment of educational issues in Heidegger's philosophy. There are however some major themes in his explorations that can make life very different for the philosophy of education and for how education as a practice is carried on. Different from what? it may well be asked. Different, in short, from what the dominant modes and tempers in Western philosophy have furnished for thought and action: different firstly from classical and more modern forms of metaphysics; different secondly from epistemology, whether in rationalist, empiricist, positivistl, or other forms; different thirdly from the Nietzschean legacies that inspire most postmodern currents of thought in contemporary educational and cultural debates. Each of these points of difference is decisive for education as a form of action that calls for insightful thinking. That is not to suggest however that one can straightforwardly elucidate the implications for education of some major Heideggerian themes. Heidegger's thinking does not easily accommodate such a scholarly exegesis. Rather, where everything that is scholarly in this exegetical sense is concerned, the radicalness of Heidegger's thinking presents itself as a confrontation. To engage in such a confrontation, or more precisely to allow one's most scholarly efforts to be so confronted, is to forgo the mannered ethos of exegesis and to experience what Heidegger himself calls "the difference between an object of scholarship and a matter of thought" (*Poetry, Language, Thought*, p. 5).

But why should one allow any such thing? Especially in the case of a thinker whose usage of language is highly individualistic and more than occasionally obscure; a thinker moreover who permitted his own thinking to join with that of the German Nazi party during a crucial period of that party's rise to power (1932–33). For many, these two well-publicized features of Heidegger's thought and life have made his work distasteful, or placed it under lasting suspicion. This is especially so where the questions of practical philosophy are concerned, not least those of the philosophy of education. In response to these reservations one could produce examples that largely dissolve the first, the individualistic/obscurity charge, as a serious objection. One could also assemble arguments that mitigate Heidegger's culpability in the National Socialist connection by pointing to his growing disillusionment with the movement during the middle and later thirties while it was still on the rise, and to the increasing suspicion of the Nazi authorities under which his works now fell. There is a sizeable literature on these matters,[1] but I don't wish to avail of any of its resources in promoting a case for the pertinence of Heidegger to educational questions. The real issue, the confrontation question referred to above, lies deeper. If Heidegger's prose were unparalleled in its difficulty, or if he ranked among the most notorious of political reactionaries, neither of these points would change the fact that his work, like that of Hume or Kant, confronts philosophy with arguments of exceptional incisiveness and insights of remarkable originality.[2] To disregard such arguments and insights, for whatever plausible reason, is to turn one's back on what is central to philosophy itself since Socrates: firstly, openness to positions that challenge one's most cherished ways of thinking and acting; secondly, perseverance in critically exploring those unfamiliar paths in the face of which one's own previous stances and outlooks proved unsustainable.

So now we might ask with more sharpness of purpose: How does Heidegger's thinking confront the conceptions of education that have been the prevalent ones in the history of Western civilization, down to our own time? In exploring this question, it will be necessary to say something about the claims of metaphysics, of epistemology, of Nietzsche, and of "the system of Catholicism," each of which figured prominently as instances of confrontation in Heidegger's thought. I also hope however to sketch something promising arising from these reflections: something of the different pathways to which thinking on teaching and learning might be beckoned.

ULTIMATE TRUTH, RATIONAL CERTAINTY, AND THE PRECONCEPTIONS OF UNDERSTANDING

That most influential of metaphysical writings, Plato's *Republic*, was interpreted and embraced by Western Christendom in such a way that some of the chief features of Platonism became defining characteristics of education.[3] These features included: firstly, the hierarchical division of knowledge into a higher *intellectual-spiritual* world and a lower *sensual* world, each with its own sub-divisions; secondly, the insistence that the higher of the two worlds was one of changeless truth while the lower was one where illusions and unworthy arts featured prominently among the accepted cultural pursuits; thirdly, the claim that the truth of the higher world, whose source was the changeless *idea of the Good*, was humanly attainable, but only by the strictly tutored "eye of the soul," and that educational effort must dedicate itself primarily to such tutoring. But the educational significance of Platonism comes properly into view only when one takes account of how this threefold philosophical scheme became overlaid in later centuries with a particular kind of theology. This had its roots in Augustine's assimilation of a religion of personal belief to a Platonist metaphysics, and then in the Christian church's acceptance of this conflux as constituting an elaborate and decisive body of doctrinal *knowledge*.

The further elaboration of this intellectual structure during the Middle Ages established a metaphysical theology as the authoritative context for the conduct of all teaching and learning, for the pursuit of all permissible research. This was made possible chiefly through the work of Thomas Aquinas, whose new synthesis of classical metaphysics and Christian doctrine drew not on Plato but on the Platonism of Aristotle.[4] The intellectual sophistication of Aquinas's philosophy marked a major advance in learning and also a significant enlargement in the scope for inquiry. Yet despite the many enduring insights in its efforts to align religious faith with the fruits of philosophical speculation about ultimate truth, its metaphysical pretensions to comprehensive knowledge eventually implicated it in various forms of oppression. The enforced uniformity and conformity that resulted from the Church's upholding of such pretensions led to recurring crises. The burning of Giordano Bruno in Rome in 1600 and the humiliation of Galileo by the Inquisition are two of the more infamous cases in point. These events served as public reminders that prompt and severe punishment could follow any attempt to break from what the all-inclusive scope of a theological metaphysics, as established truth, or-dained. Such reminders contributed to the decline into a safe and staid scholasticism of the vigorous spirit of questioning that had marked Aquinas's own work.

Luther's celebrated demand, "I want to be free," was widely taken up by thinkers who were at variance with the Vatican. It led eventually to a new philosophical climate in many of the countries of northern Europe and to the establishment and development in these countries of currents of thinking that were skeptical of or unsympathetic to metaphysics. These currents made possible some formidable challenges to the kind of ulti-mate truth metaphysics pursued and upheld. Among the more notable of these challenges were the works of Descartes in France, Hume in Scot-land, and Kant in Prussia. These works championed the claims of inde-pendent, vigilant reason, rather than the authority of the church or of in-herited tradition. Where the exercise of such reason was successful in setting the context for permissible learning, its fruits were soon to prove seriously damaging, if not fatal, to the claims to truth that metaphysics had long maintained and enforced. Where metaphysics could not provide other than speculative, or contestable, foundations for its own arguments, epistemology now demanded foundations that were grounded in critical reason, or that produced empirical evidence for each conclusion put for-ward. Such secure foundations, it was confidently argued, were the only ones that could lead the search for truth to unshakeable certainty.

But these new currents of thinking, promoted as they were by the thinkers of the Enlightenment, and by their successors to the present, did not mean that metaphysics disappeared from the world of learning. The Vatican continued to champion its cause. In 1879, Pope Leo XIII issued an encyclical, *Aeterni Patris*, paying special tribute to Aquinas and encourag-ing the study of scholastic philosophy in Catholic schools and universities. This was followed by documents containing similar encouragements is-sued in 1914 by Pope Pius X (*Doctoris Angelici*) and in 1923 by Pope Pius XI (*Studiorum Ducem*). The influence of these documents pervaded the intel-lectual milieu of Heidegger's early studies in philosophy. It is worth adding that the Vatican's support for metaphysics continues, as does its opposition to currents of thinking that are in the Enlightenment tradition, or are otherwise nonmetaphysical in character. For instance the encyclical *Fides et Ratio*, issued in September 1998 by Pope John Paul II, emphasizes with one voice the "primacy of philosophical *enquiry*" (pp. 7–8) but also speaks with Plato of the "certainty of truth" (p. 21) and criticizes the par-tiality and "philosophical pride" (p. 7) of the philosophical positions (un-named) that differ from the thought of St. Thomas Aquinas (p. 65 ff). Alasdair MacIntyre's laudatory reflections on that encyclical capture and reassert in confident voice one of the chief claims of traditional metaphysics:

> In moving beyond sense-experience towards adequacy of judgement the theoretically enquiring mind moves towards its good. It achieves that good in arriving at a perfected understanding of what things are essentially. . . . And we judge how things truly are when we think of them as they are thought by God. [5]

These historical sketches identify something of the main philosophical approaches with which Heidegger's thinking first found itself in confrontation. For Heidegger, the prominence of metaphysics in Western philosophy led to a forgetfulness of the question of Being; a forgetfulness that was rendered more intractable by the rise of epistemology (*Erkenntnistheorie*), with its confident aspirations of achieving a rationally grounded certainty and comprehensive conceptual mastery. But Heidegger's confrontations with both metaphysics and epistemology were already present in embryonic form in his letter to his theologian friend Fr. Engelbert Krebs in 1919. Here he disclosed his break with the Catholic education (as distinct from upbringing) that he had received. He explained that "[e]pistemological insights, applied to the theory of historical knowledge, have made the system of Catholicism problematic and unacceptable to me—but not Christianity per se or metaphysics, the latter albeit in a new sense" (quoted by Safranski 1998, p. 107).

The reference here to epistemological insights is to the phenomenology of Edmund Husserl, whose ever-renewed work on securing the foundations of knowledge was an inspiration to Heidegger. It was also to lead him however to the radical conclusion that the presuppositionless foundations being sought could not be securely established, and that this very search was on a wrong path. Similarly, the reference to metaphysics "in a new sense" signaled the originality of Heidegger's interest in the question of Being, a question that was to engage him throughout his life. At this early stage, metaphysics "in a new sense" marked a rejection of the scholastic philosophy that had been central to his career as a student priest. That rejection rested on Heidegger's view that the "foundations" of scholastic philosophy produced a theology that proceeded not so much from the challenges posed to faith by scripture, but from all-embracing metaphysical claims raised to the level of dogma. When *Being and Time* appeared a decade later, Heidegger's critical stance toward Catholic theology and his increasing interest in Protestant theological researches had developed to the point that he could declare as follows:

> *Theology* is seeking a more primordial interpretation of man's Being towards God, prescribed by the meaning of faith itself and remaining within it. It is

slowly beginning to understand once more Luther's insight that the "foundation" on which its system of dogma rests has not arisen from an inquiry in which faith is primary, and that conceptually this "foundation" not only is inadequate for the problematic of theology, but conceals and distorts it. (*B&T*, p. 30; *Su.Z*, p. 10)

Heidegger's rejection of scholastic metaphysics is also a rejection of a paternalistic conception of education which the "system" of Catholicism then sought to endorse, most notably through the documents of Leo XIII, Pius X, and Pius XI, referred to above. This is not to say that he discarded a belief in the possibility of objective truth about all of Being, or in its importance. Rather, it is to suggest that for him, such truth was immeasurably beyond the capability of metaphysics (or "onto-theology") to discern with concepts, and also beyond the capacity of epistemology to ground rationally. While remaining supremely important for Heidegger, truth came to be understood in his thinking as that, to which the best of human efforts might hope to draw near, but also as that which was in itself unfathomably different from what the fruits of calculative thinking might yield. Heidegger began to understand that the truth that philosophy was seeking did not disclose itself in its fullness to human existence.

LEAVETAKINGS

Heidegger's break with the "system" of Catholicism marks the start of a leavetaking—his departure not just from traditional metaphysics and epistemology but from an entire assemblage of educational assumptions, traditions, and practices. How radical this leavetaking was became evident with the shock *Being and Time* first provoked, and still sometimes does, among readers. One of the most central concepts of metaphysics, that of the *essence* of man (or the essence of the human, as it might be put today), was recast by Heidegger in a way that promptly undermined its traditional meaning. The new significance he gave it set it free from the accumulated bodies of doctrine that had historically been attached to it. Here, Heidegger's "individualistic" use of language reveals his striking originality. "The essence of *Dasein* lies in its existence" (*B&T*, Section 9, p. 67) seems at first to resemble a metaphysical statement about human nature. It may even do so if one reads it in German: "Das 'Wesen' des *Daseins* liegt in seiner Existenz" (*Su.Z*, Section 9, p. 42). Heidegger is quick to point out however that by "existence" he means not the noun sense of the word (e.g., a "whatness" to be filled in and established in place by metaphysics or onto-theology), but rather a *verb* sense: the "to-be," or "be-ing," of human existence. This be-ing moreover, he emphasizes, has in each case a mineness (*Jemeinigkeit*); it refers to a "who" rather than to any "whatness." This "mineness," or "my-ownness," differentiates the being of each person from that of others. Each human being, in other words, has his or her own be-ing as an *issue*: an issue to be faced up to or evaded, to be thought through in an authentic way or to be taken over by someone else, or perhaps by some collectivity.

As well as being important in their own right, these points counter the presumptions of metaphysics to speak universally about human existence as human *nature*. Again however, it must be noted that in giving existence (*Existenz*) priority over essence (*Wesen*), Heidegger is not making any claim (as Sartre was to do) that there is no such thing as human nature. Rather, in declining metaphysics, he also declines the unwarranted liberty it takes to speak with authority about human nature (and also the kind of liberty Sartre takes in dismissing it). Accordingly, in *Being and Time* he gives his efforts in a methodical way to an analytic of human *existence*, much as Kant gave his efforts in the first of his three critiques to an analytic of "pure reason."

Another confrontation with traditional philosophy announced in *Being and Time*, this time with epistemology, is Heidegger's critique of the philosophical status given to the individual's reflective consciousness; namely consciousness of, and questioning of, the experienced world. This primacy of status was granted to reflective consciousness in different ways from Descartes to Husserl. But individual consciousness is, on Heidegger's account, not something primary, but something secondary, or derivative (*B&T*, Section 19, Section 20). For Heidegger, to *be* at all as a human being is, first and foremost, to be-in-a-world in an "everyday" way: to find oneself already in a context of involvements with others (present or absent), with jobs to be done or avoided, with memories and expectations, with burdens and possibilities, and so on. All of this moreover is to illustrate the point that to be-in-a-world is also to have *already interpreted* that world in one way or another. It is to have one's self-understanding, one's outlooks and one's actions somehow running ahead of oneself. It is to find oneself invariably *pre*disposed, provisionally or more definitely. Heidegger's most complete break with epistemology however lies in his argument that, far from overcoming such predisposing influences through philosophical efforts to gain an understanding that is free of preconceptions, these very preconceptions are what make understanding itself possible. They constitute an active context, or significant background, within which anything newly encountered gets understood and interpreted, or for that matter, misunderstood and misinterpreted.

So where epistemology, in common with most "rational" thinking, would draw a sharp distinction between understanding on the one hand and interpretation on the other, Heidegger insists (*B&T*, Section 32) that

what is more important is their inseparability. His argument is that understanding unavoidably involves understanding something *as* something. Even where human efforts to understand fail, the "as" is still present: *as* puzzling for instance, or *as* frustrating to one's best efforts. The
"as" constitutes interpretation as a built-in feature of understanding. A
logical objection to this would charge that there is something curiously
circular in holding that to understand is somehow to have already understood, or in holding that understanding and interpretation are inextricably interlinked. Heidegger's response would be that this inescapable
circularity reveals the hermeneutic, or interpretative, structure of understanding itself; something that metaphysics never thought of looking for
and that epistemology could only contemplate as a pitfall to be avoided.
To this response he might add that the consequence, or cost, of such
avoidance is one or other contrived account of what makes understanding possible and an excessively theoretical and linear account of how it is
to be advanced.

Heidegger is quick to point out that the hermeneutic "circle" that lies at
the heart of understanding is not a vicious circle and he argues that "in
the circle is hidden a positive possibility of the most primordial kind of
knowing" (*B&T*, p. 195). To avail of this possibility however would be to
acknowledge, firstly, that one's best efforts to understand cannot be swept
clean of one's own assumptions. Secondly, it would be to acknowledge
that many more of one's own preconceptions are likely to come to light in
one's dealings with others, especially if those others are quite differently
disposed to oneself. Thirdly, it would be to take an active hand in disciplining or transforming such preconceptions through what might now
properly be called emancipatory experiences of learning.

Such acknowledgment and action would not, of course, rid teaching
and learning of differences in outlook. Indeed the suggestion here that absolute knowledge is not humanly attainable carries with it the corollary
that a conflict of interpretations will inevitably attend the pursuit of learning. Of course it can be objected that this is a curious kind of emancipation. For don't the arguments made in the previous paragraph point now
to the conclusion that the work of teaching and learning, of research and
scholarship, is condemned to endless acrimonies, where the only victor is
the ever-recurring specter of a relativism that rules over all? Doesn't the
fact that the world's academies—and individual fields of learning—are
replete with such acrimonies bear out this unhappy conclusion? To answer "yes" to this would be correct in an apparent sense, but such a "yes"
would obscure something of much greater importance. The crucial point
is that the unhappy conclusion would hold only for a standpoint that
maintained (with epistemology) that where knowledge is concerned, anything less than certainty is a deficiency that must be eradicated; or that

maintained (with metaphysics) that anything less than an all-inclusive account marks a failure. The significance of Heidegger's leavetaking of such standpoints lies firstly in his disclosure that the unattainability in question is not something that can be conquered. Rather, it is an inescapable feature of the human condition—a feature however which opens up new possibilities for how understanding itself is to be understood and advanced. Secondly, the significance of the leavetaking lies in the associated lesson (which Heidegger himself did not make explicit) that a wholehearted acknowledgment of such limitation and possibility is among the most important and enabling of educational *virtues*.

ESTRANGEMENTS: HEIDEGGER, NIETZSCHE, AND WHAT IS WORTHY OF THINKING

If Heidegger's confrontations with metaphysics and epistemology were decisive for his thinking, and for opening the way to a new understanding of how understanding itself takes place, no less decisive were his sustained encounters during the 1930s and 1940s with the work of Friedrich Nietzsche. Nietzsche's thinking has enjoyed a remarkable renaissance in recent decades, most notably in postmodern currents of thinking. As Heidegger's thought is sometimes availed of to add further weight to Nietzschean standpoints, it should be stressed that Heidegger's engagement with Nietzsche, sustained over a decade and a half (published in two large German volumes *Nietzsche I* and *Nietzsche II*, and four English ones: *N*, vols. I–IV) was, in the final analysis, more a confrontation than a concurrence or a following in Nietzsche's footsteps. As with his encounters with metaphysics and epistemology, this was a confrontation—with Nietzsche as metaphysician—from which something unexpected and fruitful was to follow, namely a dramatic turning to new pathways in Heidegger's later philosophy.

For philosophy-as-critique, Nietzsche's writings provide endless attractive possibilities for developing penetrating arguments, and almost as many different directions. This is ably illustrated in Derrida's *Spurs: Nietzsche's Styles*. Nietzsche's writings present a different complexion however if one's critique is from the start a critique with practical intent. By a critique with practical intent I mean one which interrogates practices with a view not only to detecting in them whatever is invidious or otherwise flawed, but also with a view to identifying a kind of coherent thinking that might (a) seriously tackle such flaws and (b) attempt to identify possibilities for action that could overcome them, without installing invidiousness of another kind. Although Heidegger does not describe his own work as a critique with practical intent in the sense just mentioned, it could be so described if thinking and its responsibilities are to be regarded as a form of *action*. It is worth recalling that it was an emergent awareness of such responsibilities that led Heidegger as a young man to decline a vocation to the priesthood, and then to decline the "system" of Catholicism (and later the system of National Socialism), in favor of a call to think ever anew that which was worthy of thinking's best efforts. And as Heidegger's earlier and later works show in different ways, what is worthy of such efforts is the mysteriousness/overwhelmingness/unfathomableness/ remoteness-yet-nearness of the relationship between human being (*Dasein*/mortals) and Being that is, but not as human.

Metaphysics, with its all-encapsulating gestures, its domestication of the strange, and its persistent failure to think the difference between being human and Being, does violence to this relationship in Heidegger's view. That is to say, metaphysics predisposes the thinking not just of individuals, but of whole cultures of learning and of belief, to a forgetfulness of what is most worthy of human attentiveness and reverence. But how could such criticism be pertinent to the thought of Nietzsche?

Heidegger identifies "five major rubrics" in Nietzsche's thought. These are: "nihilism," the "revaluation of all values hitherto," "will to power," "eternal recurrence of the same," and "Overman/*Übermensch*" (*N*, vol. IV, pp. 3–12). By using a term such as "rubrics," Heidegger makes clear that he views Nietzsche's thinking not as a collection of scattered and disparate observations, but as a totality with its own coherence. (Derrida's reading differs basically from Heidegger's on this matter.) But this would not make it a metaphysics. Nietzsche does not view his own work as a metaphysics. Indeed Nietzsche's famous declaration against positivism, "facts is precisely what there is not, only interpretations" (*WP*, Section 481), could apply with almost equal force against the claims of metaphysics, from Plato onward, to rise above mere interpretation. Nietzsche moves to safeguard his thinking from the charge of relativism that such a declaration makes him vulnerable to, by describing this thinking as "perspectivism." But the charge of relativism can still be made unless some criterion is found to distinguish better perspectives from inferior ones, or to give some grounding to perspectivism. "Will to power" provides this criterion and Nietzsche himself makes the connection between perspectivism and will to power in the following words: "It is our needs that interpret the world; our drives and their For and Against. Every drive is a kind of lust to rule; each one has its perspective that it would like all other drives to accept as a norm"(*WP*, Section 481). The primacy given to will to power by Nietzsche is even more pronounced elsewhere in his writings. For instance, in *Beyond Good and Evil* (Section 13) he explains "A living thing desires above all to vent its strength—life as such is will to power—self preservation is only one of the indirect and most frequent *consequences* of it." This is a recurring theme throughout that book (*BGE*, §§ 4, 23, 188, 201). In one of the later of such passages Nietzsche writes:

> "Exploitation" does not pertain to a corrupt or imperfect or primitive society: it pertains to the *essence* of the living thing as a fundamental organic function, it is a consequence of the intrinsic will to power which is precisely the will of life.—Granted this is a novelty as a theory—as a reality it is the *primordial fact* of all history: let us at least be honest with ourselves! (*BGE*, Section259)

Despite his avowal of perspectivism, Nietzsche's insistence on the *"primordial fact"* of will to power, and the connection he makes between will to power and "the *essence* of the living thing," would seem to grant this "rubric," and its four associated ones, a higher status than "interpretation"; indeed something more akin to a final explanation. The other four "rubrics" are: (a) Nietzsche's acquiescence in his own announcement that "God is dead" and cannot be resurrected in any shape or form ("nihilism"); (b) his declarations that a courageous acknowledging of will to power enables the strong (*der Übermensch*) to overcome the negative force of nihilism; (c) his view that such overcoming means being able to say "yes" again and again to a life bereft of the divine ("eternal recurrence"); (d) his proclamation that this involves the "re-valuation of all values hitherto." On Heidegger's analysis, the all-inclusive, explanatory sweep of the "five rubrics" makes Nietzsche's philosophy a metaphysics on a grand scale, albeit of a contrary kind to any traditional metaphysics. Heidegger describes it as a "metaphysical theology," and "a negative theology of a peculiar kind" (*N*, vol. IV, p. 210). Its preoccupation with power and beings proceeds, Heidegger maintains, from the nihilistic assumption that "there is essentially nothing to Being itself"(p. 211).

One of the most important conclusions Heidegger draws from his repeated explorations of Nietzsche's thinking, and from his own point of view one of the most surprising and revealing, is that Nietzsche's philosophy is not the overcoming of nihilism that it purports to be, but rather the "fulfilment" of nihilism; that it is itself a "classical" nihilism. On Heidegger's account, Nietzsche's nihilism loses sight from the start of all that is most worthy of thinking in the relationship between being human and Being.

> Classical nihilism, then, discloses itself as the fulfilment of nihilism, whereby it considers itself exempt from the necessity of thinking about the very thing that constitutes its essence: the *nihil*, the nothing—as the veil that conceals the truth of the Being of beings. (*N*, vol. IV, p. 11)

This passage, and others like it, captures the heart of the point at issue in Heidegger's confrontation with Nietzsche. The chief "practical" outcomes of the confrontation are the shifts in emphasis it provoked in Heidegger's subsequent thinking. Although Heidegger remains close to Nietzsche on the primacy of interpretation in human understanding, Nietzsche's preoccupation with human being in the context of will to power, and his precipitate shutting of the door to the kind of exploration that Heidegger viewed as most important, marks a decisive rift. The nihil, or abyss (*Abgrund*), or no-thingness, is precisely that which calls for thinking on Heidegger's view. Henceforth, in his efforts to understand better the relationship between human being and Being, Heidegger turns the focus of his philosophical attention from human being (*Dasein*) to the relationship itself as an interplay. He elucidates this interplay as one of disclosure and concealment, of bestowal and withdrawal. In keeping with this shift in emphasis (*die Kehre*), Heidegger's language begins to show less of the philosophical formality and precision of *Being and Time*, and becomes increasingly imbued with imagery and metaphor. His "Letter on Humanism" (1947) points out that this poetic turn in his thought was required by the demands of thinking itself as a responsive venturing, not for reasons of adornment or to make philosophy itself an "adventuress."

HOMECOMINGS

Will to power privileges human subjectivity and the will-fulness of its action on the world. Granting primacy to subjectivity of this kind (or of any other kind) obscures what is for Heidegger most important in being human, namely to be open in an attentive, responsive way to the truth of Being. But what does it mean to be open to the Truth of Being? Heidegger's later works suggest that to be disposed in this open way would count as a homecoming of sorts. This is not a domestication, or a homely comfort of any kind. Rather it is a drawing near to that which is impenetrably different from human being, but is that in virtue of which everything human is *as human*. This homecoming, or thoughtful hearkening, is to be accomplished (though not in any final or permanent way) by a thinking that remains faithful to that to which thinking itself, as a gift granted to humans,[6] is called or beckoned (BW, p. 196). This is why it is so important for Heidegger that ever-renewed efforts are made to overcome metaphysics and its manifold progeny.

The "Letter on Humanism" is one of the most important of such efforts on Heidegger's own part. It revisits some of the chief terms used in *Being and Time* and attempts to free them from the metaphysical connotations that had quickly been attached to them, not least by prominent philosophers. What he has to say in these clarifications also introduces further dimensions in his thinking. The clarifications are crucial then to an accurate understanding of *Being and Time*. They are also crucial to an unders-standing of how the thinking set forth in that book developed into the ma-jor themes of Heidegger's later philosophy. Especially significant among such themes is the interplay between concealment and revealment of Be-ing, in which humans, because they are *humans*, are participants. The fol-lowing extract from the "Letter on Humanism" is a good example of how the earlier themes are joined with the later ones.

> However, in the name "being-in-the-world," "world" does not in any way im-ply earthly as opposed to heavenly being, nor the "worldly" as opposed to the "spiritual." For us "world" does not at all signify beings but the openness of Being. Man is, and is man, insofar as he is the ek-sisting one. He stands out into the openness of Being. Being itself, which as the throw has projected the essence of man into "care," is this openness. Thrown in such fashion, man stands "in" the openness of Being. "World" is the lighting of Being into which man stands out on the basis of his thrown essence. "Being-in-the-world" des-ignates the essence of ek-sistence with regard to the lighted dimension out of which the "ek" of ek-sistence essentially unfolds. (*BW*, pp. 228–229)

The word "existence," from *Being and Time*, is now written "ek-sistence" to emphasize its character as a standing-out from other beings. This standing-out moreover is now described as standing in an "openness" towards Be-ing, and it constitutes the human *as* human. The openness that is native to it, unlike other living species, means that its being-in-the-world can be il-luminated rather than remaining undifferentiated or obscure. However the illuminating, or lighting (*Lichtung*), has the character not of something established or unwavering, but of something that unfolds in an interplay, or a participatory relation between human beings and Being. The passage just quoted calls attention to the point that human beings are distinct in that they are human *as* a relation to Being; a relation that is all too often overlooked, or taken for granted to the point of oblivion. But to begin to understand one's human being in this suggestive way is to rescue think-ing from established conceptualizations that "presuppose an interpreta-tion of being without asking about the truth of Being" (*BW*, p. 202). We have now arrived at the point where Heidegger's confrontations can be understood as struggles to overcome kinds of thinking—metaphysics, epistemology, Nietzsche's "rubrics," philosophical "humanism"—which cover up this openness; which do not adequately or appropriately under-stand the distinctiveness of being human.

Heidegger's later writings can roughly be seen as a succession of ex-plorations of the truth of Being, and of how human being is claimed by it, evades it, responds to it, ignores it, remains in attendance on it, rushes past it, belongs to it, or misunderstands it. All of these, it should be re-membered, are forms of learning or consequences of learning. The truth

of Being does not reveal itself fully to human thinking. Something mysterious or concealed is inherent in it. The term "unconcealment" (Greek
Aletheia, German *Unverborgenheit*), which Heidegger settled on as the
most appropriate to describe truth, does not therefore signify any permanently achieved state of enlightenment. Rather, it signifies an event of il-
lumination within a larger, encompassing mystery. In his various wood-
land images Heidegger compares it to a glade along a forest path which
enables shafts of light to shine through but which is reclaimed again by
the forest's enveloping darkness. This interplay between unconcealment
and the concealment that is a deeper withdrawal is what thinking becomes capable of experiencing only after a more man-made kind of concealment is identified and set aside in some successful degree. This man-
made concealment, Heidegger repeatedly argues, is a ubiquitous neglect,
or forgetfulness of Being. It is wrought not just by metaphysics but by
every kind of conceptuality that already presupposes some determination
of the essence of the human, or some interpretation of being human, without casting an inquiring glance in the direction of Being. It is important to
recognize that not only would metaphysical determinations like *animal rationale* and will to power count as such concealment; so also would such
antimetaphysical interpretations of the human as "existence precedes
essence" (Sartre) or as "liberal ironist" (R. Rorty). The same applies to any
mentality that has allowed itself to conceive of human action primarily as
a technology, or as some kind of "performativity."

As a kind of homecoming amid humankind's thrownness in a world,
thinking, as Heidegger elucidates it, lies among the first of humankind's
responsibilities. Embracing this responsibility moreover is not a matter of
a "theoretical representation of Being and of man" (*BW*, p. 236), nor a theoretical undertaking of any kind. It is an accomplishment, a "leading forth
into fullness," that is properly called *action* (*BW*, p. 193). As action, this
thinking is neither theoretical nor practical. It occurs before this distinction can be made. It is an attempted bringing-to-language of "the unspoken word of Being" (*BW*, p. 139). It is a finding of the way, a losing and re-
finding of the way, to one's human dwelling, or one's abode, in the
nearness of Being. There is in such action, then, from the start something
reverential, or even sacred. Insofar as it engages in confrontation, this is
not in order to make confrontation itself a virtue. Rather, it is with a view
to a safeguarding, a sheltering, of the kind of engagement that can properly, or worthily, be called educational.

An example from Heidegger's writings on art should illustrate this
point and help to show, in conclusion, how the work of teaching is, in the
first place, a form of action that answers the call of thinking. In his lengthy
essay "The Origin of the Work of Art" (*PLT*, pp. 17–87), Heidegger explores art as a work of human originality that attends thoughtfully and

creatively to the truth of Being. The work of art is a human accomplishment, or more precisely, an event of appropriating disclosure (*Ereignis*), in which human accomplishment participates (*PLT*, p. 86). As such, the work is the bearer of the interplay of lighting and concealing which enables Being to reveal something of its truth to humans, to draw humans into some nourishing disclosure of its truth. Thus it brings humans forth out of the concealments of the commonplace, out of the ambiguity of the everyday, or out of the pervasive technicity of the technological. Heidegger provides a memorable example of this unconcealing in his reflections on a painting by Van Gogh of an old and very commonplace object, a peasant's pair of boots.[7] The boots are precisely the kind of object that, from an everyday perspective in modern society, would already be thrown out as rubbish. As Heidegger writes:

> A pair of peasant shoes and nothing more. And yet -
> From the dark opening of the worn insides of the shoes the toilsome tread of the worker stares forth. In the stiffly rugged heaviness of the shoes there is the accumulated tenacity of her slow trudge through the far-spreading and ever uniform furrows of the field swept by a raw wind. On the leather lie the dampness and richness of the soil. Under the soles slides the loneliness of the field-path as evening falls. In the shoes vibrates the silent call of the earth, its quiet gift of the ripening grain and its unexplained self-refusal in the fallow desolation of the wintry field. (*PLT*, pp. 33–34)

Far from any nostalgia or escapism, the work of art here evokes remembrance and presents anew what has been repeatedly passed over in everyday experience. That is, it calls forth the familiar in an unforeseen and newly intelligible way. The work thus houses the human within the stay of the world it opens up; a world which is in greater or lesser degree already familiar, but is now also newly disclosed, yet also newly mysterious; where the familiar and mysterious are held in a mingling play.

What Heidegger says of a work of art like Van Gogh's painting can be said with no less illuminating insight of a "performing art" like teaching. Here the relationship to the truth of Being would be attempted in the relationships of learning that the teacher-as-artist thoughtfully envisages and earnestly works to bring about. The experience of every subject on a curriculum (not just "the humanities") is thus to be thought of as a bringing-to-language which opens up a world of inquiry. Such experience can attend to, or more commonly busily bypass, what is most worthy of thought in that field, whether as rudimentary experience or as an engagement at advanced levels of fluency. To regard teaching as a work of art in this way is to view teachers—and also learners—very differently than does any viewpoint that casts teaching as a technology, or as a service industry to some economic or political imperative. It is to envisage teachers, first and foremost, as active thinkers, whose work is a bringing about—often through the thoughtfulness of constructive conflict and creative struggle—of enduring and nourishing relationships to what is most worthy of the efforts of each learner. Of course this raises a host of new questions for the philosophy of education. It does, and these cannot be engaged here. Yet this engagement itself might largely be a *recasting* of questions that have been around for a long time; questions that are as recurrent and as familiar as they are seemingly intractable. What is most important to recognize then is that the kind of thinking being sketched in this reflection on Heidegger's confrontations opens up an original and promising landscape, or thoughtscape, in which educational questions themselves are to be elucidated and addressed.

NOTES

1. See, for instance, the works by Safranski (1998), Ott (1994), Dallmayr (1993) and Farías (1989) listed in the references.
2. In this essay I will be investigating the originality of Heidegger's confrontations and the promise of his thinking for the philosophy of education. To treat the lacunae in that thinking, particularly Heidegger's lack of attention to elucidating the plurality that constitutes human being-in-the-world, and human being-with (*Mitsein*), would require at least a further essay of similar proportions.
3. There is no suggestion here that there is nothing more to Platonism than the educational doctrines I am summarizing here. Rather, I am calling attention to an important dimension of Platonism which is more often passed over lightly than investigated in detail.
4. In his book *The Five Ways*, Anthony Kenny calls attention to the Platonist character of Aristotle's metaphysics (p. 71 ff). Gerard Watson, in his *Greek Philosophy and the Christian Notion of God*, points out that both Aristotle and Aquinas were Platonist in their thinking and he concludes that "the return of Aristotelianism in the twelfth and thirteenth centuries by no means implied the removal of the Platonism that had been dominant in theological speculation up to then" (p. 137).
5. These short passages are from a lecture by MacIntyre "Truth as a Good—A Reflection on *Fides et Ratio*." The lecture, presented on 23 January 2001, was jointly organized by the Faculty of Theology of St. Patrick's College Maynooth and the Faculty of Philosophy of National University of Ireland, Maynooth. It hasn't been published to date.
6. To highlight what is meant here, one could contrast thinking as a gift granted to humans with thinking as a *burden* that humans must shoulder, but which nonhuman beings are spared. For humans it could be both gift *and* burden, *and* many more things besides. For most other species of being, thinking, in the ways that humans experience it, is not an issue—to the best of our knowledge.
7. In his biography of Heidegger, Rüdiger Safranski claims that the boots were Van Gogh's own and that they were mistakenly taken by Heidegger to be a peas-

ant's pair of boots (Safranski, p. 297). This, however, adds to rather than detracts from the evocative power of Heidegger's reflection. In other words it calls forth the unfamiliar and the inexhaustible in the unremarkable life of a peasant as distinct from discerning it in the more "eventful" life of an artist.

REFERENCES

Aquinas, Thomas. *Summa Theologiae*. Translated by the English Dominican Fathers (London: Blackfriars, in association with Eyre & Spottiswoode, 1963–1974).

Aristotle. *Metaphysics*. Translated by Hugh Lawson-Tancred (London: Penguin, 1998).

Augustine. *City of God*. Abridged version for modern readers, with foreword by Vernon J. Bourke (New York: Doubleday, 1958).

Dallmayr, Fred. *The Other Heidegger*. (Ithaca, N.Y.: Cornell University Press, 1993).

Derrida, Jacques. *Spurs: Nietzsche's Styles*. Translated by Barbara Harlow (Chicago: University of Chicago Press, 1979).

Farías, Victor. *Heidegger and Nazism*. Edited by Joseph Margolis and Tom Rockmore. Translated by Paul Burrell and Gabriel R. Ricci (Philadelphia: Temple University Press, 1989).

Heidegger, Martin. *Being and Time*. Translated by John Macquarrie and Edward Robinson (Oxford: Basil Blackwell, 1973).

Heidegger, Martin. *Sein und Zeit* (Tübingen: Max Niemyer Verlag, 7. Auflage, 1977).

Heidegger, Martin. *Nietzsche*. Volumes 1–4, translated and edited by David Farrell Krell (San Francisco: Harper Collins, 1991).

Heidegger, Martin "Letter on Humanism," in *Martin Heidegger Basic Writings*. Translated with introduction by David Farrell Krell (London: Routledge and Kegan Paul, 1978)

Heidegger Martin. "The End of Philosophy and the Task of Thinking," in *Martin Heidegger Basic Writings*. Translated with introduction by David Farrell Krell (London: Routledge and Kegan Paul, 1978).

Heidegger, Martin. "The Origin of the Work of Art," in *Poetry, Language, Thought*. Translated with Introduction by Albert Hofstadter (New York: Harper & Row, 1971).

John Paul II, Pope. *Faith and Reason*. English translation of the encyclical letter *Fides et Ratio* (Rome: Libreria Editrice Vaticana, 1998; trans. publ. Dublin: Veritas, 1998).

Kenny, Anthony. *The Five Ways* (London: Routledge and Kegan Paul, 1969).

McIntyre, Alastair. 2001. "Truth as a Good—A Reflection on *Fides et Ratio*." Lecture presented at the National University of Ireland, Maynooth. Unpublished.

Nietzsche, Friedrich. *Beyond Good and Evil*. Translated by R. J. Hollingdale, with an introduction by Michael Tanner (London: Penguin, revised edition 1990).

Nietzsche, Friedrich. *The Will to Power*. Edited by Walter Kaufmann. Translated by Walter Kaufmann and R. J. Hollingdale (New York: Vintage Books, 1968).

Ott, Hugo. *Martin Heidegger: A Political Life*. Translated by Allan Blunden (London: Harper Collins, 1993).

Plato. "Republic," in *The Dialogues of Plato*. Translated by B. Jowett (New York: Random House, 1937 edition, two volumes).

Safranski, Rüdiger. *Martin Heidegger: Between Good and Evil*. Translated by Ewald Osers (Cambridge, Mass.: Harvard University Press, 1998).

Watson, Gerard. *Greek Philosophy and the Christian Notion of God* (Dublin: Columba Press, 1994).

11

Education as a Form of the Poetic: A Heideggerian Approach to Learning and the Teacher–Pupil Relationship

Michael Bonnett

INTRODUCTION

If we take "modernity" to refer to the working out of Enlightenment beliefs and aspirations in human affairs, then Heidegger's relationship to it is not straightforward. For example, he both expresses the precept of radical questioning of the commonly accepted and a desire to overthrow obfuscating tradition, but includes in this a radical questioning of that great engine of the Enlightenment itself—disengaged reason and the desire to universalize. In this sense he is thus also "postmodern" and some, such as Richard Rorty,[1] are well known for emphasizing the recognition of contingency and relativism that they detect in his work. However labelled, these strands in his thinking have strong implications for education, and themselves are open to differing interpretations. Some of these will be explored in this chapter. By way of preliminary, it is interesting to note that, while clearly intensely involved in teaching for much of his life (much of his published work was first delivered in lectures and he often gave a special status to the spoken word over the written), Heidegger rarely refers directly to ideas of teaching and education. Yet the references that he does make are very powerful and much of his writing either explicitly addresses topics of direct educational significance—in particular, the nature of thinking, understanding, and by implication, learning—or presents views on language and human being and its relationship to the cosmos which have a profound bearing on educational issues.

In this chapter, I will develop what I take to be some important insights that Heidegger's thinking offers for our understanding of learning and what would count as a full *educational* relationship between learner and teacher. To do this I will be drawing on two main sources: the philosophical anthropology of the "early" Heidegger in *Being and Time*[2] and issues associated with the distinction between "calculative" and "meditative," or "poetic," thinking which occur in the later Heidegger of, for example, *Poetry, Language, Thought.*[3]

My intention is not so much to give a scholarly exegesis of Heidegger's ideas, as to exhibit and draw upon the underlying spirit of some aspects of his thinking and to develop its potential for understanding certain central educational concerns. In particular I want to explore what a "non-technologized" (in Heidegger's sense of this term) version of learning and the teacher-pupil relationship might look like. But first, let us review Heidegger's development of certain key ideas.

HEIDEGGER ON PERSONAL AUTHENTICITY

Although only a precursor to addressing "the question of Being" and ostensibly part of a neutral description of (Western) human consciousness as the place where beings are disclosed, an important theme throughout much of *Being and Time* is the issue of personal authenticity. This is significant for education in two ways. First, in characterizing some central components of what might be meant by "human integrity," it provides a view of personhood and therefore, in a liberal tradition, a view of what must be respected and developed in the treatment of young people during their education. Second, because of the link that is made between this and the nature of human understanding, it offers a perspective on the nature of personally significant learning and the conditions that are necessary for it to occur.

Since the aspects of authenticity that I wish to draw upon are among the more familiar and accessible elements of Heidegger's thinking, I will offer only a brief résumé here.

Central to Heidegger's account is the notion of human consciousness as *"Dasein"*—"there-being" whose "own being is an issue for it." What is characteristic of authentic human consciousness is that things *matter* to it in terms of its awareness of its own existence and sense of future. Choice, and therefore a sense of responsibility, are integral to its manner of being—as is the awareness of its own finitude made apparent through a sense of "guilt" that in pursuing one set of possibilities another set is thereby denied, and exemplified most powerfully by the awareness of the inevitability of its own death. It is such awareness that individuates individuals by extricating them from thoughtless absorption in the crowd. But the angst generated by the sense of ultimate responsibility that attaches to each individual for the conduct of their own life—notwithstanding the essential contingency, uncertainties, and paradoxes of the situations into which they are often "thrown"—results in a flight from the truth of their own freedom and sense of mortality. In everydayness, awareness of such things is for the most part tranquilized by slipping into a frame of mind that Heidegger terms the "they-self"—the inauthentic understanding of the anonymous "they" whose "gossip" or "hearsay" silently covers over every call of individual conscience and every truth, substituting what is said in easy public talk for what things mean in terms of each individual's sense of their own unique existence. In this frame of mind we know and understand what *everybody* knows and understands; there is a ready explanation at hand for every occurrence and nothing is allowed to seriously disturb the self-effacing spread of averaged-off wisdom, which has something up its sleeve to deal with all contingencies. What matters is what is said in the talk, which is always ready to pass on to the next thing whenever there is a danger of its all-knowing demeanour being brought into question; diverting ephemeral sensationalism and titillation standing substitute for genuine concern and inquiry.

It is clear that in general terms such an account acquires particular force in a society where much of the everyday is dominated by consumerism, and could serve as an intellectual counter to those forces which seek to convert us into essentially passive recipients of trivia. In a parallel way it raises some crucial issues for education. For example:

- How much learning in schools essentially has the character of "hearsay"—amounting to little more than the acquisition of what is said in the talk rather than being carefully interpreted and evaluated in terms of the learners' sense of their own existence?
- What is the role of education in initiating individuals into the nature and truth of their own freedom and their own mortality?
- How is "real" learning from others—and therefore in education—possible? Will it not always insinuate elements of the levelled-off public understanding of things that will be tending constantly to subvert the unique and authentic individual perspective?
- How should we conceive of knowledge and truth in education and how they are acquired?
- What implications do these issues have for the teacher-pupil relationship whose prime concern is with authentic learning?

Clearly there is a range of questions here that invites a thorough analysis and evaluation of current practices. But perhaps what emerges most powerfully is the importance of learners having the opportunity, encouragement, and support to decide how they will *value* what they learn, to decide how it should affect their outlook and their actions.[4]

This has extensive implications for the character of educational learning and the teacher-pupil relationship, which we will explore shortly. First, it is important to note that on this account authenticity is not "primal" in the sense that it is the natural state, or that it can simply be assumed present. Personal authenticity is an *achievement*. We have to extricate ourselves from the frame of mind that constitutes the "they-self" and which proximally and for the most part conditions our perceptions. Yet also, it needs to be recognized that there are inherently passive elements to authenticity. One important aspect of this is illustrated in Harry Frankfurt's notions of "unthinkability" and "volitional necessity," and another in Charles Taylor's discussion of the role of 'horizons of significance' in authentic choice.

Through his introduction of the notions of "unthinkability" and a corresponding "volitional necessity" into personal authenticity, Frankfurt makes the point that we have cares and concerns that are nonvoluntaristic and which provide a *necessary* framework for an individual's choices:

> Unthinkability is a mode of necessity with which the will sometimes binds itself and limits choice. This limitation may be an affirmation and revelation of fundamental sanity. . . . The will of a rational (sane) agent need not be . . . empty or devoid of substantial character. It is not necessarily altogether formal and content less, having no inherent proclivities of its own . . . it is precisely in the particular content or specific character of his will . . . that the rationality (sanity) of a person may in part reside.[5]

This notion of there being underlying substantive purposes and preferences in terms of which choices are articulated echoes a criticism that Maurice Merleau-Ponty made of Sartre's notion of consciousness as essentially empty and capable of "criterionless choice," which was the only true expression of its freedom.[6] For Merleau-Ponty, such criterionless choice is both unknown and incoherent. There is always a "sediment" of established concerns, commitments, and predispositions in an individual consciousness which it acquires over its history and which must condition (but not *determine*) present choices. In voluntary deliberation we are going over the possibilities in an attempt to make explicit a decision that was already *implicit*, for how else could there be a weighing up? Freedom must be "buttressed by being" if a person's choice is to be *their* choice. This sediment provides a necessary framework for unifying the self and for giving intelligibility to the idea of personal choice.

In a parallel vein, Charles Taylor[7] has argued (very much in Heidegger-ian fashion) that the self develops *dialogically* and that the "horizons of sig-nificance" which our culture provides are essential references for our sense of ourselves, the choices that lie before us, and the demands and tensions with which we have to contend. A notion of self-determining freedom that denies the significance of such a normative context trivializes our predica-ment by yielding "a flattened world in which there aren't very meaningful choices because there aren't any crucial issues."[8] By "horizon of signifi-cance" Taylor means a valuation system of a historically grown commu-nity—the authoritative principles, rules, values, and norms that are ex-pressive of the socially prevalent conception of the good life. The necessity of reference to such an element, which lies beyond any individual, again reveals the tension that exists within authenticity between being active and being passive and makes it clear that in the educational context both ele-ments must be taken into account. Furthermore the rich view of authen-ticity that begins to emerge here, that gives a place to guilt as awareness of negation and acknowledges both an internal structure of concerns and a superordinate cultural normative framework, directs the focus of discus-sion away from the notion of the authentic individual as somehow operat-ing in splendid isolation from the real world and places it instead on the quality of his or her relationship to the world. This brings us up against the nature of this world and the character of authentic learning.

POETIC THINKING

During his ruminations on the question of Being in his later works, Hei-degger develops a seminal distinction which, in the educational context, can be seen to relate well to the idea of personal authenticity in education and, I believe, has the potential to contribute to our understanding of a teacher-pupil relationship in which authenticity of both learning and the individual would flourish. I refer to his distinction between "calculative" thinking which "challenges forth" and "meditative," or "poetic," thinking which "brings forth."[9] Since the character and significance of the latter is perhaps most readily understood against the backcloth of what Heideg-ger perceives to be the growing dominance of the former, I will begin with "calculative" thinking.

For Heidegger, "calculative" thinking is the kind of thinking that is in the ascendant—indeed, approaches its zenith—in the modern age. (One might say that for him its ascent is the grand narrative of modernity.) It is that kind of thinking which seeks to reckon everything up in terms of its own instrumental purposes—to master, to possess, to exploit all that it encounters. It encompasses everything in a "world picture," where what is meant by "world picture" is not merely a picture of the world, but a framework of instrumental relationships in terms of which *the world first appears*—in which things first have their being for us—and which therefore determines *how* they appear in terms of their meaning and their value, the quality of their occurring. The world picture as a "horizon of significance" conditions what we perceive and how we understand, presenting everything as nested in a web of technical-instrumental motives and connections. Much of this is made explicit in his essay *The Question Concerning Technology*[10] in which Heidegger argues that the essence of technology is not to be confused with its products such as cars, computers, atomic bombs, and genetic clones, which, with varying degrees of plausibility, it is possible to perceive as existing to serve us. For Heidegger, closer to the *essence* of technology than any machinery is a frame of mind, a way of seeing things—or what he aptly terms "a mode of revealing"—that expresses a certain relationship between human beings and the world. This means that technology is badly misunderstood if it is, in its essence, regarded as a neutral means to ends, a sort of protean tool at our disposal. If its essence is a mode of revealing it has, as it were, become internal to our consciousness—we have become *technologically minded*. It is a way of relating to things in which we are caught up and carried along. Thus, for Heidegger, there is a fundamental sense in which it is less a case of us using technology and more a case of *technology using us*. We increasingly think and act in accordance with the world picture it provides. Along with the "they-self," in the modern era, technology is a dominant aspect of our everyday selves.

So, what is it to be technologically minded in this sense? Characteristic of the technological mode of revealing is a fixation of things by categorizing them and representing them to ourselves in thought through abstract categories, thus making them manageable and capable of being efficiently manipulated—a demand to which the fluid and the ill-defined remains inconveniently resistant. Thus we "enframe" things by turning them into *instances*—understanding them in terms of the objective properties attributed to members of the category to which they have been allocated. At this point, I offer what might sound a quaint interpretation of this phenomenon in the aftermath of the "linguistic turn" in philosophy and the current preoccupation with the postmodern portrayal of everything as relative to contingent human practices that gives any reference to "things themselves" an archaic ring.

In this processing of things in order to intellectually possess them, the uniqueness of individual things is lost—they no longer have their own meaning, only that which we allocate to them according to where we place them in our calculations. Calculative thinking is thus essentially self-assertive, setting everything up as something to be exploited—a resource—and this attitude expresses a fundamental lack of respect for things themselves in their many-sidedness. For Heidegger, the real motive expressed in modern technology as calculative thinking is Nietzsche's "will to power," and increasing immersion in this self-assertive/calculative frame of mind alienates us from things themselves, for things thus "organized" do not—*cannot*—show themselves as they are in their uniqueness, their sheer "suchness," their 'here and now.' A consequence of this totalitarianism over things (which of course includes ourselves, for we too are challenged forth and must assume the position and value allocated to us in the instrumental world picture) is that we are insulated from inspiration in the sense of the enrichment and refreshment afforded by encountering things afresh and in their inherent strangeness. Our view of the world becomes pre-formed, one track, closed off, and thinking becomes "constipated." Thus, as the technological way of relating to the world gains ascendancy—which of course is central to its masterful nature—so we move along a road whose ultimate destination is nihilism in the sense of an empty meaninglessness resulting from an inability to receive meaning from outside ourselves, our "self"-centered plans, calculations and definitions. (I put "self" in quotes here, as in this context clearly it arises in a singularly cabined sense.) It is under the influence of such thinking that the shining of a color can be transformed into a wavelength, and the quiet, highly nuanced, presence of a wild flower in the grass can be transmuted into a crude (if highly precise) set of objective properties as it is slid into a scientific database. In each case the potential richness of the original experience is left behind as we move from participatory celebration to rational explanation, from receptiveness to emergent things to manipulating defined objects of thought. In a refusal to be held in the sway of the primitive and elemental—one is tempted to say in a certain sense, the "eternal"—we fall under the sway of the pre-specified, ever preferring ingenuity to creativity, ratiocination to that primal thinking relationship with things which Parmenides once called a "letting-lie-before-us and taking-to-heart." To use Heidegger's language, we become "forgetful of Being."

Shortly, I will explore some of the resonances of this with contemporary educational practice that organizes itself around a prespecified curriculum in the pursuit of standardized goals, but, because of its salience to learning and the pupil-teacher relationship, I will pursue one element of Heidegger's critique of technology just a little further.

The notion of responsiveness to things themselves is well illustrated in the contrast that Heidegger draws between the quality of making something in modern manufacturing as compared with that of the craftsman. The former challenges nature to provide the materials required by a blueprint that specifies in advance every detail of the finished product.

Everything is then wrought to play its part efficiently—for example, "natural" materials, animate or inanimate, are reengineered as necessary to achieve maximum yield. For Heidegger, such fabrication is quite different in spirit to the making undertaken by the craftsman who works *with* his materials within a tradition to bring something into being. He brings out the figure slumbering in the wood, the luster inherent in the metal, the texture of the stone, by assuming a role of *co-responsibility* with the creative physical attributes and cultural powers which give the work meaning and in which they are revealed and expressed. Thus the material is not simply "used up" in such production, but helped to show itself in the work piece. It comes into its *own* as an ongoing receptive-responding rather than a challenging-imposing characterizing the process of making. Things made in this way inherently express authentic dwelling and open up the human world. In this sense the process and the product are "poetic" and the integrity of all is preserved.

Thus Heidegger claims that for the ancients a temple could both reveal its materials and its surroundings, gathering them in their human significance (which is nonetheless not thereby human-*centerd*) thereby rooting a people in their world, expressing their dwelling:

> Standing there, the building rests on rocky ground. This resting of the work draws up out of the rock the mystery of that rock's clumsy yet spontaneous support. Standing there, the building holds its ground against the storm raging above it and so makes the storm itself manifest in its violence. The lustre and gleam of the stone, though itself apparently glowing only by the grace of the sun, yet first brings to light the light of the day, the breadth of the sky, and the darkness of the night. The temple's firm towering makes visible the invisible space of the air. The steadfastness of the work contrasts with the surge of the surf, and its own repose brings out the raging of the sea. . . . The temple-work, standing there, opens up a world and at the same time sets this world back again on earth, which itself only thus emerges as native ground. . . . The temple in its standing there, first gives to things their look and to men their outlook on themselves.[11]

It seems to me that in Heidegger's characterization of what I will term poetic thinking, making and building is highly suggestive for an understanding of a nontechnological form of education. Also, it sensitizes us to the ways in which education has already fallen under the sway of the essence of technology. This is starkly illustrated by the market and managerial models of education that increasingly set the tone for so much that has come to be regarded as educational reform. Consider the following significant "calculative" features: a radical separation of means and ends which enables those external to the teaching-learning situation (and sometimes with little interest in it above and beyond what it is seen to produce in instrumental terms and with what economy of resources) to set the criteria for success; prespecification of essential content and teaching approach independently of individual learners and teachers; modularization of curricula; accountability through periodic testing and inspection with the publishing of results in standardized forms which leads to a preoccupation with tangible outcomes which can be captured through measurement-based assessment; increasingly, a focus on highly instrumental and sometimes narrowly vocational aims. In all, a system highly "enframed" and "enframing" in Heidegger's sense, in which it becomes entirely natural to regard education primarily as an economic resource. And in which the development of genuinely individual perspectives and personal ways of making sense of experience appear as a frothy luxury.

AUTHENTIC LEARNING AND THE
TEACHER–PUPIL RELATIONSHIP

> To learn means to make everything we do answer to those essentials that address themselves to us at any given time.[12] . . . Teaching is more difficult than learning because what teaching calls for is this: to let learn.[13]

In the light of the theme of personal authenticity and the analysis of technology discussed in the previous two sections, I think it is possible to retrieve a view of the educational process that may be very timely. There is, of course, a long tradition of celebrating an ostensibly honorific conception of education that sharply distinguishes it from notions such as "training" and an instrumental preparation for the "world of work." The idea of "liberal education" is one such conception in which the freedom and enrichment of the mind are held to be of intrinsic worth and in which the idea of education is held to possess its own inherent values. In many ways, this has been an abiding preoccupation in the philosophy of education: from Plato to John Dewey, Richard Peters, Israel Scheffler, and thereafter. Thus, for example, from a conservative perspective, Michael Oakeshott [14] has made the point very forcibly that it is not for education to simply dance attendance upon whatever demands happen to be most prominent in current society, whose bustle is preoccupied with immediate practical gain. Rather it should remain steadfast in its central duty of initiating each generation into those great traditions of thought and sensibility which constitute our "civilized inheritance" and which is largely *unfamiliar* to everyday life. Oakeshott holds that it is only within the space opened up by these traditions that what it is to be properly human is articulated and evolves, and in which "self-disclosure" and "self-enactment" of the individual truly can occur. On this account, schools may take on something of a monastic character where "excellences may be heard because the din of worldly laxities and partialities is silenced or abated." While a subsequent postmodernist generation of philosophers of education would no doubt be quick to expose the pretensions, ethnocentricity, and generally unacknowledged relativism that they would see to be rampant in this account, it nonetheless stands as a reminder of the possibility of a noninstrumental view of education which would therefore operate according to a set of internal rather than external norms. It seems to me that this is a key—and highly problematic—issue for education in the modern/postmodern age and I believe that the elements of Heidegger's thinking with which this chapter has so far been concerned offer an important perspective. I have elsewhere[15] characterized it under the rubric "teaching as poetry" and in what follows I will attempt to refine and defend this as a view of what an *educational* sense of learning and the teacher-pupil relationship would be.

As the quote that heads this section suggests, for Heidegger, learning and teaching are highly demanding enterprises. They are demanding because they require thought in the demanding senses which he elaborates in his characterization of personal authenticity and his critique of technology: thinking as an engagement with things which is both personal in its commitment and transporting through its openness to things themselves; thinking which involves true responsibility for self and towards things, in which contingency and the many-sidedness of things is recognized and the nonhuman powers involved in the arising of things is sensed and responded to. This is thinking as *poiesis*—bringing forth. Such thinking, arguably, is fundamental to authentic human consciousness, for it is ultimately central to the notion of—and *experience* of—*truth*, without which human life becomes unintelligible. Truth, understood in a Heideggerian sense of our awareness of things as they are in their presencing and our expression of this through fitting language—the word or other expression which seems best to reflect that which addresses itself to us and thus, in a sense, brings it into being for us—orients everything which is human, and never more so than when it is being subverted or forgotten. If such a "poetic" relationship[16] with things is a constituent of human essence then it would seem that the process of education should reflect this.[17]

So, how does a concern for the poetic translate into education and, in particular, learning and the teacher-pupil relationship? Basically it seems to me that it invites us to view education, in its essence, as an ever-evolving triadic interplay between teacher, learner, and that which calls to be learned. It thus locates the teacher-pupil relationship at the very heart of

education—indeed, as maintaining the space in which education suc-
ceeds or fails. Furthermore, it implies a relationship that is radically noninstrumental in the sense that it evolves according to its own norms and
is destroyed if made subservient to any set of external norms that attempt to prespecify what it is to achieve and how it is to proceed. Clearly
there are resonances here with Dewey's attempt to give intrinsic direction to education by means of those internal norms of "growth": "interaction" and "continuity."[18] And the issue therefore arises as to whether it
is subject to a similar objection, namely, that far from providing sufficient
internal direction, it simply assumes an external value framework. However, the case stands somewhat differently with Heidegger since the
whole thrust of his work is to retrieve a way of relating to things which
is fundamental to human consciousness as a whole, including its implicit
cultural dimensions (as, for example, previous reference to "horizons of
significance" makes clear). Thus if education is conceived as initiation
into what it is to be human in some founding sense, poetic thinking is intrinsic to education in the sense that its restoration becomes a central,
"internal" educational purpose—one which stands regardless of the demands and pressures which happen to be current in everyday society
and which may wish to impose their purposes upon education.

This relates to a second objection: Does not the lack of prespecified
overarching norms mean that learning undertaken in this way will lack
discipline and rigor? This objection is itself interesting for the deeply
mechanistic assumptions that it makes about learning; namely, that rigor
must be a product of some kind of enframing, of adherence to some set of
prespecified rules, and that order cannot be conceived without (external)
control. The riposte to this is that, to the contrary, the rigor of poetic thinking and practice is greater than any to be generated by following an ex-
ternally imposed framework, for it requires constant and close attention
to the signs which are its way, to a sense of that which is as yet withdrawn,
not yet manifest. It requires a genuine *listening* to that which calls to be
thought in the evolving situation—which means, in terms of the triadic
relationship, the engagement of the learner with that which concerns
him/her and the teacher's sensing of this and of the integrity of the subject matter itself as a tradition of concerns and perspectives.[19] Thus poetic
thinking generates its own intimately context-relative interpretations of
criteria which express a receptive-responsive openness to things—constitute a whole-hearted engagement—such as vitality, perceptiveness, apt-
ness, empathy with subject. To continue the theme of the Heidegger quotation which opened this section:

> The teacher is ahead of his apprentices in this alone, that he has still far
> more to learn than they—he has to learn to let them learn. The teacher must

be capable of being more teachable than the apprentices. The teacher is far less assured of his ground than those who learn are of theirs. If the relation between the teacher and the taught is genuine, therefore, there is never a place in it for the authority of the know-it-all or the authoritative sway of the official. It is still an exalted matter, then, to become a teacher—which is something else entirely than becoming a famous professor. That nobody wants any longer to become a teacher today, when all things are downgraded and graded from below (for instance from business), is presumably because the matter is exalted, because of its altitude.[20]

The teacher can never be sure of his ground because it cannot be specified in advance, nor can any authority or official source do so without disrupting the educational process—the ongoing invitation to think (in the demanding sense, the sense in which "science does not think").[21] So the teacher-pupil relationship is not to be conceived as a vehicle for the attainment of some set of prespecified standards in education—in effect as a management tool—but as a genuinely creative, because genuinely open, encounter in which the teacher attempts to sense both the quality of the learner's current engagement and to help him to hear for himself the call of what calls to be thought in this engagement—to sense what is on the move in the domain with which he is engaged and to attend to the withdrawn (the as yet *un*thought, the incipient) that alone draws thought forward. This quality strikes a sharp contrast with "effective thinking" in the calculative mold which conceives mystery as an unnecessary obfuscation and is driven by a need to get things rapidly sorted out and made manageable. A thinking whose consuming goal becomes blind transparency—"blind," because in its refusal to stay with things, always looking past them to further purposes, it loses sight of them. Only thinking of this character could impose a standardized curriculum on education and fail to notice that individual learners and teachers have dropped out of view. Perhaps it is that *because* they are no longer visible, the harm that is done them can go unremarked. "Educational" standards are "met" or "not met," prespecified learning goals are "achieved" or "failed in," teaching and teachers are accounted "effective" or "ineffective," and the authentic life of the mind is likely either bypassed, or worse, destroyed.

Again, in contrast to the machinery of periodic monitoring and standardized assessment of learning to achieve quality, the poetic teacher-pupil relationship would be highly reciprocal and based on *trust*, which preserves both the integrity of the learner and of the material. In such a relationship it will never be the task of the teacher to take over the learner's problems and hand them back sorted out, for this would simply be to displace the learner from his unique engagement, to leave him free-wheeling—disengaged and dependent. Yet such learning will require emotional support, for it involves *risk* and on occasion will bring into question beliefs which may be deeply constitutive of one's personal identity and which significantly shape one's outlook. Thus the teacher has an important role to play in supporting the *experience* of learning and thinking. Through her own experience of engaging with issues within the domain "from the inside" she may be able to empathize with the frustrations, seeming incomprehensibility, and deadness which are as much a part of thinking as the excitement and satisfaction of feeling underway. She, toward her pupil, and he, toward what is to be learned, are involved in a relationship that at a primary level is *dis*interested, but never *un*interested. Both are required to invest something of themselves in the process in a way that has nothing to do with ego satisfaction and everything to do with the personal fulfillment that comes from genuine receptivity.

Perhaps such a "poetic" teacher-pupil relationship can best be characterized as an "empathetic challenging" in which, from out of her sensitivity to the concerns of the learner and the potential of the domain with which he is attempting to engage, the teacher can suggest, challenge, provoke in ways that both respect the integrity of this engagement and deepen and refine it. Also, through the judicious revealing of her own sense of what is important, problematic, analogous, fascinating, a source of wonderment, she can exhibit—to the extent that she is authentic—what an honest engagement might mean and how it becomes integrated into a human life, making a difference to what is seen and felt. In such a relationship, no *one* initiates the work, is wholly responsible for it, controls it. Progress is the result of a set of constantly evolving mutual relationships and what it is to *be* a teacher or learner in the occurrent sense is a function of the different locations which actors may occupy at different times in this interplay as they respond freely and responsibly within it. They are no more prespecifiable independently of this relationship than is the learning which is its outcome.

To summarize: A Heideggerian account sees learning as a highly demanding and participatory affair which requires the full engagement of the learner and is certainly not something that could be instilled from without through a heavily didactic process. Nor, indeed, on this account, could it be conceived of in terms of the achievement of a prespecified set of detailed learning objectives as set out in some standardized curriculum. If the teacher has to *let* the pupil learn rather than impose learning upon her, far from being wholly passive in character, it requires that the learner submit herself to the demands and rigor of thinking in the active sense of listening for and attending to what *calls* to be thought from out of the unique learning situation in which she is involved. This is far removed from an education that mechanizes (and thus tranquilizes) thinking by attempting to enframe it in prespecified and often highly instrumental structures, thus closing down its open possibilities. For

Heidegger, genuine thinking is not the assimilation of a series of gobbets of prespecified information and ideas, nor the acquisition and application of free-floating "thinking skills," but an exciting and demanding journey into the unknown. It is deeply rooted, being drawn forward by the pull of that which is somehow incipient in our awareness but has yet to reveal itself, and the fundamental achievement of education lies in learners coming to feel for themselves the call of what is there to be thought in this unthought: the harmonies, the conflicts, and the mysteries. In this chapter, I have attempted to sketch an account of learning and the teacher-pupil relationship that reflects this.

NOTES

1. Richard Rorty, *Essays on Heidegger and Others* (Cambridge: Cambridge University Press, 1991).

2. Martin Heidegger, *Being and Time*, translated by J. Macquarrie and E. Robinson (Oxford: Basil Blackwell, 1962).

3. Martin Heidegger, *Poetry, Language, Thought*, translated by A. Hofstadter (New York: Harper Colophon, 1975).

4. The lack of this in the context of the UK National Curriculum has recently been noted by, for example, Triggs and Pollard, who, reporting on a survey of children's views on how they were being taught, observed that a theme which ran through their school experience was: "a sense of time as a scarce resource. They were aware of the pressure to 'get things done'; felt there was not enough time to do things properly, not enough time to learn as they would like, often not as much time as their teachers might like to give them. They were being urged to hurry up and learn because it was necessary to 'get on.'" P. Triggs and A. Pollard "Pupil experience and a curriculum for life-long learning" in *How Shall We School Our Children? Primary Education and Its Future*, edited by C. Richards and P. Taylor (London: Falmer Press, 1998).

5. Harry Frankfurt, *The Importance of What We Care About* (Cambridge: Cambridge University Press, 1998), 189–90.

6. Maurice Merleau-Ponty, *Phenomenology of Perception*, translated by C. Smith (London: Routledge & Kegan Paul, 1962), pt. 3, ch. 3.

7. Charles Taylor, *The Ethics of Authenticity*. (Cambridge, Mass.: Harvard University Press, 1991).

8. Taylor, *Ethics of Authenticity*, 68.

9. See, for example, Martin Heidegger, *Discourse on Thinking*, translated by J. Anderson and E. Freund (New York: Harper & Row, 1966).

10. Martin Heidegger, "The Question Concerning Technology" in *The Question Concerning Technology and Other Essays*, translated by W. Lovitt (New York: Harper Colophon, 1977).

11. Martin Heidegger, "The Origin of the Work of Art" in *Poetry, Language, Thought*, translated by A. Hofstadter (New York: Harper Colophon, 1975), 42–3.

12. Martin Heidegger, *What is Called Thinking?* translated by J. Glenn Gray (New York: Harper Colophon, 1968), 8.

13. Heidegger, *What is Called Thinking*, 15.

14. Michael Oakeshott, "Education: The Engagement and Its Frustration" in *Education and the Development of Reason*, edited by R. Dearden, P. Hirst, and R. Peters (London: Routledge & Kegan Paul, 1972).

15. Michael Bonnett, *Children's Thinking* (London: Cassell, 1994), ch. 14. Also Michael Bonnett "'New' Era Values and Teaching as a Form of the Poetic" *British Journal of Educational Studies* 44 no.1 (1996).

16. I use the term "poetic" here rather than "meditative" as the former seems to more comfortably encompass practice as well as "pure" thinking. It also, perhaps, better conveys the sense of creativity inherent in such thinking and the frame of mind it sustains through its connotation of "bringing forth."

17. At this point it is worth noting a reservation arising from Richard Bernstein's claim that Heidegger distorts the human-thing relationship by focusing on Aristotelian *poiesis* and ignoring *praxis* and *phronesis*, which, if incorporated would reinstate a broader and more human world-as-it-is-lived dimension. (Richard Bernstein, *The New Constellation*, Cambridge: Polity Press, 1991). This would then take proper account of everyday human realities such as the suffering and hardship caused by what Heidegger would regard as "inessential" aspects of life—aspects which are simply symptoms of the workings out of deeper metaphysical motives or "destinings." Viewed only from the Heideggerian heights, such aspects of life are left unaddressed in their own terms. Rorty, too, criticizes Heidegger's seeming disdain for a concern for mere human comfort. Heidegger's elevation of the view of the Thinker and the Poet on occasion might call forth the rejoinder that: You can't eat poetry! This is a serious objection which deserves (and has received) more consideration than space permits here. But for present purposes there is a powerful retort: It is surely an important consequence of Heidegger's analysis that phronesis and praxis have been transformed in the modern age into forms of the calculative and therefore need to be looked beyond and to be reconstructed. Such reconstruction becomes a central duty for an education that is truly to respond to the need of our time, a time that has "forgotten Being." See Michael Bonnett "Education in a Destitute Time. A Heideggerian approach to the Problem of Education in the Age of Modern Technology," *Journal of Philosophy of Education* 17 no. 1 (1983). Reprinted in *Major Themes in Philosophy of Education*, ed. P. Hirst and P. White (London: Routledge, 1998).

18. John Dewey, *Experience and Education* (New York: Collier Books, 1972), ch. 3.

19. See Michael Bonnett, "Teaching Thinking, and the Sanctity of Content," *Journal of Philosophy of Education* 29, no. 3 (1995).

20. Heidegger, *What is Called Thinking*, 15.

21. Heidegger, *What is Called Thinking*, 21.

Index

About the Contributors

Valerie Allen is associate professor of English at the John Jay College of Criminal Justice, City University of New York. She previously taught at the University of South Florida and at the University of Stirling, Scotland.

Ares D. Axiotis practices law in New York City and is formerly a research fellow of Clare Hall, Cambridge, and lecturer in philosophy at the University of Stirling, Scotland.

Michael Bonnett is senior lecturer in philosophy of education, Homerton College, Cambridge. He is the author of numerous journal articles and contributions to collections, which explore the implications of a Heideggerian perspective on the purposes and procedures of education. He is also author of the book *Children's Thinking* (1994), which develops these ideas in the context of promoting thinking and understanding in the primary school. Current areas of particular interest (and the subject of recent publications) are the principles and values that should inform environmental education and the impact of ICT on our understanding of the idea of quality in children's learning.

David E. Cooper is professor of philosophy at the University of Durham and director of the Durham Institute of Comparative Ethics. He has been a visiting professor at several universities across the world and his many books include *Existentialism: A Reconstruction, Heidegger*, and *World Philosophies: An Historical Introduction*.

Patrick Fitzsimons is senior lecturer at the James Cook University, Australia. He was formerly senior research officer for the New Zealand Council for Educational Research of New Zealand. He has published nationally and internationally on education policy, critical social theory, and poststructuralist approaches to education philosophy and social policy.

Ilan Gur-Ze'ev is senior lecturer at the faculty of education, University of Haifa, Israel. He is the author of *The Frankfurt School and the History of Pessimism* (1996), *Philosophy, Politics, and Education in Israel* (1999), and *Destroying the Other's Collective Memory* (forthcoming). Also, he is the editor of *Education in a Postmodern Era* (1996), *Critical Theory and Education* (1998), *Modernity, Post-modernity, and Education* (1999), *The Israeli Condition* (forthcoming), and *Conflicting Philosophies of Education in Israel/ Palestine* (2000).

Pádraig Hogan is senior lecturer in education at the National University of Ireland at Maynooth. He is an assistant editor of the *Journal of Philosophy of Education* and a former president of the Educational Studies Association of Ireland. He is author of *The Custody and Courtship of Experience: Western Education in Philosophical Perspective* (1995), editor or joint editor of a number of other books, and author of numerous articles.

F. Ruth Irwin is a New Zealand Bright Futures and Sasakawa Scholar in the faculty of education at the University of Glasgow currently researching for a Ph.D. She has published articles and contributions to edited collections on Nietzsche, Heidegger, and poststructuralist theory. Her emphasis is on the environment, technology, and ethics in relation to education.

Bert Lambeir was educated at the Catholic University of Leuven where he graduated in educational sciences. His M.A. thesis was on "Critical Thinking as an Educational Aim: Just Another Brick in the Wall?" He holds the position of research fellow at the center for philosophy of education (KU Leuven) and is preparing a Ph.D. thesis on the implication of new technologies for the concepts of "learning" and "identity" within an educational relationship. His work is situated within the Wittgensteinian tradition but also takes up continental philosophical insights.

Michael A. Peters is research professor of education at the University of Glasgow. He also has a personal chair at the University of Auckland and is adjunct professor of communication studies at the Auckland University of Technology. He has research interests in contemporary philosophy and public policy, with a special emphasis on education. He is the author and/or editor of over twenty books, including most recently: *Poststructuralism, Marxism, and Neoliberalism: Between Theory and Politics* (2001), *Richard Rorty: Education, Philosophy, and Politics* (2001) (eds.), *Nietzsche's Legacy for Education: Past and Present Values* (2001) (eds.), *After the Disciplines: The Emergence of Cultural Studies* (2000) (ed.), and *Wittgenstein: Philosophy, Postmodernism, Pedagogy* (1999) with James Marshall.

Paul Smeyers is professor in the faculty of psychology and educational sciences at the University of Leuven in Belgium, where he teaches philosophy of education and qualitative research methods. He has published widely in Anglo-Saxon and European journals on issues related to a Wittgensteinian philosophy of education. With Jim Marshall he co-edited *Philosophy and Education: Accepting Wittgenstein's Challenge* (1995) and with Nigel Blake, Richard Smith, and Paul Standish he co-authored *Thinking Again: Education after Postmodernism* (1998) and *Education in an Age of Nihilism* (2000).

Paul Standish is senior lecturer in education at the University of Dundee, where he teaches philosophy of education. His recent books include *Education in an Age Of Nihilism* (2000), co-authored with Nigel Blake, Paul Smeyers, and Richard Smith, and *Lyotard: Just Education* (2000), co-edited with Pradeep Dhillon. He is editor of the *Journal of Philosophy of Education*.

Iain Thomson is assistant professor of philosophy at the University of New Mexico, specializing in Heidegger's philosophy. He has published articles on Heidegger in *Inquiry, The International Journal of Philosophical Studies, Philosophy Today, Enculturation,* and the *Journal of the British Society for Phenomenology.* He is currently working on a book on Heidegger's philosophical development, titled *The End of Ontotheology: Understanding Heidegger's Turn, Method, and Politics.*